D0163411

Doing Business with South Korea

Doing Business with South Korea

A HANDBOOK FOR EXECUTIVES IN THE PUBLIC AND PRIVATE SECTORS

Larry M. Hynson, Jr.

Q

QUORUM BOOKS
New York • Westport, Connecticut • London

Library of Congress Cataloging-in-Publication Data

Hynson, Larry M.
  Doing business with South Korea : a handbook for executives in the
public and private sectors / Larry M. Hynson.
    p.   cm.
  Includes bibliographical references.
  ISBN 0–89930–509–1 (alk. paper)
  1. United States—Commerce—Korea (South)—Handbooks, manuals,
etc. 2. Korea (South)—Commerce—United States—Handbooks, manuals,
etc. 3. Foreign trade promotion—United States—Handbooks, manuals,
etc. I. Title.
HF3127.5.H96   1990
658.8'48'095195—dc20   90–30015

British Library Cataloguing in Publication Data is available.

Library of Congress Catalog Card Number: 90–30015
ISBN: 0–89930–509–1

First published in 1990

Quorum Books, 88 Post Road West, Westport, Connecticut 06881
An imprint of Greenwood Publishing Group, Inc.

Printed in the United States of America

The paper used in this book complies with the
Permanent Paper Standard issued by the National
Information Standards Organization (Z39.48–1984).

10 9 8 7 6 5 4 3 2 1

Copyright Acknowledgments

The author and publisher gratefully acknowledge the following sources for granting
permission to use copyrighted material:

Nora Lockwood Tooher, "Rhode Island Business Plays by South Korea Rules," *The
Business Providence Journal Bulletin*, September 13, 1988, p. 1, © 1988 by the Providence
Journal Company. Reprinted with permission. All rights reserved.

Philip A. Spanninger, "Winning Government Approval of a 100% Foreign Investment:

The Goodyear Experience," *East Asian Executive Reports*, September 1988, pp. 9, 15–17.
Courtesy of *International Executive Reports* and Philip A. Spanninger.

Table 3.1 and 3.2 are from Frederic Hiroshi Katayama and William Bellis, "The
International 500," *Fortune*, August 1, 1988. Courtesy of *Fortune* magazine.

To Mr. Yoon-Ho Ham

A recognized expert in international trade and law, an exceptional, able consultant, one who understands not only the Korean market but also successful U.S. export strategies. Without his guidance and encouragement, this book might not have been written.

Contents

Figures and Tables

FIGURES

TABLES

Preface

It has been accurately predicted that what Japan was to the 1970s, Korea may well be through the 1990s. Korea is already on its way to becoming the next major front in world trade and international commerce. Those individuals and business executives wise enough to get in on the ground floor of this activity should realize amazing profits.

Of late, Korea has enjoyed high visibility. The 1988 Olympics showcased Korea via global television. Special conventions in America, such as the 1988 Oklahoma World Trade Conference, selected "Export to Korea" as a theme. Special articles in *The Wall Street Journal*, *Barron's*, and *Forbes* have profiled the commercial bonanza developing in Korea.

My own involvement in Korea dates back to 1963, when I served as an Army artillery and intelligence officer in the Demilitarized Zone. So naturally each time I return to South Korea, those early images remind me of the magnitude of economic change. At the recent Oklahoma World Trade Conference, I spoke about that economic change and how businesses can take advantage of it. The flurry of current activities—headlines about export opportunities to Korea, occasional Korean trade missions, conferences on economic changes in Korea—only underscore my impressions. Little wonder that Korea has achieved its international status.

Despite all this attention, however, precious little has been published in book form about the precise steps to follow in order to establish an active export operation to Korea. Because of this, I have set forth in the following chapters a specific plan for expanding trade with Korea. This book is written both for business people who want to expand their export operations and for professionals who study and analyze international trade. The focus is on company evaluation, product selection, overseas business practices, local customs, and Korean outlets.

Part I (Evaluate Export Capacities) begins with an analysis of company strategies and how to market products to South Korea. Part II, the second major topic division—Select These Products—discusses opportunities in Korea, the products that sell, and relates them to the Korean economy and U.S. trade. Part III (Know This People) places trade into a social context. Since exporting trends are moving toward joint ventures, these cultural considerations become all the more important. Whether exporters establish long-term ventures or not, traders must observe certain cultural practices (Part IV). These include an understanding of how the Korean import market works, how U.S. suppliers compare with Japanese, how to gain access to the Korean markets, and how insiders view Korean practices. The last two major sections emphasize both Korean protocol (Part V) and outlet procedures (Part VI). Readers also see how to practice the last step of exporting: getting into the distribution systems.

Readers also will find a selected bibliography and an appendix. The entries are designed for those who want to go into more depth or establish a library of reference materials. The bibliography should be an asset for those deliberating important issues of international trade, doing market research, seeking market contacts, or getting involved in cross-cultural training.

Professionals need information about practices and procedures that can be applied to particular companies, scholarly endeavors, or international policies. And while this book will be of value to market researchers, trade associations, government analysts, and university students, its primary purpose is as a sales tool. This book is pragmatic. It teaches the ins and outs both of how to identify products needed in Korea and how to gain a market share in expanding global exports. I have paid particular attention to creating networks, reviewing business surveys, understanding Korean etiquette and business relations, projecting future market needs, and evaluating market trends. These facts, however, do not ensure success.

Some exporters are successful, others are not. What is the difference?

American firms have access to their own resources, but they often over-look their networks. Whether overlooked or not, the process of suc-cessfully exporting to Korea demands intense coordination of professionals located inside and outside any company. This theme—exporting within a social context—makes sense for executives sensitive to intermediaries and end users. That advice also comes from a recent survey of Korean importers working with American exporters. Their concerns are described in this book because they significantly impact American exporters.

The Korean economic situation has only recently developed and rad-ically changed. As a result of that change, our assumptions (and corollary images) of Korea must also change. Most Americans still associate Korea with the 4077 Mobile Army Surgical Hospital (MASH) and village life—bright folk dresses, old men in white wearing tall black hats and puffing on long-stem pipes. Others associate Korea with strong military gov-ernment rule, student unrest, and military aid. Obviously many of these exotic images do not fit today's scene. Changes have occurred as recently as 1986, when South Korea had its first substantial foreign-trade surplus.

That event has been followed by others: open elections, trends toward democratization, hosting of the 1988 Olympic Games, an improved econ-omy, and a new constitution, which should reduce fraud and corruption. Korea, a newly industrialized country, has long been associated with, even described as a satellite of, the United States. But former images of Koreans as patrons must now give way to images of them as partners. For that reason, former American images, along with those of economic development and increased exporting activities, need updating.

The underlying premises of this book are: (1) aggressive exporters should study the markets in South Korea, especially those with the right product or service mix; (2) exporting is a process of networking not only within a company but also outside a company; (3) a responsive marketing strategy works best; (4) appropriate information increases profits by avoiding painful pitfalls and isolating open markets; and (5) business decisions begin and end at the bottom line.

It is obvious to anyone reading this book that it is a joint effort in-volving many different people. For their assistance I owe much. I cannot begin to remember everyone. But I do want to acknowledge some Ko-reans and Americans interested in this project. Dr. Soo-Chul Kim, my colleague for years and a visiting scholar at Oklahoma State University (OSU), discussed and defined many Korean terms. Dr. Bill Shaw—a Fulbright Scholar, Harvard University professor, and reference librarian at the Library of Congress—gave suggestions and references. The Ko-rean Embassy staff and commercial officers in Washington, D.C., also provided references and new insights. The Korea Foreign Trade Association, the Korean Economic Institute, the Korea Ministry of Trade, The Association of Foreign Trading Agents of Korea, and The Korea Trade Promotion Corporation all provided data for tables.

I found assistance and obtained many documents from the U.S. Department of Commerce, especially the Korean desk officers—Karen James Chopra and Ian Davis. Karen even travelled to Tulsa to assist us in the 1988 Oklahoma World Trade Conference, and in March 1990 Ian participated in an Oklahoma City conference on exporting to Korea. The contributions of these desk officers have been many. The Library of Congress staff (Dr. Kim) allowed me to xerox many valuable, hard-to-get articles. And finally, the U.S. Chamber of Commerce provided information about legislation and trade issues developed in Seoul.

The OSU Center for International Trade Development staff gave me more than moral encouragement. They supported my writing of a business monograph, one which lead to serious work on this project. The then executive director, Dr. Duane Hall, and his assistant, Brian Gauler, provided sound advice on trade issues. To Amy Tuncel I owe a special thanks for sharing the script from one of her televised programs. I could never have completed this task without the help of Mr. Jeff Levy. Mr. Levy, now at the University of North Texas, was the business librarian at OSU. He spent hours tracking the latest sources. His guidance and encouragement are greatly appreciated. Thanks also to my family for allowing me to spend time for writing. Thanks also go to my sponsoring editor, Eric Valentine, not only for his encouragement to write this book but also for many a conversation on how to make it better and to both the production editor, Alicia S. Merritt, and the copyeditor, Marie Smith, for making the text much stronger as a result of their perceptive critiques.

In conclusion, I want to thank the members and officers of the Tulsa World Trade Association for their encouragement. I appreciate their professional dedication to international trade efforts. This trade association and other trade groups make exporting work. I've learned much from them. Finally, I wish to express my gratitude to Wade Watkins. While in Washington, D.C., he introduced me to important Koreans and gave freely of his time.

Evaluate Export
Capacities

Company Environments

American companies have only begun to establish export operations to South Korea, yet in 1989 U.S. exports totalled $12.3 billion for the year. For those doing business in the Pacific Rim, South Korea ranks second in U.S. export volume behind Japan. Based on annualized U.S. Department of Commerce statistics, U.S. exports to Japan totalled $40.5 billion (1989), while exports to South Korea totalled $12.3 billion. Taiwan ranks third in U.S. exports ($10.2 billion), followed by Australia ($7.7 billion), Singapore ($6.6 billion), Hong Kong ($5.8 billion), People's Republic of China ($5.4 billion), and Malaysia ($2.6 billion).

Combining export and import figures, we find that overall Korea is the United States' seventh largest bilateral trading partner ($31 billion, 1989). As an international trading nation, South Korea imports good and services that totalled approximately $124 billion in 1989. By analyzing the total import volumes into South Korea, we find that the United States controls about 25 percent of that market (Japan, 31 percent). The good news for U.S. exporters is this: imports into Korea should increase 400 percent in the 1990 decade, reaching $200 billion in goods and services.

Besides that, the South Korean government policy is one which encourages Korean importers to buy U.S. products. Getting the right products and setting up for exports create money-making opportunities. How can this market best be tapped?

The immediate problems facing a tool and die company in Indianapolis or a wine merchant in San Diego or a beef breeder in Austin are language, culture, distance, import restrictions, and trade laws. These barriers to exporting seem so ominous that many companies never give a second thought to opening export avenues.

Robert Rubini, Vice President of Marketing at Cissell Manufacturing in Louisville, Kentucky, is a business executive who knows the monetary value of creating exports to nations like Korea. Rubini's company has established export operations to 96 foreign countries. Currently, 40 percent of Cissell's production is sold to foreign consumers.[1]

"We treat our foreign customers just like our customers in the United States," says Rubini. "This requires a team effort that includes advertising, engineering, and marketing. If we see that a plan we've developed for a customer in Denver, Colorado, will not work for a customer in Bangkok, Thailand, then we develop a new plan that will work in Bangkok. Our growth rate has been unbelievable."

You may think that's all well and fine. But how did he get those contacts in the first place? Cissell Manufacturing attends international trade shows to establish contacts with foreign buyers. They want to know four types of information: what products are needed in these foreign countries; what products cannot be produced locally or grown in that climate; what companies are seeking a cooperative exchange of goods with a U.S. company; and what the upside potential is for introducing the populace to advanced technology, leisure products, and fashion items. That's only the beginning.

Having gained an understanding of a nation's commercial potential, Rubini's staff studies the demographics of the country and its business traditions. They compile lists of cities according to population, chief business activities, location, and access to transportation routes. They study how people work and live, noting ways in which their existing U.S. products can be modified to meet the needs and desires of the foreign consumers. Finally, they evaluate differences in particular markets to find product fit. In shipping the staff asks, "Should we use the indirect selling, say with an Export Management Company (EMC) or Export Trading Company (ETC)? Or should we go with a sales representative or send directly to end-users?"

Their initial Korean encounters would go smoother if they learned about business practices, the market potential, and distribution channels. Still marketing executives wonder about Korea. They worry about import requirements for auto parts and finding office space in Seoul, about rising labor costs and student unrest. Getting the right information for their Korean Marketing Plan (KMP) at two differnt levels of analysis takes considerable effort.

The KMP should identify two levels of product and market potential for Korea—macro and micro. Understanding the macroenvironment—economy, demography, technology, social, cultural—is necessary as an external data base. This level is useful for marketing research systems in supporting recommendations. The microenvironment level is perhaps more useful. It deals with lifestyles and Korean laws as they influence future decisions. It shows U.S. presence and highlights opportunities. It also suggests economic accessibility and stable market trends over the next three to five years.

Naturally, no emerging nation will remain static in its growth, needs, or development. Nevertheless, adjustments to product demand are no more difficult for foreign clients than they are for domestic ones, once the commercial exchange and connections have been solidly established.

That's the first step. And you need to take it now. Tom Peters, author of *In Search of Excellence* and *Thriving on Chaos*, has his own ideas about priorities of international markets. "Every U.S. firm over $2 million in revenues should take first steps to examine international-market-creation opportunities. Every firm over $25 million should be alarmed if it is not doing 25 percent of its business overseas."[2]

No matter what your motivation may be—reduced manufacturing costs overseas, balance of trade, expanded outlet for goods, increased profits—there has been no better time than now to enter into international trade.

THE FOCUS ON KOREA

Of all burgeoning overseas markets, Korea shows the greatest potential. Per capita income has increased drastically from thirty-five years ago (the annual per capita income of $87, 1953). In 1990 the per capita GNP should be $5,000. By the year 2000 projections suggest an annual per capita income of $10,000. For the past five years, Korea's economy has grown almost 12 percent compared with Singapore (4.7 percent/year), Hong Kong (7.23 percent), Taiwan (9 percent), Japan (3.6 percent), and the United States (3.5 percent).

Favorable statistics spell opportunities now. At his 1988 State of the Union Address, the Korean president, Tae-Woo Roh, emphasized one major point—his commitment to open markets. He wants greater trade and investment access, favorable foreign exchange rates, and more capital market reform. Additionally, the Korean president wants to reduce the government's role in the economy, to increase Korea's imports from the United States, and to liberalize the financial sector.

"Korea is one of the most promising markets in the world for U.S. exports," says Ian Davis, Korean desk officer, International Trade Administration, U.S. Department of Commerce. Risks and uncertainties still exist. Korea is certainly not a market to jump into without extensive preparation. In 1988 one southeastern U.S. firm attended an international trade show and was able to sign a $1 million export contract. Rather than a blessing, it proved to be a disaster. This U.S. firm had neither foreign representatives nor international managers on site in Korea; it had no written plan for product delivery and distribution to end users; and it had not even talked to its engineers about calibrating the company's products. The excitement of landing a million dollar client had blinded company executives to the need for advance preparation. By contrast, Cissell Manufacturing taught us all one profitable lesson. The research and legwork come first; contracts come later.

It takes much more than opportunity to sell Kansas wheat in Inchon. The distance from Kansas wheat fields to Korean western hills is affected by shipping deadlines. Managers need an elaborate yet flexible KMP. Such a plan gives exporting staffs time to adjust to uncontrollable, ever changing, sometimes stressful, foreign markets. Therefore, a good KMP lists objectives along with contingencies. It also allows for tight planning and a long-range strategy to realize profits (in one to three years).

SIX STEPS TO SUCCESS

Export ventures are sometimes overwhelming, but six steps can lead to export success. Step One is to narrow the product line. Examine your company and decide which products are of value to the Korean markets. You may increase your range of product offerings, but for a start offer goods that will generate instant acceptance.

Step Two is to target your consumers. Rather than say, "I want to ship to Korea," say instead, "our steel-toed safety boots would sell best in Seoul with its continual construction," or "our software programs would be perfect for small manufacturers in mid-size cities where firms need inventory control and cash flow management." Learning to be sensitive to Korean sentiments and values makes sense economically. Emotional preference affects life styles and sales of consumer goods.

Step Three is to assess your long-range potential for this market. Examine your marketing philosophy; analyze your pricing needs; project your future market mix and range of products for the Korean market; determine your publicity, advertising, and public relations strategies. Look at industry trends and estimate how much lag there is between the United States and Korea.

Determine your domestic strength in relation to your industry as a whole. Then decide how you will fend off competitors and cope with the demands of meeting domestic customer needs while you create export openings to Korea. You want to identify target markets and develop strategies for each market. Only after you are armed with appropriate facts can you confidently answer all the questions your superiors may ask. Only then can you guide most discussions around legitimate road blocks.

Step Four is to secure expert advice. Resourcefulness keeps companies from spending money unnecessarily. Expert consultants are available who can meet the need for metrification, packaging for Korean consumers, writing and printing in the Korean language, taking part in trade expositions, preparing export documentation, diversifying product use, and reducing manufacturing costs. Help can be obtained through private consulting firms, industrial trade associations, university professors, and the U.S. Department of Commerce. They give expert advice about the Korean markets, tax advantages of exporting, trade exhibitions, export documentation, and the Korean consumers.

Step Five is to understand the Korean culture. It is important for potential exporters to visit Korea and to tour its cities and countryside. It is wise to read books about the nation's history and to attend orientation classes that are held in-country. It is vital for an "outside" trader to know the Korean value system, Korean tastes, Korean laws and heritage, in order to meet commercial needs.

Invest whatever is necessary to accommodate, not to offend, the tastes of Koreans. And that may mean seeing a product line, a marketing strategy, or distribution channels from a different perspective than your own. Cultural sensitivity correlates with the right actions to elicit preferred responses from consumer groups. Additionally, by obtaining a first-hand sense of the economic conditions of the country, you will have a more natural feel for when, where, and how to market your specific goods.

Step Six is to initiate your export operations. Having defined your product offerings, you target a consumer market, acquire proper advice on market entry, and then you make your move. If difficult decisions arise, as they will, just weigh your options, choose a course of action, and forge ahead. As each new success comes along, do not pause to rest on your laurels, but strive to maximize each gain. Within two to five years you should already be seeing substantial returns on your efforts and investments.

NEGOTIATION FOR KOREAN MARKETS

International training pays off. To forget international professional development could be fatal. Professor Franklin R. Root (Wharton School

of Business) says that international managers have the primary responsibility of engaging foreign markets, which means the people. Develop
the necessary skills for comprehending and negotiating in this unique
Korean culture.

Exporters who negotiate with Korean nationals should consider three
factors that impact Korean business transactions. These factors impact
promotion, sales, and profits.

1. *Symbols of Power*. Symbolic leaders and politicians affect imports. Korean
   symbols of power should be known before U.S. suppliers fly to Korea. That
   knowledge helps suppliers cut through red tape, eliminate ambiguous talk,
   and identify Korean leaders with the power to close deals and make decisions
   (see Parts I and III).
2. *Context of Channels*. U.S. strategists gain a competitive edge by negotiating
   sales, delivering on time, and getting the work done. In an era of international
   uncertainty, strategists have few doubts about either their marketing objectives or how to reach them (see Parts II and VI).
3. *Meaning of Products*. Koreans play *changgi* as Americans play chess. Koreans
   enjoy forcing their opponents into checkmate. Their preferences for U.S.
   products, like their preferences for changgi, are different from Americans'.
   The utility and value of some U.S. products may be greater or lesser for
   Koreans than Americans. High-tech toys may be in great demand in America,
   but of almost no value in Korea. Drugstore supplies and health-care products
   may be commonplace in America, but a luxury to Koreans.

Negotiators should be sensitive to meanings Koreans give to U.S.
products. Products symbolize security, safety, prestige, or happiness to
consumers. If so, exported products should be marketed with a social
conscience and a spirit of international cooperation. Exporters communicate on deeper human levels by asking the "why" as well as the
"what" of their business purposes (see Parts IV and V).

This information should be factored into various projects, whether for
an American company or the U.S. Government. Although no two companies have the same Korean export potential, all begin at the same
place. They start with the sales program—the marketing philosophy,
product mix, pricing, and advertising/promotion plans. They then move
toward international marketing, to include target markets and strategies
for negotiating in a setting for business deals. Take a close look at (1)
symbols, (2) context, and (3) meaning, but keep these insights from your
competitors. Such insights on Korean markets should increase your confidence and profits.

RESOURCES FOR FIRMS

Profits prompt companies to Korean markets. But there are several
other reasons—expansion, size, competition, costs. Some enter Korean

markets to expand their product lines. Others do so when they reach a certain size. Still others demand reciprocity. The logic goes, "Our competitors do well there; why can't we do well there?" And finally others look at excessive manufacturing costs as their reason for expanding into international markets.

Whatever the reasons are for firms to export—increased profits, increased growth, additional markets, extended product cycles, increased number of customers, tax advantages, added product lines, improved competitiveness, and favorable publicity—they need pertinent export information. Some know nothing about the Korean game plan and only now are exploring the possibilities. Some have exported to Korea, and now they are studying other options for expansion. They need information on customary business methods and established channels of distribution. And some readers are international managers with large firms. They're seasoned veterans with written plans that evaluate their products (strengths and weaknesses) and Korean distributors.

Several resources are available for firms evaluating their environments and potential for exports. One resource may come from a firm's reorganization. Eastman Kodak reorganized because of inadequate financial returns. Realizing how much international markets were changing, top executives abandoned their old functional organizational concepts— manufacturing, marketing, R&D. They formed matrix systems and focused on product business units. As a result, profits immediately increased. Managers attributed their economic successes (triple profits for 1987 over 1986) to these changes.

"What we've done is establish the business unit manager's position as a truly global one," said Philip Samper. He was responsible for making the international divisions work. As a smart manager, he made others responsible for their product performances. "We have designed a process whereby the business is driven by a worldwide business unit and implemented by a geographic unit," he said.[3] Within the international units there were five general managers, one for the Asian, Africa, and "Austrasian" regions, one for the European region, one for the Japanese region, one for Latin America, and one for Kodak Canada.

Another resource is information technology. Corporate executives no longer cable messages to Seoul intermediaries, they use fax machines. Those without global strategies may lose not only their international markets but possibly their domestic ones as well. Texas Instruments established extensive communication networks to meet global challenges. Firms like this switch to integrated systems that combine voice, data, text, and video services. Some video systems are so exact that viewers can detect colors, fabric, and patterns of clothing.[4]

Information technology introduces new options for international managers. Three recent systems are data support (DS), executive support systems (ESS), and database management systems (DBMS). According to consultants, exporting managers need all three for five reasons.[5] (1) Geographic spread of global markets necessitates this type of sophisticated coordination. (2) Organizational structure evolves from needs. These support systems allow for greater flexibility. (3) Matching skills and abilities to global and local situations is easier through these systems. (4) The systems also allow for special data on culture, laws, and the politics of each country. (5) Through these systems, managers can cut down on the amount of uncertainty typical of international markets.

Each system has its own advantages. DS compares export versus offshore investments, forms of investments, products currently manufactured, financial policies, and so on. ESS analyzes a specific country, such as Korea. It describes where to go and who to see. It profiles customers and information on competition. DBMS models marketing production, planning, and serving needs. It assesses impacts of various products and organizations.

Since manufacturing costs are accelerating, this next resource should help. Flexible computer-integrated manufacturing facility (FCIM) keeps costs down. Called a microfactory, the system operates on a time share basis. It is an economical way to manufacture products through cost sharing. The U.S. Department of Commerce and the Assistant Secretary for Productivity, Technology, and Innovation (Dr. Merrifield) are working on the concept of expanding company resources. Their plan is to aggregate the manufacturing process, thereby expanding a firm's capability.

"The quality, productivity and just in time delivery from supplier to factory [are much easier to obtain]," Dr. Bruce Merrifield said. "Once you have the one facility, you can clone anywhere in the world."[6]

Many consultants give costly advice. Smart exporters get expert advice free from the U.S. Department of Commerce. The Korean desk officers and the Republic of Korea Government (ROKG) sponsor "Export Now— Korea" seminars. These joint efforts highlight the growth of Korean markets. Export opportunities grew by 43 percent in 1988. This seminar covers trade promotion programs designed to facilitate U.S. exports to Korea. The seminars provide updates on Korean policies, laws, tariffs, and economic outlooks. "The implementation of the *Export Now-Korea Program* will provide exporters with the tools necessary to penetrate Korean markets and to expand existing market share."[7]

WHAT COMES NEXT?

In the following chapters, you will find information on Korean financial institutions, marketing practices, distribution networks, and governmental agencies. One recurrent theme is how much business outcomes reflect social settings. Koreans find meaning in culture. The values, behavior, attitudes, and practices of the people do not alter greatly from family setting to social life to the corporate arena. As such, skilled American business negotiators coordinate marketing skills with regional philosophy and match commercial efforts to local pace. There are specific strategies for accomplishing this.

If you catch yourself wondering if all the effort will be worthwhile, consider the words of Emery Olcott, President of Camberra Industries of Connecticut, a company that exports $60 million of its production annually. "Once we made the decision at Camberra to emphasize foreign sales, we elevated exporting to a very important activity. We think and plan long term. The domestic market may be easier, but it is also limited. We now do 55 percent of our yearly sales to foreign countries and we plan to increase that continually."[8]

What goes through the minds of doubtful, even skeptical, exporters as they approach their decisions about export commitments? "How much time will this take?" They know that delicate international relationships require strong commitments of time. Decision making never ends; new challenges arise.

One management guru, Tom Peters, answered the question about time: "If you're not prepared to spend six weeks a year overseas, don't bother to start." What is generally true of the Europeans is especially true of the Asians. Personal encounters are cultural traditions. Successful exporters discovered the mystery about Korean connections. To them it's no secret what it takes to be successful.

Success also belongs to those who develop their products incrementally and distribute them flexibly to Inchon. But more important than these prerequisites is one more. Success belongs to those who work well together as a professional team. It takes everyone working together, wholeheartedly committed to getting the job done.

Emery Olcott agrees: "What happens if you don't have a good support staff for your exporting operation is that your sales people devote most of their attention to the much easier domestic market."[9] Doing what comes naturally will not work in Korea either.

Ki-Jung Kim said this: "Businesses are successful because someone makes the sacrifices others are unwilling to make."[10] The opportunities for U.S. firms to conduct trade differ now from what they were after World War II.

At one time U.S. companies didn't worry about international business; they didn't have to. For one thing, exports took too much time to reach their destinations. But the limitations of travel time have changed. So too have international marketing opportunities. Today, with satellite communications, supersonic transports, Fax machines, and global computer relays, the whole planet is a free market. With so many technologies, why not increase overall sales? Profits from exports are easier now than ever before. But exports require a single mindedness over the long haul.

Obviously learning about Korea is the first step, exporting is the next. An exporting firm hired a consultant who gave them some good advice: "Start advertising three ways—on radio, on TV, and through personal contacts."

Most agents, indigenous leaders, and effective interpreters spell export success with a capital "ES." It is absolutely "(ES)sential" to use meaning in culture—the values, practices, and attitudes of the people. Begin by seeking assistance on industry/product research and by gathering pertinent information about Korea.

To conclude, hear what the Koreans (the white-clothed people) have to say. Listen to those living in Korea (the land of personal encounters). As you enter their land, Koreans says, "May you come in peace." That is also my wish. May your exporting prosper as you enter Korea.

NOTES

1. Katherine Glover and Bill Scoutone, "50 Firms Share Export Techniques," *Business America*, September 12, 1988, 23. Throughout the book, I either describe case studies or give specific examples of successful U.S. exporters. These stories were written by Katherine Glover and Bill Scoutone for *Business America* (U.S. Commerce). I use them to illustrate some basic principles of exporting. Because of their usefulness, I owe much to those who collected them. Other stories are taken from other sources. And in those cases, the specific citations are given. Materials without citation are taken from government documents; others have specific citations.

2. Tom Peters, *Thriving on Chaos* (New York: Harper & Row, 1988), 150.

3. Rena Grossfield, "Kodak's Matrix System Focuses on Product Business Units," *Business International*, July 18, 1988, 221–22.

4. Raja K. Iyer and Lawrence L. Schkade, "Management Support Systems for Multinational Business," *Information & Management* 12 (1987):60.

5. Iyer and Schkade, 63.

6. Ann Blumberg, "Factory of the Future: Time-Share Manufacturing," *Business International*, December 19, 1988, 395.

7. Ian M. Davis, "Export Now—Korea Seminars are Planned by Commerce Department," *Business America*, December 5, 1988, 27.

8. Glover and Scoutone, 19.

9. Glover and Scoutone, 19.

10. Henry O. Dormann, *The Speaker's Book of Quotations* (New York: Fawcett Columbine, 1987), 24.

2

Expanding Sales and Marketing

The world is both bigger and smaller; both trends mean greater international trade and profits. Firms sell to an increasing number of Asians, some 3 billion. Many in Japan buy U.S. products. This highly developed economy accounts for 70 percent of the economic activity in the Pacific Rim. But newly industrialized countries (NICs) such as South Korea and Taiwan also represent an economic force. The Bank of America expects that the Pacific Rim will average 4.8 percent annual growth over the 1990–92 period, compared with 2.7 percent for Western Europe, and 2 percent for North America.

The world also seems smaller and more manageable. Firms can use advances in transportation and communication systems to extend operations. The growth of merchandise and business service trade continues in Japan and South Korea. In fact, trade within that region totals $240 billion. It is growing at an annual rate of 25 percent. International trade experts estimate that the Asian Pacific region constitutes a more powerful grouping than does the European community.[1]

As Korean and U.S. companies become increasingly linked together in this global economic network, U.S. exporters increase profits from net sales and licensing agreements. Over the next fifteen years Korea-Pacific Chemical company will pay Union Carbide $5.8 million down and 3.9 percent on net sales for technical information, as well as data on the production of low-density polyethylene. Similarly, Pizza Hut licensed their fast-food production to Dong Shin Food Company for $200,000 down and 3 percent of net sales for five years.[2]

Even though the pace of Korean economic growth has declined somewhat, Korea still remains "one of the world's fastest expanding economies while offering an increasingly attractive investment site and marketplace."[3] Bob Petersen, Director of Development for American National Metric Council, argues that firms should expand their markets. U.S. businesses already operate in an international context. These companies no longer exist as isolated economic entities. Integrated world systems preclude geographic isolation. Competition for consumers is worldwide, whether American executives accept this fact or not. In order to strengthen domestic markets, Petersen advocates what the Koreans, Japanese, and Taiwanese are already doing: let U.S. businesses expand their sales through carefully devised international marketing strategies.

U.S. firms could evaluate each phase of the exporting process by soliciting ideas from significant others, for example, product champions. "What a person thinks on his own without being stimulated by the thoughts and experiences of other people is even in the best case rather paltry and monotonous," Einstein said.

Some CEOs did this by organizing the U.S.-Korea Business Council (1988). Business executives from both countries (twenty-seven Korean members and forty-two U.S. members) organized to discuss trade issues. Dr. Nam (Duck-Woo), the mastermind behind the Korean economic success story, leads the Korean group; David Roderick, Chairman of the Board and chief executive officer of USX Corporation, heads the U.S. team.[4]

Their dialogue is both fascinating and revealing. At one gathering, both sides went back and forth on issues. Mr. Roderick voiced concern over both Korea's expanding exports to the United States and Korea and Japan's seeming lack of concessions to U.S. firms exporting to either country. "The worse argument . . . is to ask for great tolerance and patience," he said. "The reason that I don't think it's respected any longer in Washington is that I think they feel they've been deceived by it, in at least one economy [Japan], for about 25 years."[5]

Trade imbalance problems are discussed by the U.S.-Korea Business Council. "Patience doesn't sell well when you have a $120 billion trade deficit," Roderick lamented. "That's not the time for patience but for insistence."[6] Both sides, however, grappled over key trade issues.

Koreans want to globalize their domestic markets while at the same time they diversify their export markets. They're worried about hiking wages, curbing inflation, reducing the external surplus, increasing private investments, providing more equitable income distributions, and balancing growth. The Koreans also would like more partnerships and joint ventures, especially in new technologies.

The U.S. members want action. They advocate mandatory investigation of, even retaliation against, any Korean violators of intelligence rights (copyrights, patent rights, and trademark). Furthermore, they're concerned over Korea's lack of enforcement of antidumping laws. As U.S. exporters, they want full participation in the wholesale and distribution of their products; they're troubled over how Koreans link imports to exports. Additionally, they like neither the layered system of import taxes nor the foreign exchange rules. And finally, they asked their Korean counterparts to restrict the authority both of private trade organizations and of customs and quarantine officers. U.S. members believe these Koreans often have an anti-import bias, one that shows.

Trade issues are complex, but the fundamentals of strategy (the grand design) must be remembered.[7] Winning football coaches realize the importance of game strategy. The secret to the success of Bud Wilkinson, former University of Oklahoma football coach, was simply "his insistence upon organization, well-run practices, and a positive mental attitude."[8] The same for Penn State coach Joe Paterno: "Football games are won or lost on five or six plays," he said. "The trouble is you never know when they're coming."[9]

Exporting to Korea is like playing football. Sometimes managers worry about which rules count and whether others play fair. They ask: "Is the General Agreement on Tariffs and Trade (government agreements on rights and obligations for conducting multilateral trade) the rule book for everyone?"

This chapter is about game plans. Few coaches planned better than the best blackboard coach in football, Tom Landry. "More important than merely setting goals," said Landry, "is discovering the best way to achieve those goals, and then sticking with the plan—even through lean times—until success is achieved."[10] And finally, among great strategists, Bear Bryant possessed one asset over others. He routinely fit his strategies to the uniqueness of his teams, not the other way around.[11]

EXPORTER'S SQUARE

The fundamental strategy is to find a market fit. This is accomplished by aligning company resources to Korean needs. The objective is to create a win-win scenario, or what has been described as the " best fit" formula. In considering the best fit formula, pay attention to the basic

Figure 2.1
Exporter's Square

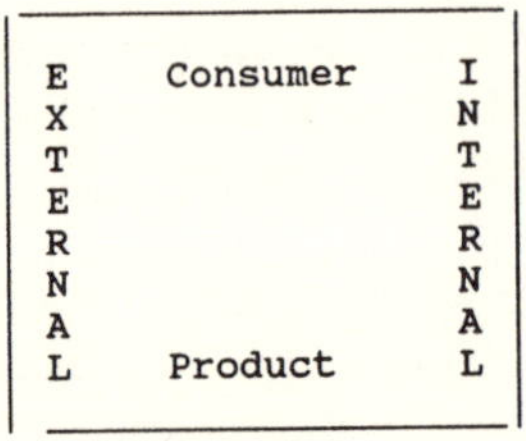

```
┌─────────────────────────┐
│ E     Consumer     I    │
│ X                  N    │
│ T                  T    │
│ E                  E    │
│ R                  R    │
│ N                  N    │
│ A                  A    │
│ L     Product      L    │
└─────────────────────────┘
```

elements of exporting (see Figure 2.1). Note, however, the process of exporting to Korea—as well as Taiwan or Japan—is much more complicated than the model implies.[12] Its simplicity could cause you to overlook the role of the ROKG, which dominates public trade policy and private sector initiatives.

Even though the models on export are limited, they are useful. Note that the exporter's square has four sides labelled "consumer," "product," "internal," and "external." These four concepts represent, in simplistic form, the process of international marketing. On the one hand, this figure is a useful variation of the marketing four Ps—product, place, promotion, and price. On the other hand, it gives a frame of reference from inside your company. Once you understand it, you, as an exporter, can adapt it to progressively more complex environments. So evaluate it by the criterion of utility, not validity. It is a heuristic device, not an isomorphic description of all exporting practices.

Figure 2.1 can benefit you in two ways. First, this model can be applied to various stages of exporting. International marketing is more complicated than it appears. Exporting sometimes follows Murphy's law: "if something can go wrong, it will." Some agree with Patrick O'Toole, who thought Murphy was an unrealistic optimist. Second, this model summarizes the major tasks at three stages: initial assessment, early development, and trial markets. The framework, like an accordion, clarifies marketing expansion and marketing mix. At times export managers must reassess foreign environments, consumer interests, and product usefulness. While this model provides data on neither Koreans' food preferences—*pulgogi* and *kalbi*—nor on Korea's growing sense of nationalism, it does suggest that exporters should think globally, yet market locally. The model allows for these adaptations even as word processing programs provide windows for various analyses. The windows of this model—internal, external, consumer, product—stay the same.

For this first exercise, we'll use the square functions as a discovery device. This is not a text given to complex issues of international marketing.[13] However, it could be useful as a tool for initially sketching out the square and answering these four questions:

- How much do we know about our Korean clients?
- What specific products do we want to sell to them?
- What internal changes will be called for in order to prepare products for Korea?
- What external arrangements must be made in order to set up the deals?

This sort of initial brainstorming improves focus as you establish specific goals. From your diverse product line, select those that have great sales potential in Korea. From your staff, select key people as liaisons. And finally, consider time elements, cultural differences, cash flow concerns, and customer satisfaction. How you view potential customers (misconceptions or myths about Korea) could hinder any realistic assessment of this market potential. "Korea is [not] an underdeveloped nation, politically unstablized [sic] and just leaning on Americans for assistance. What very wrong perceptions."[14]

A MODEL BRAINSTORMING SESSION

Does this discussion have practical applications? Let's see just how you might use it. A model brainstorming session similar to one you may consider will outline some focal points for concentrated marketing strategies.

Reaching Consumers with Your Message

Koreans travel throughout Seoul from 4 A.M. to midnight. Some take the taxis. Thousands prefer the mass transit system—Seoul metro-commuter lines. They can get a ride every five minutes for about 300 *won* (about 45 cents). To get the right train, they watch for color coded signs, indicating four lines—downtown, Olympic complex, Seoul Railroad, or Sadong. Some ride the surface electric train down to Inchon. While riding on this mass transit system, Koreans notice what's on the walls. Along the walls of these commuter routes are hundreds of posters that advertise hotels, cosmetics, restaurants, newspapers, movies, food, and clothes. By putting your advertisement on these walls, you would gain high visibility at a reasonable price. This is one way to launch an advertising campaign for your products or services. Reach Koreans by asking questions about their life styles. What products do they buy? How are they used? Where are the products bought? Try to discover markets overlooked.

Creating Products Koreans Will Buy

Determine which of your products will fill a void in the Korean economy. Who will buy them, why, and for what price? How will your products be packaged so that their size, color, language, and names will appeal to Korean buyers? It will be important to talk about a general marketing strategy and what sort of benchmarks will be used to gauge success or failure.

Itaewon is a famous shopping district in Seoul that is comprised of 1,300 shop owners who average U.S. $300 in sales each day. In 1989 some 1.5 million tourists visited Itaewon.

Because many shops in Itaewon sell leather goods, it is an excellent place to sell skins and hides. Many of these leather products—coats, shoes, pants, pocketbooks, dresses, and shirts—use a poor grade of leather. It is difficult to find the good quality leather they want. U.S. suppliers could export more skins and hides to Korea, were the prices right.

Revamping Your Internal Production Practices

Once implemented, marketing plans require job responsibilities and procedural changes. They specify agents' responsibilities. Your Korean marketing plan may require you to revamp procedures to include new purchase orders, billing statements, and sales letters printed in Korean. You may have to devise letter/order acknowledgments, deal with distributor/agent application forms, and contract price lists and terms (sale and payment). Your plan should include briefings for local bankers, insurance agents, and legal advisers, as well as forwarders and accountants.

The Crocker National Bank at 250 2-ga Taepyong-ro (Seoul), along with fifty foreign banks, performs business services. Foreign branches can do limited business. Yet their scope of responsibilities is greater than those of representative offices and officers, which is another type of legal business operation in South Korea.

The Ministry of Finance regulates the financial sector. This ministry coordinates the Korean banks that conduct international transactions by selecting their general managers, Korea's regional banks (one in each of the provinces), and other financial institutions (finance companies, investment and trust companies, credit unions, and mutual credit associations) for short-term loans. Only recently have U.S. insurance companies entered this Korean market. Because of these banking limitations, U.S. firms may revamp their internal production practices by using one of eight specialized institutions—the Leasing Companies. They provide a leasing package for foreign operations. U.S. foreign

Figure 2.2
Expanded Market Model

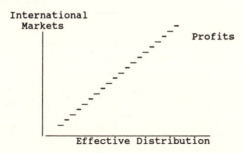

operators can even choose one of thirty firms that sell securities and other services, as in capital markets.

Revamping Your External Transaction Procedures

Targeting specific Korean locales as test markets for export market expansion safeguards unreasonable expansions. If you adapt test markets, be prepared to develop procedures for obtaining bills of lading, packing lists, and other documents (certificate of origin and insurance). U.S. exporters and Korean importers form a nexus of interaction, that necessitates locating intermediaries, selecting personnel, signing international contracts, estimating office costs, establishing office procedures, and contracting for delivery.

Whether you obtain technology licenses or form stock with a small Korean firm makes a difference. In 1987 the government granted over 500 licenses. The ROKG wants more technology for small to medium companies. Stock companies, similar to those in the United States, gave Koreans the investments. The ROKG gave incentives; however, this practice has subsided considerably except in the case of high technology investments. These investments still receive depreciation allowances, value-added taxes, and special customs procedures.

Focusing on the Factors Related to Exports

Having begun with the Exporter's Square Model, we now continue with the Expanded Market Model. The Expanded Market Model (Figure 2.2) isolates two crucial activities that could be developed, enacted, and monitored.

Two key ingredients for successful profits are to develop both your international markets and distribution systems. Affluent Korean professionals work and live much as their American counterparts. The tech-

Figure 2.3
Exporter Strategy

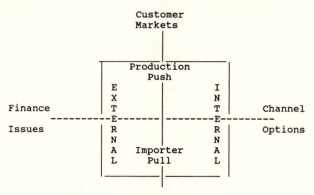

nology they use is similar; only the business and government protocols differ. Some international experts argue that successful marketing depends on neither consumers' boundaries nor their life styles.

Koreans buy IBMs and Americans jog in Korean-made tennis shoes. The expansion of international markets considerably increases the potential buyers with similar needs. "For market research, their [consumers'] needs can be analyzed more in terms of group or clusters with similar habits and tastes than in terms of nationalities."[15] That is what expanded markets are about: finding groups of Koreans who want the products or services that American exporters can provide.

Combining All Accumulated Data into One Planning Model

Having continued our model building with the Expanded Market Model, let's now combine the two models. We gain yet another perspective by overlaying the Exporter's Square on the Expanded Market Model. This gives us a total Exporter Strategies figure (Figure 2.3), which encompasses several factors. It has the four elements of the Exporter's Square and two dimensions of expanding international markets. Note, too, the dynamics of this model are the product push and the importer's pull. The product push springs from international competition even in domestic markets. The importer pull, as we'll see later, comes from both Korean consumers and ROKG officials who prefer U.S. products over other countries'.

COMPANY STRATEGIES

It is risky business not knowing exactly what products to develop, especially for some technologies that take long-term planning and developmental work. Such is the case with robots. Presently, Japan has more robots than any other nation in the world, over 14,000 industrial robots and 62,000 simpler robots. Korea is a decade away from these developments.

Until 1987 Korea had few industrial robots.[16] Currently Japan supplies nearly all of Korea's robotics, about 60 percent of the import market demand. Four major Korean companies work in this area—Daewoo Heavy Industry, Hyundai Heavy Industry, Samsung Aerospace Industries, and Lucky-Goldstar. These firms—along with the Korea Institute of Machinery and Metals, Seoul National University, the Korea Advanced Institute of Science and Technology—supply about 45 to 70 percent of domestic needs, excluding imports.

Korean suppliers meet the domestic needs for arc and spot welder robots. Foreign exports of robots to Korea will increase, but only Japan is engaged in this market. Once Japan exported 3 percent of their production. Now they export 16 percent. By the early 1990s, they should export 20 percent. As productivity increases, so will robot demand, since robots are more efficient than people in some operations. As Korea enters an era of higher labor costs, robots can do dirty, routine jobs, freeing skilled workers for cleaner, more challenging ones. In the case of nuclear development, robots can accomplish tasks too risky for people.

U.S. suppliers could penetrate this market if they advertise and promote their products extensively. The Japanese competition, however, is stiff. But U.S. companies could target large Korean conglomerates that have the resources and interest to purchase robots.

This market is growing. By 1992 some 2,500 units, totalling $136.9 million, will be utilized in Korea. Those units include several types of robots: spot welders, arc welders, coaters, assemblers, material handlers, metal working apparatus, loaders/unloaders, and educational robots. Adequate production, however, depends upon two key technologies—drawing technology and major parts manufacturing technology.

Work out some agreement on training the Koreans in the skills, then sell them certain products. To penetrate the market, U.S. manufacturers should plan how to reach the end users found in these Korean industries: auto, heavy industry, and mechanical industries. Locally, Hyundai Motors Division uses robots in car assembly factories. Nationally, 238 units (56 percent) were found in the auto industry, 128 units (30 percent) were in electric and electronics industry, and 59 units (14 percent) in heavy industry (1987).

AN EXPORT STRATEGY

Companies can develop their Korean markets using carefully devised, individual strategies. The process of exporting to Korea can come under

Table 2.1
Integrated Export Strategy

Customer Markets	Channels Options	Finance
Pull of Sales	Internal Packing	Terms of Payment
direct	pack	cash
indirect	crates	Letter of credit
trade leads	marks	S/D, D/P, D/A**
FTI, ADS, WTDR*		
Push in Promotion	External Shipping	Credit
program	mail	date of drafts
materials	shipping	F.C.I.A.
trade shows	consolidation	OPIC ***
publicity	containerization	

```
*    Foreign Traders Index (file overseas customers)
     Agent/Distributor Service (search for interested reps)
     World Traders Data Reports
     (background reports on foreign firms)
**   Payment to distributors and sale channels which
     use credit responsibly. Two types of sight drafts:
     documents against payment and documents against
     acceptance time of title passage
***  Foreign Credit Insurance Association
     Overseas Private Investment Corporation
```

three main headings: (1) Customer Markets, (2) Channels Options, and (3) Finance (Table 2.1).

Each of these major divisions also has several subtopics. The six cells and the three major categories are discussed in later chapters. The Korean market has it own dynamic—it comes from the pull of an expanding economy and the push of aggressive U.S. exporters.

This push-pull theme is explored throughout the book. The other two topics (channel distribution and financial issues), which deal with export trade mechanics and logistics, are found in later chapters. Two chapters, 15 and 21, describe several Korean distribution channels. International pricing and financing, always pressing concerns, are presented in Chapter 23.

To think through your Korean Marketing Plan is to begin an export operation to Korea. Naturally, as with all business plans, you'll revise, modify, and adjust your export strategies as new opportunities arise. To keep up with the Koreans, you'll need to work hard. Korean businessmen enthusiastically tackle seemingly impossible jobs. "I'll do it anyway" (*ockji*), they say. That willingness to work hard economically propelled them to where they are now. Eduardo Lachica found evidence of that same determination. "The Japanese come to Silcon Valley to shop for U.S. know-how; the Russians to steal it if they can. But the Koreans are here to learn it the hard way—by starting their own companies in this hotbed of high technology."[17]

FINAL COMMENTS AND CONCLUSIONS

Korea's GNP is equivalent to $169.2 billion. It is driven by a 12.2 percent average rate of economic growth. The 1990 per capita income in U.S. dollars was $5,000. As their Presidential Commission stated: "Korea is expected to play a new role and bear more responsibility in the international community."[18] To conclude, economic restructuring issues have prompted the ROKG to establish new guidelines of international cooperation and trade. Future economic policies, while historic in their pursuit of unity within diversity, suggest that the prospects for Korea's economy look good. Korea's investments in high economic growth should encourage U.S. exporters to consider expanding their exports and marketing their products to Korea. American companies could develop Korean markets by using carefully devised, individualized strategies. Each marketing step can lead to profits, but only for those who start off right. In the next chapter you'll learn how to stay right on target by properly and patiently implementing your Korean Marketing Plan.

NOTES

1. Amy Albertson Tuncel, "Doing Business in the Pacific Rim," National University Teleconference Network, February 8, 1990.

2. Patrick G. Marshall, "Pacific Rim Challenges," *Editorial Research Reports*, April 7, 1989, 15.

3. Mark Michelson," Business Outlook: Korea," *Business Asia*, February 1, 1988, 42.

4. Stephen Lande, "A Private Forum for Reducing Frictions," *Business Korea*, March 1989, 28–30.

5. Lande, 30.

6. Lande, 30.

7. Leila J. Gainer, "Making the Competitive Connection," *Training & Development Journal*, September, 1989, S5–S30. An excellent analysis of the strategic organizational process.

8. Hank Nuwer, *Strategies of the Great Football Coaches* (New York: Franklin Watts, 1988), 60.

9. Nuwer, 110.

10. Nuwer, 123.

11. Nuwer, 102.

12. For additional information on Korean sources, consult the Appendix and Chapter 16.

13. International managers worry about initial involvements (entry and expansion strategies), competitive marketing and pricing, and the functional matters of integrating and coordinating their game plans. Exporters, like everyone else, look for examples and case studies about the Steve Jobs or Lee Iacoccas who struggle with similar problems. International marketing planning tools—

Boston Consulting Group and General Electric—are useful not only for comparisons but also as checklists.

Even with timely information and planning tools, marketing strategies follow their own course over time. They must first be developed, then revised to fit particular regions. The perennial issues include debate over basic organization, type of authority structure, distribution strategies, and types of market research. Obviously to discuss these would be a book in itself. Our focus is on Korea. And these chapter ideas (Expanding Sales and Marketing) are basic to our analysis of international marketing and management. Such models serve two purposes: (1) to stimulate thinking about product lines and Korean markets and (2) to serve as an organizing principle in developing other chapters.

14. Philip R. Harris and Robert T. Moran, *Managing Cultural Differences* (Houston, Tex.: Gulf, 1987), 409.

15. Kenichi Ohmae, *Beyond National Borders* (Tokyo: Kodansha, 1988), 83.

16. Pacific Consultants Corporation, *Profile of Industrial Robots in Korea* (Seoul: The U.S. Department of Commerce, the Embassy of the United States of America, March 1988). Successfully exporting this product requires long-term planning and development. Those interested should contact the Korea Institute of Machinery and Metals Robotics Laboratory, 66, Sangnam-dong, Changwon City Kyungnam, Korea, or the Korea Advanced Institute of Science and Technology, 39–1, Hawologok-dong, Songbuk-gu, Seoul, Korea.

17. Harris and Moran, 408.

18. The Presidential Commission Report on Economic Restructuring, *Realigning Korea's National Priorities for Economic Progress* (Washington, D.C.: Korean Economic Institute, 1989).

3

The Olympic Showcase

Historians are prophets in reverse. They interpret patterns after they've already happened. Historians might now note an interesting parallel. In 1964 the Olympic Games were held in Tokyo. That next decade Japan drew global attention to itself by becoming a leading industrial nation. In 1988 the Olympic Games were held in Seoul and, ever since, Korea has rapidly been emerging as the newest Asian leader in global commerce.

Momentum began even before the Olympic Games. Just over five years ago, Koreans panicked over their ever increasing, all-time-high debt of $46 billion. Today, with reduced foreign debts, Korea is now a creditor nation. How did this happen and what are the results?

The first question is about money used for an economic face lift. Some capital came from the Asian Development Bank (ADB). Korea joined in 1970, borrowing $6.8 million to build a highway from Seoul to Inchon, Korea's major port. Since that time Korea has borrowed seventy-nine times for more than $2.3 billion (1968–88).[1]

Other monies have come from elsewhere. Over 436 loans have come from various major sources, including one hundred loans from the U.S. totalling over $5.2 billion. Note that just over half of that money ($2.7 billion) has been repaid. The total loan amount ($23.2 billion) is slightly larger than that amount which has been distributed ($19.6 billion).

The second question is about the results. Let's look at just two—the projects themselves and the accumulation of returned surplus. Of the 70 projects funded, 66 have been completed. The projects were used to develop banks, water supply, transport, agriculture, industry, and urban sectors. Only in 1986 did Korea first report a surplus of $4.8 billion in foreign trade. By 1987 Korea recorded a $10 billion foreign trade surplus and changed from a debtor to a creditor nation. The year 1986 was the beginning of what has been a steady annual growth rate of 12 percent increases in foreign trade. As of January 1989 Korea is a creditor nation with foreign assets exceeding foreign debts. The Economic Planning Board reports that Korea's overseas assets now reach $31.5 billion, which includes $20 billion in foreign debts. Since 1953 the real income has grown 1,200 percent.[2]

Can supply technology to Korea lead to commercial benefits now that citizens demand more consumer goods, better wages, and a fairer distribution of the accumulated wealth? Perhaps, but these are just some of the reasons why Koreans hail the Olympic Games as a symbol of economic emergence and a new era of prosperity.

Korea's advancing wealth status is in two positive directions: (1) Korea has become a more prosperous and stabilized country and (2) Korea has vast new pools of money with which to order additional goods from countries like America. Proving these speculations to be realities is the fact that in 1988 Korea increased its importing of U.S. goods by a whopping 20 percent ($9.7 billion).

Even the most conservative of economic forecasters believes that the Korean economy will continue to grow at the rate of 8 percent each year for the remainder of this century. Securing these growth rates are a variety of known factors: reduced tariffs; reduced import licensing restrictions; declining oil prices; a stronger evaluation of the Korean won against the U.S. dollar; high public morale; a strong labor force; and cooperative governments.

U.S. exporters of electronics components are reaping huge profits. Other exporters must follow suit, since Koreans are seeking a variety of consumer goods. This fact, coupled with the Korean government's efforts to improve unfair trade practices, points to export opportunities. American businesses that are prepared to meet these needs and desires will find an eager market of buyers. While other countries are also eager for American goods, the *chaebols*—large Korean corporations—are an index for showing how far South Korea has come.

CHAEBOLS

Finding wealthy Koreans who import American goods isn't that difficult. They work in or own the most prominent of Korea's two-tier system of commerce.[3] They are either in the large, dominant businesses or own the small to medium ones. Large business groups known as *chaebols* control the bulk of the Korean economy. As private corporations, they promote each other's efforts at entrepreneurship and global competitiveness. Although their production and marketing strategies may differ from corporation to corporation, their overall track record is impressive enough to put several of them into the *Fortune* International 500 list. These corporations have had Korean government sanction and endorsement.

But if the chaebol can provide unity and strength, it can also produce some negative factors. A powerful chaebol can put pressure on banks to meet its needs for risky loans; even government agencies can be made to show favoritism or provide subsidies for a chaebol with important directors. Sometimes this proves to be disastrous, as in the situation in 1987 when the Korean government wrote off $1.36 billion in debt owed to it by four chaebols it was forced to dissolve. The government also had to reschedule 5.83 trillion Korean won owed by other chaebols, so that they could have an extra thirty years to pay off the debt.

Naturally, the publicity associated with such government bailouts only works to confuse the populace regarding the financial stability of the chaebols. According to its 1987 financial report, the Daewoo Corporation of Korea lost 69.4 billion Korean won. Workers, however, were not convinced of the problem, so they went on strike demanding a 55 percent increase in wages. Such demonstrations have caused the Korean government to reexamine its stance on supporting financially troubled chaebols. In March 1989 the Ministry of Trade and Industry worked out plans to reschedule Daewoo's 250 billion won debt with new loans totalling 150 billion won. Koreans worry that they will pay this bill with increased taxes.[4]

As private corporations chaebols promote entrepreneurship and competition. While their strategies differ, they are all powerful entities to consider either as competitors to any export venture or as partners in them (Table 3.1). Critics express concern over them. Often these conglomerates operate with favoritism, alliances with banks, government subsidies, and government bailouts. Yet they have their supporters. These companies have brought Korea to where it is; they provide jobs for many Koreans. Their ascendancy parallels the Olympic Showcase, partly because they are one and the same. These large corporations contribute to the high standard of living. Yet they also compete with any American imported products. As such their influence is both positive and negative, depending upon the viewpoint.

Table 3.1
The 1988 Eleven Largest Korean Corporations

RANK KOREAN	INTERN'L 500	COMPANIES	SALES MILLIONS	NET INCOME MILLIONS	ASSETS MILLIONS	EMPLOYEES NUMBER
1	20	SAMSUNG	$21,053.5	$249.3	$14,558.7	$160,596
2	32	LUCKY-GOLDSTAR	14,422.3	180.7	10,268.5	88,403
3	35	DAEWOO	13,437.9	36.8	19,680.8	94,888
4	90	SUNKYONG	6,781.6	91.0	3.521.1	17,985
5	153	SSANGYONG	4,582.7	74.5	4,741.7	16,870
6	181	KOREA EXPLOSIVES	3,563.8	33.9	3,505.9	18,291
7	186	POHANG IRON & STEEL	3,533.2	85.1	6,457.1	19,329
8	191	HYUNDAI MOTOR	3,437.4	72.3	2,335.2	29,000
9	206	HYOSUNG	3,257.8	58.8	2,276.2	24,000
10	225	HYUNDAI HEAVY INDUSTRIES	2,964.5	19.3	3,291.3	48,200
11	430	DOOSAN	1,478.2	35.0	1,517.8	14,793

Source: *Fortune*, August 1, 1988.

ENTREPRENEURS IN KOREA AND THE UNITED STATES

Both the United States and Korea value business entrepreneurs. Both countries encourage business ventures, so it is not surprising to learn about risk takers like Art Fry and Sang-Sik Wee.

Art works for 3M and leads the church choir. On Sundays his markings in hymnals, loosely placed between the pages, often fell out. He solved the problem by using an adhesive developed in the 3M lab. The product is "temporarily" permanent and works for marking hymns on office memos (Post-it Notes).

Sang-Sik is one of 3,500 furniture shop owners. Unless someone is especially innovative, that Korean industry is bleak. But this president firmly believed Borneo International Furniture could compete internationally. With a design for function, durability, and quality, he developed overseas markets and made it big.

When asked what motivated them, Art Fry said: "Over the years, 3M has been extremely careful to develop a remarkable habitat for its creative people. At 3M, each division is run as a separate company with its own profit and loss statement."[5] Sang-Sik Wee said: "I firmly believed in success to begin with, since I had confidence in all the products we put the BIF Korea label on."[6]

"As an inventor," Fry said, "developing a successful new product is about as close as you can come to achieving immortality."[7] With sixteen franchise showcases and seven retail stores in California, Wee profited $20 million (1987).[8]

In Korea the government pursues aggressive and talented entrepreneurs who want to expand their businesses. Koreans, like their counterparts in the United States, value those business executives who are the key players in economic growth.

"They are the resource converters, acting and re-acting to the dynamic and volatile domestic and international environment," says Professor Chang. Not all of them succeed in the sense that Art Fry or Sang-Sik Wee did, but they are allowed to try. That's what is important to Korea, trying. Some barely succeed; others greatly prosper.

"Several are quite successful and have established giant enterprises called *chaebol*, which can be translated as conglomerates," according to Chang. In Korea, as in the United States, successful individuals actually depend on others who value them. In Korea entrepreneurs depend on three institutions: "Korean management system, relationships of family, alumni, region, and the government relations to business are critically important."[9]

Ju-Yung Chung founded Hyundai group. Now his seven sons, known as the seven princes, are quite influential. Five of his sons are now managers of their own divisions. Byung-Chul Lee founded Samsung group. The founder's son, In-Hoi Goo, founded Lucky-Goldstar group. His other son, Ja-Kyung Goo, is now the senior executive. In the Miwon group only family members are considered worthy of key positions. What works for Korean families works for outsiders in other relations as well.

These companies recruit from similar universities. In a Confucius society education is more than getting a degree. It includes membership in the alumni groups and networks of associations. The Daewoo group has recruited nine of its key executives from Kyunggi High School. Seoul National University, the highest status university, counts among its alumni the largest percentage of executives in the best chaebols. Over 84 percent of Korean executives come from the Seoul National, Yonsei, and Korea universities.

Regional factors are also valued. Koreans make special places for people from their hometowns. Even government ties remain quite valuable to Korean enterprises. Many of these large firms have recruited executives from the government: ruling party, National Assembly, Economic

Table 3.2
The 1988 Largest Corporations by Country

COUNTRY	RANK	TOTAL NUMBER	LARGEST COMPANY
Japan	1	157	Toyota Motor
Britain	2	73	British Petroleum
W. Germany	3	54	Daimler-Benz
France	4	41	Renault
Canada	5	29	General Motors of Canada
Sweden	6	20	Volvo
Taiwan	7	13	Chinese Petroleum
Australia	8	12	Elders IXL
South Korea	9	11	Samsung

Source: *Fortune*, August 1, 1988.

Planning Board, and Ministry of Finance. These former government officials make the right connections and bring in the profits to the chaebol. Such associations—military experiences, hometown contacts, family members—extend throughout the Korean culture, which is a tightly connected and rigidly controlled society.

INTERNATIONAL 500

At present the chaebols seem like a force to be reckoned with. Four Korean companies rank in the top 100 of the *Fortune* International 500 list. Ten Korean companies rank in the upper 50 percent of the list. Statistically though, Korea's chaebols appear only as a noticeable element compared with Great Britain and Japan.

Compared with leading international companies of the world (Table 3.2), the chaebols are small. Nevertheless, their numbers are growing. The top ranked corporations represent a worldwide trend toward big business as shown in Table 3.2.).

The *Fortune* International 500 list includes companies from all industrial nations of the world, except U.S. companies. Korea has 11 entries, while Japan dominates the list (157) even over Britain (73). Germany is not far behind with 54 of the largest companies, then France (41), Canada (29), Sweden (20), Taiwan (13), and Australia (12). Mr. Ju-Yung Chung, Chairman of Hyundai Business Group and Chairman of the Federation of Korean Industries, expressed this view: "Large Korean corporations competing with corporations of the United States, Japan and other advanced countries, are nothing but the world economy's kindergarten children in terms of sales and profits."[10] That may be true, but these children are growing up fast. They influence increased consumer demand. Their exports have also been the major driving force behind Korea's economic success. The export volume for the 1962–87 period rose 827 times, from $55 million to $46.2 billion, which is a growth rate averaged at 31.6 percent. Imports also increased 90 times from $0.42 billion to $37.9 billion.

THE STEADY CLIMB

Koreans work at international success. Six Korean firms number among the $17 billion or larger corporations. The five largest chaebols listed in Table 3.1 had sales of over $62 billion (1988). These five conglomerates accounted for almost a third of the gross output for Korea. They began in steel, shipbuilding, and textiles but diversified into electronics, computers, service activities, and construction. Now they have over 600 affiliates operating overseas.

Scholars note that chaebols invest heavily in developing countries. Economists say that about 40 percent of Korea's federal development investments (FDI) outflows go to developing countries. Koreans used their community movement, much as they did the Olympics, to showcase economic accomplishments. Dignitaries were regularly invited to Korea to observe community development programs. Now Koreans go to other countries to spread their technical know how. Among the largest recipients are Indonesia, Saudi Arabia, Pakistan, and Malaysia. The objective of over half the projects is to import raw materials and petroleum back into Korea.

These giants invest as a way of accessing natural resources. It makes sense considering that Korea has few such resources. They import raw materials, then export them back to third world countries. With rising productivity and wages at home, Koreans can also take advantage of lower labor costs abroad. The Korean Development Corporation gives loans to domestic businesses wanting overseas expansion. Since most overseas manufacturing projects require investments of less than $2 million, these firms venture out short distances from their home base. Asia accounts for more than half of the projects.

Korea's manufacturing investments to its neighbors are carefully orchestrated toward labor-intensive or technologically standardized products (textiles, unsophisticated product lines of electric and electronic appliances). This pattern served Japan, as it now does Korea. Some firms even transfer technologies they originally acquired from developed market economies. They adapt them to less industrialized countries.

These strategies account for Washington's hesitation to give technological license for sophisticated military hardware. Such weapons could possibly end up in developing countries. Already the Thais manufacture and assemble Korean semiautomatic weapons originally copied from Japanese and European models. Dae Dong Corporation formed joint ventures with Thai partners to product diesel engines. Other companies used technology acquired from Japanese partners to establish plants for assembling electric meters.

This international strategy works. Why should the ROKG interfere? Monitoring has, therefore, been limited. After all, these industrial engines drive the financial and cultural advances of Korea. Even with the recent pressure to redistribute income domestically, the ROKG can't easily harness these "wild tigers." The situation is similar to an elderly couple being supported by a high-spirited child. They would like to discipline him, but they are afraid that he might retaliate by cutting off their support funds. So about all they try to do is coax him in the right direction, without, at the same time, being too critical.

Economic analysts believe outside pressures will ultimately bring chaebols into check. Already numerous countries pressure Korea to liberalize markets. Too much pressure could disrupt the chaebols' privileged status. The law of supply and demand would create fairer price competitions for trading partners internally.

In 1985 Canada began exporting to Korea. Its volume was less than 2 percent of Korea's total imports. Nevertheless, once in, Canada gained amazing momentum, and eighteen months later it was doing $709 million of annual business with Korea.

The ground swell for the Olympics, like trade with Canada, began in 1985–86 (Table 3.3). Those years marked the rapid change of Korean imports by volume and country. Japan was able to position herself quite well (1985, $7.56 billion) and she consistently (1986, $10.87 billion) increased market share. By contrast the United States shows slight increases during this period (1985, $6.49 billion; 1986, $6.55 billion). But these countries were not the only ones getting in on the act. Others (Table 3.3) included Malaysia, West Germany, Australia, Indonesia, Canada, U.A.E., France, Oman, Ecuador, the United Kingdom, and Saudi Arabia.

Total imports remained constant ($31.46 billion, 1985 versus $31.58 billion, 1986). What changed dramatically were Japanese export volumes. They seized more of the market share.

A STRUGGLING CULTURE

Those at the Olympics observed a rugged, yet beautiful country, a quaint place, yet one gaining in sophistication. For Koreans to continue

Table 3.3
Imports by Country

Rank	1985 ($ mil., %)			1986 ($ mil., %)		
	Country	Volume	Comp Ratio	Country	Volume	Comp Ratio
1	Japan	7,560	24.3	Japan	10,869	34.4
2	U.S.	6,489	20.3	U.S.	6,545	20.7
3	Malaysia	1,234	4.0	West Germany	1,216	3.8
4	Australia	1,116	3.6	Australia	1,080	3.4
5	West Germany	979	3.1	Malaysia	902	2.9
6	Indonesia	669	2.1	Canada	709	2.2
7	U.A.E	664	2.1	France	706	2.2
8	Oman	661	2.1	Saudi Arabia	635	2.0
9	Ecuador	653	2.1	United Kingdom	454	1.4
10	Saudi Arabia	640	2.1	Oman	440	1.4
	Subtotal	20,665	65.8	Subtotal	23,556	74.4
	Total Imports	31,136	100.0	Total Imports	31,584	100.0

their twentieth-century advancement, however, they must purchase both the natural resources they lack and the technology they need.

The Korean peninsula borders Manchuria and Eastern Siberia on the north and extends southward to within 70 miles of Japan. It's a tiny peninsula, just 1,000 miles from either Beijing or Tokyo. For centuries Korea's culture depended upon China, then Japan, now the United States. This small East Asian country, roughly equivalent in size to Great Britain, has a strange mix of East and West. Since 1945 the peninsula remains divided into two zones—The Republic of Korea and North Korea—with 5,400 miles of coastline. Three seas encompass the Korean peninsula: the Sea of Japan eastward, the narrow Korean Straits southward, and the Yellow Sea westward.

Hills and scenic mountains extend down the east coast, covering 70 percent of the land. Because of the mountainous terrain, the rivers and hills give the impression of massiveness and grandeur that has earned the region the nickname "Switzerland of Asia."

In rural areas thatch roofed houses are still prevalent. Mud brick walls may appear inadequate for the cold winter temperature; however, centuries ago Koreans discovered radiant heating systems. Through a series of vents beneath the floor, the stone floor is kept warm and comfortable, but not without toil. The warm house—along with fields of rice, vegetables, and fresh fruit—give evidence of the farmer's hard work. Yet old images are giving way to new ones, especially as Koreans record higher standards of living and greater selections of imported goods and technology.

As stated earlier, by the year 2000 per capita average income should be around $10,000. Modern Koreans hope to leverage this capital into homes with long-term mortgages and consumer credit. They are rapidly moving toward a capitalistic, enterprising way of life. In Itaewon, a famous shopping area of Seoul, buyers find an unusual mix of Eastern and Western cultures and old and new life styles. You can buy footballs or Japanese sake in a *karoke* or sing-along bar, or American Miller Lite as you listen to Grand Ole Opry, Western-style music. Growing up for Koreans is not easy. Korea blends East and West, thus Korean identities are blurred. Foreign suppliers import merchandise, making affluence a Korean way of life. But what about jobs?

A win-win scenario works best if American companies hire local Koreans as their employees. Universal Data Systems of Alabama has hired Korean nationals to serve as distributors, negotiators, and general troubleshooters. George R. Frumbles, UDS President, claims it has saved the company years of time in cutting red tape. It also has created a lot of good will.

Besides, "you have to work through nationals," he says. "If you send U.S. folks into a foreign country, you have to expect it will take a couple of years for them to find their way around. Instead, you have to find people who are embedded in the local economy." This process speeds everything up.

Frumbles believes in any process that accelerates profits. Yet he's realistic enough to know that all the flanks of exporting must still be covered, especially in Korea. That is why he advises exporters to "carefully select distributors [who] help companies cope with trade barriers and the special requirements of highly monopolized postal, telephone, and telegraph companies, and who give preferences for locally manufactured products."

But where do you find those distributors? And where do you hire locals as representatives? Where do you locate these Koreans? These are good questions. One possible answer comes from Warren, Michigan, and the Menlo Tools Company (MTC) located there. President Frank M. Kastelic, Jr., uses the services of the U.S. Department of Commerce—Trade Opportunities Program (TOP). TOP provides sales leads of overseas firms seeking to buy or represent U.S. products; these leads are available electronically to the private sector. The Agent/Distributor Service, a customized search for interested and qualified foreign representatives, will identify up to six foreign prospects who examined the firm's literature and expressed some interest in the product or services it offers.

Those who use this service seem satisfied. MTC exports to forty-seven countries, including Korea. Their volume for exporting comprises 10 to 20 percent of their total revenues. Their sales strategies epitomize what it means to reevaluate company resources and to consider exporting to Korea.

Korea was a sport's showcase during the 1988 Olympics. "Hodori," the tiger mascot of Seoul Olympics, exudes confidence. So do the Koreans. For after serving as the site of the games of the 24th Olympiad, the Koreans are now planning new international economic games. Now Korea's strategy is to globalize its own domestic markets, thereby increasing trade bilaterally. It makes sense. For Korea to continue its exporting strategy, bilateral policies are essential. With current appreciation of the won (15 percent increase annually), it's a good time both for Koreans to invest outside their country and for Americans to export to it.

During the 1990s Korea is destined to be a global business showcase. It will continue to export goods. But one practice is bound to change. The social order of international trade demands, through its norms of reciprocity, fair play from one country to another. For U.S. exporters, it is a chance to export more products and services to Korea, even as they export liberally and without tariff constraints to the United States. For Koreans, it is a chance to gain greater respect and admiration for their accomplishments.

But this time more people than those representing the 161 nations of the last Olympics will be watching Korea. More will watch the Koreans as they strive to win both international profits from increased export trade and bilateral respect from fair trade practices. As the international game of trade is played fairly, say with compliance to the General Agreement on Tariffs and Trade (GATT), their success is surely to be long term. The norms of reciprocity work in practice, not just in theory.

NOTES

1. Keiko Hagihara Bang, "A New Era at the Asian Development Bank," *Korea Business World*, May 5, 1989, 64.

2. Bang, 64.

3. While still depending on these large conglomerates, ROKG is beginning to shift its policies toward the small to medium sized companies. Two policies—decentralization and localization—are designed for this purpose. Such policies have implications for U.S. exporters seeking new markets. See Chapter 5 for details.

4. "Critical Condition," *Korean Business World*, May 5, 1989, 46–47.

5. "Lessons from a Successful Entrepreneur," *The Journal of Business Strategy* (March/April 1988):20–25.

6. Kwang-Hee Lee, "Fledgling Furniture Makers Look to Better Days Ahead," *Korea Business World*, November 1986, 71–73.

7. "Lessons," 23.

8. Lee, 72.

9. Chan-Sup Chang, "Chaebols," *Business Horizons* (March/April 1988):51–57.

10. Frederick Hiroshi Katayama and William Bellis, "The International 500," *Fortune*, August 1, 1988, D7–D37.

4

An Export Checklist

Good checklists help us verify, compare, and order relevant issues. They also sensitize us to requirements, procedures, and actions. Such lists are safeguards against neglecting either critical stages in a long process of events or some timely resource readily available but easily overlooked.

In evaluating the Korean market for particular products, decision makers must make value judgments: "The Korean market is good for International Incorporated because. . . ." Or it could be the opposite evaluation: "Korea is a poor investment climate for us right now." Executives need to validate their decisions to export to Korea. Superiors use documentation to justify decisions. Making judgments is something business executives do every day. They judge people's performance, policies, world events, and yes, executives even judge lists against their experience.

How do you judge the claim "exporting to Korea is profitable"? It hinges on the assumption that profits are to be made. Yet that assumption should first be tested against a set of valid criteria. To use them increases chances of exporting profits; to neglect them decreases them.

Stories about small export firms that succeed sometimes surprise us. Eleven years ago, a group of graduate students did something quite incredible. They, along with their professors and trade specialists, working with Baker Instrument (Fort Collins, Colorado), developed a plan for exporting high-voltage test equipment. "We offered good service. We did what we said we were going to do," said Tom Baker, Chairman of the Board. As practical business executives, they accepted this philosophy as a guide for exporting ever since that first attempt. They're satisfied with the result. They now export to seventeen countries. That volume, increasing 300 percent every five years, represents 35 percent of their profits.

One of the graduate students working with Baker was David Schump. Dave is now the President of this Colorado exporting firm, which won the Governor's Excellence in Exporting Award.

KOREAN IMPORT PROCEDURES

Practitioners know that getting the product into Korea itself is only the first step. Fortunately, we do have a Korean checklist for the established importing procedures. Figure 4.1 shows The Chart of Import Procedures. To begin the process, exporters must have import contracts with a Korean trading agent. After signing contract agreements, suppliers request permission to import any items currently restricted by ROKG. They also apply for the import license as they complete arrangements for sales and transportation. Next they establish a letter of credit (L/C) through a foreign exchange bank. After arranging payments, exporters must obtain a receipt of transport documents before shipping the goods. Finally, they ship or mail the goods to Korea. Once on Korean shores, the goods go through customs. All of these steps are shown in Figure 4.1.[1]

U.S. exporters have trouble with the Harmonized System (HS), just as they did the Customs Cooperation Council Nomenclature (CCCN). Both are similar to the Brussels Tariff Nomenclature (BTN). Neither classifications fully specified all items. In these cases item customs classifications are shown in neither the tariff schedules nor the dutiable status of goods. So if U.S. exporters have these items or questions about procedures, they should attach them on the written application to the Collector of Customs (Seoul). They must do that before advance shipments. It's not mandatory that samples go with the application. Should this be impractical, then photographs, specifications, and descriptions should be used. It would also be prudent to forward these with the export applications.

Figure 4.1
The Chart of Import Procedures

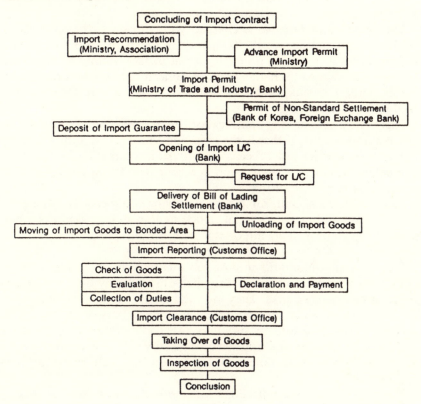

Conclusion of Contract

Export requirements are changing, yet restricted imports, reduced in scope, still exist. Requirements come from the Foreign Trade Law, the Foreign Exchange Control Law, and the Tariff Law with reference to the "Export & Import Notice" issued by the Ministry of Trade and Industry (M.T.I.).

Items can be exported to Korea unless specifically prohibited and/or the method of payment contradicts the Foreign Exchange Control Law (FECL). The purpose of this act was to control foreign exchange for Korea and other foreign entities. Through the FECL, Koreans gained three economic advantages. First, they gained an equilibrium in the balance of payments position. Second, they obtained greater stability for the value of their domestic currency. And third, they achieved an effective utilization of foreign exchange currency.

The Ministry of Finance is charged with foreign exchange control, subject to cabinet approval. Its agency is the Bank of Korea, which executes that function in principle, if not in fact. Acting with the authority of the Korea Exchange Bank, American banks—the Chase Manhattan Bank, Citibank, N.A., and Bank of America—are authorized to deal in foreign exchange.

Import Recommendation. Some export items could be on Korea's restricted imports list. If that is the case, the M.T.I. must authorize their entry. The exporter must receive an import recommendation from the competent authority or association in accord with the applicable import procedures before exporting.

Some items must conform to special public announcement. Again the M.T.I. must authorize a special notice to that effect. This does not, however, include a freely importable item, since no recommendation is required.

Import License. Nontariff import controls include an import license, obtainable from the Korea Exchange Bank or from any one of the Class A foreign exchange banks. They are valid for six months. Such licenses are required for every transaction, even before letters of credit may be opened in favor of foreign suppliers. All commodities may be freely imported unless they are included on a negative list. Former restrictions are now liberalized. In other words, 90 percent of all import licenses will be granted.

Remember that all applications for import licenses must be accompanied by the firm's offers issued by a foreign supplier. In most cases that comes through the supplier's qualified local agent. Such pro forma invoices are then checked by agents to see whether the offer prices exceed the maximum import prices set by ROKG. Only firms that are registered as foreign traders are eligible to receive import licenses.

Those who import capital goods approved under the FCIA are required neither to obtain a trader's license nor an import license. In the case of counter trade, an import license must be obtained directly from the M.T.I. In all cases the president of the foreign exchange bank issues an import license.

Other than in those cases, the actual importation does require licenses. Entities wanting to perform export or import activities in Korea must, by law, obtain an export-import license (trader's license). Such an applicant must: (1) have paid-in capital of more than 100 million won and (2) receive U.S. $300,000 worth of export letters of credit.

This license still has restrictions. To retain this trader's license, holders must continue to record U.S. $1 million of exports each year, except for the first calendar year the license is obtained. Joint-venture companies approved under the Foreign Capital Inducement Act (FCIA) have to obtain a trader's license for either the export of joint-venture products or the import of raw materials used to manufacture those products. Moreover, they do not have to meet import status maintenance requirements.

U.S. suppliers, as foreign firms, may arrange for sales and transportation of needed overseas materials. But only joint venture companies can be legally established in Korea. This provides for a supply agreement between the foreign company and a Korean one. Such supply agreements are subject to the Fair Trade Committee, especially if the terms exceed one year.

A growing number of manufacturing firms export their products and are also registered traders. "Offer agents" for foreign suppliers must have paid-in capital of not less than 10 million won (approximately $14,700, 1989). They submit their agency agreements to the Ministry of Trade and Industry for registration. To remain qualified, registered offer agents must earn a minimum of $30,000 in annual sales commissions.

Establishment of Letter of Credit. Once foreign importers receive their import licenses, they must immediately establish letters of credit. Usually the time period is specified by a foreign exchange bank. U.S. suppliers or Korean importers should carefully arrange the L/C to match the same information as recorded on the import authorization form.

The amount of the L/C neither exceeds the authorized amount nor alters the type of currency, as indicated on the import authorization form. Such deviations would only delay exports.

There are three methods of payment. First is the standard method:

- Import against a general L/C.
- Import on D/P (document against payment).
- Deliver import commodities in third countries.
- Pay part of import settlement after performance test.

A second method is the nonstandard settlement. To use this type of payment, exporters must have an advance permit from the Ministry of Trade and Industry. And finally, a third method is to import on a deferred payment basis through either a Usance L/C, D/A (document against acceptance), or limited raw materials for export and capital goods (180-day limit).

Receipt of Transport Documents. U.S. exporters next obtain receipts of transport documents. To ship the goods, they must comply with the conditions of the L/C. After receiving the L/C, the foreign exporter negotiates with the exporter's bank a documentary bill, issued only after the exporters use the transport documents as security.

The responsibilities now shift to the bank used by the exporter. That bank next sends the transport documents to the bank that issued the L/C. The "L/C opening bank" verifies that the conditions of the transport documents are consistent with the ones of the L/C. This bank settles the account of the import transaction and transfers the transport documents to the Korean importers.

The importers then submit the bill of lading (B/L) to the shipping company and collect the importer freight. If, however, the freight has arrived without the transport documents, importers can still get the freight. Importers may take special action. After receiving a letter of guarantee (L/G, prepared under fixed conditions) from the importer's bank, the importers may present this L/G to the shipping company and receive the freight in advance.

Three documents are required for nearly all surface shipments to Korea: (1) a full set of clean, on board, ocean bills of lading, made out to an exchange bank designated by the importer; (2) a marine insurance policy or certificate, in duplicate, endorsed in the bank for 110 percent of the invoice value (for CIF shipments); and (3) signed commercial invoice in quintuplicate and packing list in duplicate. Duplicate copies (certificate of origin), however, are required only for shipments of certain selected goods. Such certificates are issued by a Korean Consulate and show the marks, numbers, commodity descriptions, quantities, prices, and the country of origin. Exporters should remember that before importers open letters of credit, they must possess notarized pro forma invoices legalized by Korean Consulates. The exception is for pro forma invoices that have been issued to importers by an authorized local agent of foreign suppliers.

Exporters are urged to use extreme care in preparing their shipping documentation. Reshipments (say to correct unessential shipments on an order) may result in double payment of customs duties and additional delays. To minimize delays in the clearance of livestock imports, it is also advisable to obtain certain quarantine certificates issued by appropriate Korean governmental agencies.

Customs Clearance. One final step has to do with customs and clearance. After having either the receipt of transport documents or the letter of guarantee, the importers unload the imported freight from the ship. They then place it in a bonded area, while they submit a report of imports to the superintendent of the customhouse. Note that customs clearance reports are prepared only by a consignee (importer) who employs a certified customs specialist or a certified customs clearance corporation.

The ROKG designated two free export zones for the bonded processing of imported materials into finished goods for export. The free export zones are specially established industrial areas where foreign invested firms can manufacture, assemble, or process export products. Such firms can use freely imported, tax-free raw materials or semifinished goods.

Also provided here are generous tax incentives for foreign investments. The ROKG constructs various facilities, including plant sites or factory buildings, for sale or lease to initial occupant industries. The Masan Free Export Zone (1971) is located near Pusan. Located on the Western coast is the Iri Free Export Zone (1975), a place where Koreans actively recruit for foreign occupants.

After the receipt of this import report, the customhouse inspector verifies the contents. The contents must correspond to the descriptions found in the import authorization form. This confirms to the inspector that the documentation is in order. The inspector then calculates the customs charges and levies the appropriate tariffs. The inspector presents an import of approval to those so designated. Now the imported merchandise may be removed from the bonded area and transported to another destination.

STRATEGIC EVALUATION CRITERIA

Experienced exporters recognize two strategies. First, they know that what happens between international organizations (suppliers, importers, distributors) affects profits. Second, they also know that the process of evaluation within their particular organization is equally important. To evaluate firms' export capacities, exporters should evaluate business issues.

Professor Michael Porter of Harvard evaluates marketing strategies for major U.S. industries. He tackles the tough economic, global issues exporting managers face. He combines timely research with practical suggestions. After conducting extensive research on corporate strategies of thirty-three large U.S. companies, he concluded that corporate survival depends upon understanding "what good corporate strategy is."[2]

Two ideas might assist export managers. Porter's first idea is about the concept of corporate strategy; his second one concerns criteria for evaluation. Corporate strategy is a daring attempt to gain a competitive edge. Corporate executives determine strategies, but business units implement them. These units give the corporation its competitive advantage. According to Porter, (1) competition begins at the business unit, not anywhere else, and (2) diversification adds costs and constraints to business units, which must be absorbed, not ignored.

Now let's turn to Porter's checklist. Before shipping products, exporters should examine the conditions that make such decisions financially acceptable. Porter recommends three tests: (1) The attractiveness test: Korea either has need of or would benefit from certain U.S. products. (2) The cost-of-entry test: The cost of Korean market entry does not "capitalize all or too much of the future profits." Do expenditures of money and staff make exporting efforts worth it? (3) The better-off test: Would the firm be better if this venture were successfully implemented?

This chapter on an export checklist is designed to provide valuable information on both exporting procedures to Korea and criteria for evaluating marketing strategies. Once Korean markets were unattractive because of the high cost of entry (high dollar versus low won, high tariffs, import restrictions). The country market did not pass the better-off test. Many obstacles have been eliminated; others are scheduled for elimination.

Having discussed the Korean import procedures and strategic evaluation criteria, let's see how marketing fits with CEOs. It's a good idea to not misjudge your CEO's actual commitment or to overrate your ability to avoid the common export mistakes.

CEO's CHECKLIST OF ACTION

Exporting requires realistic assessments. Professor Porter encourages his corporate clients to identify interrelations among business units, select the core business activity of joint ventures, create a horizontal mechanism to facilitate this core, pursue diversity in a shared capacity, pursue the transfer of skills, restructure the operations, if needed, and reward those involved.[3]

Based on findings from 236 U.S. firms, two marketing professors discovered how low marketing professionals rate. They are not fully appreciated. Most CEOs give more attention to other functions than they do to international marketing. Among respondents were CEOs whose overseas markets generate one-half of their revenues (Texaco and Ford), or 40 percent (Hewlett-Packard and Norton), or a fourth of their total sales volume (1,000 large U.S. firms).

As important as market analysis may seem for America to remain internationally competitive, that factor ranked low on CEOs' checklists. Their highest priority items were corporate growth and profits, factors that CEOs predict won't change in the future. These CEOs gave less time to market analysis than to all other executive functions: financial planning, product development, personnel, R&D, customer relations, labor relations, and production manufacturing. Experts claim that these eight factors directly affect American competitiveness. Since marketing ranks the lowest among those CEOs surveyed, the researchers expressed concern: "Our findings may indicate some serious roadblocks to substantial improvement of American global performance."[4]

Evidently CEOs' commitments to international markets give way to other, more pressing, matters. This seeming lack of CEO involvement means that the marketing department's analysis is all the more weighty. It becomes useful not only in market analysis but also, and more importantly, in implementing the market procedures once decisions are made.

THE TEN MOST COMMON MISTAKES OF EXPORTERS

Two final checklists conclude this chapter. These are, first, the ten most common mistakes of potential exporters and second, the best, most reliable resource people to contact for particular questions about exporting to Korea.[5]

1. Failure to obtain a qualified export counsel and to develop a master international marketing plan before starting an export business. *Business America* lists guides for export assistance (Subscriptions $40/year: Superintendent of Documents, U.S. Government Printing Office, Washington, DC 20402).

Assistance is available from The International Trade Administration or its offices: Overseas Posts, Country Desk Officers, Trade Development Industry Officers, Export Trading Companies, Travel and Tourism. There are also resources from other Commerce Export Services: Export Licensing Assistance, Foreign Requirements for U.S. Products and Services, Minority Business Development, Foreign Metric Regulations, Fisher Product Exports. Other resources include:

a. U.S. Export-Import Bank, 811 Vermont Avenue, N.W., Room 1203, Washington, DC 20571 (Export Credit Insurance, Working Capital Guarantee, Direct and Intermediary Loans, Guarantees, Small Business Advisory Service, and Briefing Programs). Use for small business export loans.

b. Small Business Administration, 1441 L Street, N.W., Washington, DC 20416 (Export Counseling, Small Business Institutes, Contact Programs, Export Training, Financial Assistance, Legal Advice, and Regional Offices).

c. Department of Agriculture—Foreign Agricultural Service, Washington, DC 20250. Use to strengthen farm exports to Korea.

d. Trade Policy—The U.S. Trade Representative is in the Executive Office of the President, 600 17th Street N.W., Room 100, Washington, DC 20506. This staff of international experts represents the U.S. at the GATT. Exporters can register trade complaints. This gives business executives considerable political leverage, but only if unfair practices did, indeed, occur.

2. Insufficient commitment by top management to overcome the initial difficulties and financial requirements of exporting. International markets, more than domestic ones, require long-range goals.

3. Insufficient care in selecting overseas distributors. Export Services in Commerce can help on these matters: export counseling, agent services, commercial news, comparison shopping, foreign buyer programs, trade opportunities, world traders data, trade fairs, and matchmaker events.

4. Chasing overseas orders instead of establishing a basis for profitable operations and orderly growth. Distributors only support those who give them incentives; therefore, give Korean distributors training on key features of products or services. Because of this added effort, experts recommend that firms concentrate on a few geographical regions at a time.

5. Neglecting export business when the U.S. market booms. This is especially problematic if exporting becomes a way out of the slump.

6. Failure to treat international distributors as equals with domestic counterparts. This applies to advertising campaigns, discount offers, sales incentives programs, special credit terms programs, warranty offers. A practice of discriminating will sap the vitality of any overseas efforts.

7. Unwillingness to modify products to meet regulations or cultural references. The Korean Bureau of Standards (KBS) reports to both the Industrial Advancement Administration and the Ministry of Trade and Industry. As a signer of the International Agreement on Technical Barriers to Trade (popularly known as the Standards Code), Korea is responsible for notifying the Secretariat in Geneva of any proposed regulations that might have an adverse impact on trade. KBS now has a certification program with the mark "KS" for Korean Standards.

8. Failure to print services, sales, and warranty messages in locally understood languages. Even though many Koreans can read English, it is still better to translate product labels and instructions directly into the Korean language. Since Koreans now live in just about every major city in the United States, it should not be too difficult to find Korean residents to do this.

9. Failure to consider the services of an export management company (EMC). If firms cannot afford their own export department, then experts recommend using an EMC. These organizations act as the export department for several manufacturers of noncompetitive products. They solicit and transact business in the name of the manufacturers they represent for a commission, salary, or retainer plus commission. Many EMCs carry not only their own financing but also a full line of services such as translating materials into Korean.

10. Failure to consider licensing or joint-venture agreements here or there. Korea's Pohang Iron and Steel and U.S. Steel have a California plant and market. Many such ventures exist in Korea. Yet Korea still has import restrictions on some items, such as agricultural products and

foods, as well as insufficient staff in some areas and limited product lines. These barriers are coming down as Korea seeks partners in the automotive industry, textiles, electronics, and computers. Don't dismiss export opportunities to Korea. Licensing and joint ventures may be an alternative exporting plan. For more information, contact the Korean Government, private economic organizations, Offer Agency Association, market research agencies, or business consultants.

NOTES

1. *A Guide to the Korean Import Market* (Seoul: KOTRA, 1989), 55–57.

2. Michael E. Porter, "From Competitive Advantage to Corporate Strategy," *Harvard Business Review* 45 (1987):43–59.

3. Porter, 58–59.

4. Richard T. Hise and S. W. McDaniel, "American Competitiveness and the CEO—Who's Minding the Shop?" *Sloan Management Review* 29 (1988):49–55.

5. U.S. Department of Commerce, International Trade Administration, *A Basic Guide to Exporting* (Washington, D.C.: U.S. Government Printing Office, 1981), 84–85.

_____ **II**

Select These Products

5

Opportunities in Korea

This chapter marks a transition. So far we've focused on how firms evaluate their export capacities by using individualized marketing strategies. Success depends on key decision makers working together on two broad sets of variables—internal strengths and external opportunities. Now we will shift our attention to export products and government incentives. You'll learn about the Omnibus Trade and Competitiveness Act and import liberalization. You will also see how governments create conditions that reduce the likelihood of export failure, while at the same time increasing the probability of success.

SEIZING THE OPPORTUNITY

Opportunities must be seized with great vigor for two reasons. First, Korean economic growth in particular industries may not last. Second, it is through perseverance that exporters eliminate the possibilities of frustrating failures.

Finding your niche depends upon several factors: what is in the marketplace, what is evolving there, and how your company can adjust to market changes. Even with adequate planning, there is not enough time to seize all the opportunities. Scenarios and forecasting about Korea must be monitored. The competitive picture changes for particular market segments, especially in the international arena. International managers need indexes from which to plot changes.

After three years of negotiations with Korea officials, Goodyear was satisfied. Philip A. Spanninger, former Director of Technology and Venture Management for the Goodyear Tire and Rubber Company, successfully negotiated a $100 million project. To the negotiating team's credit, the proposed facility is to be wholly owned by the U.S. firm.

As the Korean economy expands, so do U.S. opportunities for large-scale projects. But cutting through the bureaucratic red tape and competing with foreign companies is not easy. It is one thing to know opportunities exist—nuclear power plants, fossil-fuel power plants, railroad constructions, telecommunications projects, water and sewage treatment facilities, solid waste disposal projects, airport expansions, subway lines expansions in Seoul and Pusan are all possible moneymakers. It is quite another to sign, as Goodyear did, a contract for increased participation.

This type of direct investment comes as a result of favorable opportunities. U.S. investments are on the rise. Presently they exceed $1 billion. The process of gaining approval for investments may not go as smoothly as U.S. firms expect because of the barriers of language, culture, distance, and trade laws. Those problems can be solved.

REDUCING THE RISK OF FAILURE

Exporting to South Korea carries fewer risks of failure because of new U.S. regulations and recent Korean policies. Markets look more attractive, as the possibility of failure declines. In cases of unfair trading practices, business executives now have alternatives. These minimize risks. If a company thinks it has experienced unfair trade practices, managers can now seek redress of their grievances under the provisions of the 1988 trade act ("Super 301").

Through the Omnibus Trade and Competitiveness Act of 1988 (P.L. 100–418), Congress will monitor the implementation of certain provisions, especially Section 301 regarding unfair foreign trade practices. Congress is primarily concerned about macroeconomic policies: policies that affect exchange rates, options for solving developing country debts, possible restrictions on foreign investment in the United States, and export promotion and controls.

Yet U.S. firms can assemble a trade weapon by citing and substantiating unfair trade practices. Countries with the most citations are "prioritized" under provisions of Section 301. Until now trading problems were handled individually on a commodity basis. Now the law strikes at the web of obstacles that hamper fair trade for U.S. firms. Once offending countries have been identified, they must institute policy changes over a three-year probationary period. Otherwise they suffer U.S. trade sanctions.

Among those countries already cited, Korea tops the list. Korea is mentioned in twenty-one petitions of grievance. That figure compares with seventeen for Japan, ten for India, eight for Taiwan, seven for Brazil, and five each for the European Community and Thailand. All together some forty-eight countries are listed as potential violators. Fortunately, Korea made many concessions and did not come under Super 301 sanctions for 1989.

But Super 301 did come under attack at the GATT's most recent council meeting. Virtually all members expressed concern. During the June 1989 meetings, U.S. Trade Representative Carla Hills said the United States did not agree with the conclusion that this procedure is retaliation. She said it characterized a negotiation process.

RESPONDING TO U.S. PRESSURE

Just as the U.S. government has reduced the risk of failure in Korea, so has the Korean. The ROKG has liberalized imports and reduced barriers for imports and investment. These changes have created favorable conditions for business success.

The ROKG has responded to U.S. concerns about closed markets and has taken actions. It has opened up new business opportunities not only encouraging trade but also promoting it. Here are some policies: (1) import liberalization, (2) tariff reduction, (3) foreign investment decontrol, (4) financial liberalization, (5) protection of intellectual property rights, and (6) an import source diversification policy.

These Korean policies come in batches. One set of Korean import policies—import liberalization, tariff reductions, the liberalization of foreign investment, financial changes—was designed to accommodate U.S. exporting requirements. Another set dealt with the red tape in getting import licenses. Import procedures were drastically reduced by a simplified approval format that takes applications thirty to forty days.

As of June 1988, the foreign direct investment in Korea, on an approval basis, totalled $5.3 billion. Of that amount U.S. direct investment ($1.5 billion) equalled 28.3 percent of the total amount. The ratio of liberalization extends to almost 94.7 percent (1988), a figure close to those found among other developing countries. Of the total 10,241 items in the classification system, only about 547 items do not receive automatic approval. ROKG has extended the projects for liberalization. Consequently new liberalization policies (1989–91) should reduce tariffs even more.

Exporters expressed concern about financing costs and protecting intellectual property. The Korean government responded to these complaints by enacting two policies, one on financial liberalization and one for the protection of intellectual property rights. The liberalization of the financial factors should be completed in 1990, when capital markets will be totally liberalized.

Under the revised Patent Act (July 1987), the law protects patents for eighteen years, not the old fifteen-year limit. This includes intellectual protection of product patents, computer software, copyrights, and trademarks. The Korean government provides protection for certain U.S. patents on a retroactive basis. The big issue is enforcement under provisions of the Universal Copyright Convention, the Geneva Phonogram Convention, and the World Intellectual Property Organization. Korea belongs to these organizations.

The import source diversification policy redresses the trade imbalance problems, which result from selling too much to the United States and buying too much from Japan. To attain a more balanced trade, Korea adopted import diversification. ROKG plans several strategies to restrict imports from Japan and encourage imports from U.S. firms. The Korean government requires that Japanese imports must be recommended by various trade associations. Next government authorities forced importers in the process of obtaining an import license application to shift buying sources from Japanese to U.S. firms. Finally, they requested importers to deposit 110 percent import guarantee money in advance.

Simultaneously, the government provides financial incentives for Korean companies both to buy U.S. products and to seek supplier relations. The Korean government raised special import funds amounting to $5 billion in 1988. Of this amount $3 billion was used to finance importers who buy raw materials and capital goods from the United States. The most favorable and lowest interest rates (10 percent) were for those Koreans complying with the policy. Usually such rates varied from 12 to 15 percent. Other invisible and indirect favors were given to those importers who switched. This included quick import license procedures and easier financing approval for other projects and so on. Government and trade organizations jointly selected the 335 transferable items. Finally, the Korean government and Korea Foreign Trade Association jointly sent buying missions to the United States between 1987 and 1990.

These Korean incentives, such as ROKG funding, suggest that this is the time and Korea is the place for exporting. Also to be considered are the favorable exchange rates for that region. The first comparison is the high yen and weak dollar. This condition is attractive to Korean importers. A survey of 199 leading Korean importers—those with 1986 total Japanese imports valued at $3 billion—revealed that imports could be shifted to U.S. suppliers. According to them, 285 of 335 items (85 percent) could be imported from the United States, not Japan.

The second favorable comparison is the strong won and weak dollar, a condition ideally suited for exporting. The Korean won has been going up continuously. In 1986, 860 won equalled one U.S. dollar. The 1989 rate, 680 won to the dollar, reflects both a 14 percent reevaluation and an acceleration of imported U.S. goods.

A third comparison is between current rates of inflation and possible rates of inflation. To restrain inflation—caused by an excess of foreign exchange reserve—the Korean government encourages an open-door policy of international markets. If Korea buys more U.S. goods and products, the threat of U.S. protectionism should ease. Because of the external factor of a trade imbalance, more Koreans are buying U.S. goods. That external factor is compounded by an internal one. Improved living standards are leading to demands for foreign-made quality products and services. Foreign exporters at the Olympic Games realized the demand for imports of foreign-made goods.

MATCHING COMMODITIES REQUIRES PLANNING

At a recent foundry exporting seminar, participants discussed the opportunities for exporting U.S. casting abroad. The American Foundry Society vice president Alvin Singleton, agreed that "exporting of casting is an idea whose time has come."[1] It does seem that small to medium sized businesses can be as profitable as large ones. According to experts, if global economic conditions remain stable, the dollar should be competitive internationally for some time. Given these assumptions, U.S. firms could take advantage of the opportunity to export profitably and to establish foreign market operations.

Nevertheless, Alvin Singleton qualifies his statement on exporting opportunities. "Devaluation is a plus, but that alone doesn't make exporting possible. Foundries must learn to export."[2] The climate is right for exports to Korea, but good planning is absolutely necessary. "It takes more than the devaluation of the dollar to make exporting work, but we made it work and so can you," said Robert Reesman, Vice President and General Manager of Auburn Foundry in Indiana. "The competition worldwide is not that awesome," he said. But this executive, like his counterpart, Singleton, warns firms about the lack of quality products. "The quality has to be there or you'll have problems," says Reesman. "If you have quality problems, don't ship overseas. If you have rejections, the freight on the returns will kill you."[3]

That planning begins by knowing about specific export products. One good export area is agriculture, a primary sector of commodities. In 1988, this sector grew by 9.8 percent due to the record crop of rice and grains.

Since the United States is the world' largest exporter of agricultural products, it is not surprising that Korea represents an attractive export market. The value of total agricultural exports for 1988 ($35.3 billion) overshadows what Korea purchased from the United States. But agricultural products sell quite well. Korea is the fifth largest importer of U.S. agriculture products. Korean purchases exceeded $1.2 billion (1987). This figure should increase because of two government actions—the liberalization of the ratio of imported agriculture products (80.2) and the gradual market expansion encouraged by government policies. Such policies, to include transferable import items from Japan, should increase that 1987 figure even more. Presently there are over 235 export items that belong to this category. If interested, the readers can obtain the 1986–87 tables to compare product line, volume, date, and source (primarily Japan and U.S.).

Basic food commodities produce an excellent output for some exporters. But the two biggest volumes are found in nonelectric machinery and electronics and electrical products.

As for electronics, U.S. exports to Korea represent about a third of those from Japan. In 1988, U.S. total exports to Korea figures $11.29 billion compared to $37.73 billion for Japan. Of that volume for Korea two sectors figure high—electronics and nonelectrical machinery. In 1988 the total export volume of machinery and electronics exceeded $5.9 billion and $5.4 billion, respectively. Of these amounts, U.S. firms exported $1.4 billion of machinery and $1.2 billion of electronic components. That meant that the U.S. share projected for the full year would be $2.6 billion (17.3 percent) for these two sectors. In 1988 the manufacturing sector posted a 13.9 percent volume increase over figures for 1987. During that same period, the electronics industry recorded a 12.6 percent increase. It is evident that the Republic of (South) Korea has moved to establish both the electronics and aerospace industries.

ELECTRONICS COMPONENTS

In 1989 the American Electronics Association (AEA) planned to name Korea as a "Super 301" country as defined by U.S. law. Through the Omnibus Trade and Competitiveness Act of 1988, Congress monitors Section 301 provisions regarding unfair foreign practices abroad. AEA did not have to make that appeal. Because of the responsiveness of the Korean electronics industries (Electronics Industry Association of Korea), William Krist, Vice President of AEA, is optimistic about Korea. "The main job ahead," he said, "is to encourage U.S. companies to learn more about market conditions in Korea and to take a closer look at opportunities there."[4]

As an organization, AEA is comprised of 200 semiconductor members and 735 members who represent the software industry. Since these U.S. companies export about 18 percent of their products, these members worry about unfair practices. But now they see Korea, in contrast to Japan, as an ideal country for exports. Already the U.S. industry is becoming too dependent upon Japan, a market that according to William Krist "ought to be absolutely, totally open to U.S. suppliers."[5]

As a result of these recent negotiations and trade developments, U.S. exports in electronics should continue to grow at a rapid pace. That fact is underscored by the fact that ROKG sees this sector as the core of its industrialization program. Korea's export-oriented electronics industry is also expected to continue expansion in response to more sophisticated electronic consumer and industrial products. As this Korean sector improves and expands, this should reduce U.S. dependency on Japan.

U.S. exports of electronic components to South Korea exceeds $700 million a year and should grow at about 10 percent yearly. Products with high potential for U.S. exporters include ceramic capacitors, other fixed capacitors and parts, relay fuses, connectors, switches, printed circuits, some types of variable and fixed resistors, cathode-ray tubes, silicon transistors, silicon diodes, large-scale integrated circuits, electronic microcircuits, mounted piezo electric crystals, lead frames for semiconductors, and light emitting diodes.

The Korean electronics industry currently produces at levels exceeding $11 billion. It consists mainly of consumer electronics ($3.5 billion), industrial electronics ($2.2 billion), and can components and parts ($5.5 billion). Not only is Korea a major producer and exporter of electronic products, it also is a major importer. Imports of integrated circuits and semiconductors have doubled in the past five years, reaching above $3.5 billion in 1988, and should continue at an annual rate of at least 15 percent through 1990, thus justifying U.S. participation at such events as the Korean electronics show in October of each year. Through these means, U.S. exporters should get a larger share of the market.

Another related product sector with strong sales potential in Korea is that of computers and peripherals. Since the first computer was introduced in Korea twenty years ago, substantial commercial expansions (number and scale) have produced more sophisticated EDP (electronic data processing) technology. All government agencies use computers not only for basic accounting and bookkeeping, but also for advanced, innovative applications and procedures.

The trend is toward networking and decentralization among advanced private sector computer users. This will also spark significant demand for other types of computers and peripherals. There are wide ranges of applications, particularly in the commercial business fields. It is this, together with the gradual opening of public telecommunications facilities planned by the ROKG for commercial data communications services, that should result in substantial growth markets. U.S. sales of large and other computers and peripherals could serve as the main host computers.

Thus the ROKG and industry are the primary customers for the local computer market. Their demands are expected to grow by 10 percent annually through the 1990s, reaching a level greater than $1 billion annually. The trend is already there, for U.S. exports have doubled over the last few years.

Since 1986 (when the figure was $250 million), U.S. exports of computers and peripherals to Korea have grown about 10 percent annually. Japan once served as the leading foreign supplier, accounting for over 50 percent of the import market. Now that supply route is being transferred to the United States. The U.S. share has been about 40 percent. Japanese suppliers have also dominated the supply of peripherals such as floppy disk drives and printers. Japanese dominance is changing, making both U.S. software and hardware more attractive. Already U.S. suppliers dominate the market for computer hardware. Products in this sector have particularly high potential for U.S. exporters. Look to computer hardware, main storage units (e.g., magnetic disks and magnetic cards), auxiliary storage units (e.g., floppy disk drives and hard disk drives), magnetic media key entry devices, graphic displays, high-speed printers, plotters, and specialized terminals such as on-line bank teller terminals for the big sales.

The combination of strong Korean demand and lower trade barriers could result in substantial increases in U.S. exports of computers and peripherals. If you are interested, check out the U.S. Computer and Office Automation Equipment Show scheduled in Korea each January through the 1990s.

AEROSPACE INDUSTRY

United Technologies Corp. (UTC) builds and repairs engines for Korea's industry. Working with Daewoo Sikorsky, UTC designs helicopters for the Korean Army. Earlier they provided thirty-six F–16s with F100 engines to the Air Force. As the eleventh largest U.S. exporter to Korea, this firm, along with Korea's Samsung Aerospace, overhauls and repairs the F100 engines in the Pacific. These transactions make sense. "We are most willing to transfer technology to the Korean partners," says UTC Chairman Robert Daniel.[6] And why not? In 1986 UTC's business in Korea equalled $200 million. By 1988 that figure doubled to $400 million of which $60 million came from its firms located in Korea.

Korea wants some new fighter and commercial aircraft. The government wants a licensed production of 120 FX aircraft. Most of these would be produced in Korea, not the United States. Until now resistance came from buy-back provisions and the desire of Korea to produce these aircraft in Korea.[7]

But with tight budgets and political uncertainties, Korea will take a greater role in its own defense. Already the annual joint military U.S.-Korean field exercises have been scaled down. The cost for war simulation runs over $33 million. Now military spending is down and anti-American sentiments are up. During these military exercises the combined force uses the most recent aircraft available. The 7th Air Force has an inventory of seventy-two F–16D/Ds, three F–15s, twelve A–10s, and twelve OA–10s now based in Korea. But deployment comes from the northwest region of the United States.[8]

While these exercises may scale down in the future, they do demonstrate two aspects of the aerospace industry in Korea. First, it is big business, involving not only general officers, but also CEOs of the largest U.S. and Korean companies. Each day over 1,000 sorties fill the skies of the Republic (Korea). This is a lucrative market that takes large investments up front. Already Korean Air, Samsung Aerospace Industries, and Daewoo have together invested over $230 million in this field. In the United States such firms as Boeing, McDonnell Douglas, and Lockheed control about 70 percent of the market. Parts alone throughout the 1980s account for a $40 billion expenditure.[9]

Second, U.S. defense and political strategies are shifting in this region. Until now the United States has limited Seoul's offset policies. ROKG wants to change that for three reasons: (1) greater Korean industrial participation, (2) more buy-back programs where Koreans operate under a licensed production agreement, and (3) the momentum for change is there, especially with reduction in U.S. armed forces.

What that means to U.S. exporters and Koreans on joint ventures is this: lower profits for the former, higher for the latter. For U.S. firms the days of direct benefits averaging 50 percent are gone. U.S. industrialists should expect 20 percent or less in direct benefits tied with an additional 20 percent ascribed to technology transfer. For Korean firms, the future looks good. They will gain key technology for military and commercial use. That is the same strategy the Japanese are using to gain high technology for the vital industrial sector. What role ROKG finally plays is debatable. But one fact remains certain: look for more joint ventures between U.S. and Koran companies in the aerospace industries.

CONCLUSION

As a newly industrializing country Korea has joined the ranks of industrialized countries and is assuming greater responsibility for world trade. One major issue facing Korea, according to Koreanologists, is the trade issue.

Korea is taking responsibility for the burgeoning surplus with the United States. In March of 1989, Seung-Soo Han, Minister of Trade and Industry, released a publication titled *Free and Fair Trade: Korea's Record and Commitment*.[10] As a policy the ROKG encourages buying missions, import reform, and joint ventures with U.S. firms. The ROKG also accepts the rising expectations of its citizens, who accept economic growth as normal patterns. They adjust by wanting even better, higher quality products and higher standards of living. As educated people, their interest coincides with opportunities for more U.S. products. The Korea Development Institute predicts economic growth (7–8 percent) through the year 2000, with Korea showing increasing exports ($173 billion) and imports ($168 billion).

There are labor strikes, but wage increases should subside now that workers' salaries are up. Overall the export markets should remain high for the following items in descending order: machinery; nonelectric, electronics, and electrical products; chemicals and chemical products, crude oils; iron and steel products; transport equipment; aircraft; ships; raw hides; leather; logs and wood; pulp and paper; coal; grains; and raw cotton.

Export opportunities are also there in the industrial, service, and energy sectors. But other countries know that as well. In 1988 U.S. exports to Korea increased by 46 percent, while Japan's increased by 17 percent, and the European Community's by 31 percent. In terms of market share, the U.S. controls about 24 percent; Japan, 31 percent; and the EC, about 13 percent; followed by the Middle East, 4 percent; and others 29 percent. In 1988 total exports into Korea were up about 26.3 percent, representing a total figure of $51.8 billion.

NOTES

1. Paul M. Bralower, "Climate Right for Exports—But Good Planning Is Necessary," *Modern Casting*, August 1988, 34.

2. Bralower, 34.

3. Bralower, 34.

4. William Krist, "Electronics Export," *Business Korea*, December 1989, 75.

5. Krist, 75.

6. Robert F. Daniell, "Fueling Korea's Aerospace Liftoff," *Business Korea*, December 1989, 63.

7. "Tight Budgets, Political Uncertainties Cloud Future of Team Spirit Exercises," *Aviation Week and Space Technology*, April 24, 1989, 71.

8. "Tight Budgets," 72.

9. Young-Ho Lee, "Korea's Aviation Industry Ready for World Takeoff," *Korean Business World*, April 1987, 58.

10. Two important publications are *Free and Fair Trade: Korea's Record and Commitment* and *Responsive and Responsible: Korea's Trade Partnership with the United States*. Contact Reid and Priest, 111 19th Street, N.W., Washington, DC 20036.

6

Products That Sell

It is ingenious what some business and government leaders do to export to Korea. Donald W. Baumgartner knew his company had reached its domestic potential. Analyzing sales trends, this president (Paper Machinery Corporation, Milwaukee) saw potential for Asian markets. He developed this potential when three Japanese printers and packaging firms ordered thirty paper cup dispensing machines. If the Japanese need them, so do other Asians, he reasoned. So he established joint ventures with Japanese and Korean firms. Now this firm sells 40 percent of its production directly to Koreans and others in twenty-five countries.

Koreans need international education and want international travel. On the west coast, San Diego established a Korean academic program. On the east, Florida asked for joint ventures. Both are doing more than promoting Sea World, oranges, and beaches. Both are appealing to Koreans' basic needs. By meeting Korea's needs, several states hope to close business deals.

Through the University of California, San Diego residents hope to increase the number of Koreans living there. They invite Koreans to "come here to study at UCSD's Graduate School of International Relations and Pacific Studies (IR/PS). This unique program focuses on Korean business economics, politics, and culture."[1] It works. The Korean population in San Diego increased from 5,000 (1986) to 20,000 (1988). To show their long-term commitment, Californians also built a Korean Heritage Library.

Their ultimate goal is business economics, at least that is what Alfredo Bautista, Deputy Director in the California governor's office, says. "Our ultimate goal is to increase trade relations with Korea through a better understanding of Korea," says Bautista.

Now for the east coast. Florida is also promoting stronger ties with Korea. Some 33 state delegates recently visited Korea (1989). They offered Koreans a chance to visit Disneyworld and meet business leaders. They offered low taxes, young workers, and joint ventures. They prepared for long-term relations—the kind the Koreans prefer. By promoting friendship first, Bobby Brantley and business leaders hope for more. As lieutenant governor and secretary of Florida's Commerce Department, he believes the opportunities for Korean exports are limitless. So his proposal goes: "We want to be to Korea what Georgia is to Japan," says Brantley. As a state Georgia has aggressively pursued Japanese investments. "What we have seen in Korea is very impressive and we are very pleased," he said. "We hope to be able to do business in Korea."[2]

Alabama, Alaska, Florida, Georgia, Idaho, Indiana, Texas, Utah, Virginia, Wisconsin, and North Carolina have representatives in Korea. The Korean-American Chamber of Commerce (North Pacific Coast) is located at 160 Indian Road, Piedmont, California 94610. Over 100 business organizations are affiliated with this chamber.

As international traders, you know your products. Knowing is first, selling is second. Combine your individual sales strategies for particular locations in Korea. Just as Donald Baumgartner, Alfredo Bautista, and Bobby Brantley maximized their gains, so can you. It all starts with Korean needs.

BEST EXPORT PROSPECTS FOR U.S. FIRMS

Once agricultural commodities represented the largest export volume. In 1984 exports to Korea totalled $5.7 billion, of which the largest sector was agriculture. Corn, cotton, and wheat were the major U.S. export items, followed by electronics components, parts for aircraft, and telecommunications equipment. Agriculture has not decreased so much but

Table 6.1
The Best Export Prospects for U.S. Firms

Category Description	Specific Products
Grains	Soy beans
Fuels/distillates	Petroleum and bituminous products
Inorganic chemicals	Aluminum, chromium and titanium oxides, phosphates and phosphate borates, silicon carbide.
Organic chemicals derivatives,	Styrene, hydrocarbon halogenated
	ethylene products, propylene, cerephalic acid, acrylonitrile, heterocyclic compounds and nucleic acids, epoxides, ketones, saturated polyesters.
Plastic materials	Polymerization products, polyethylene, ethylene, copolymers, polystyrene
Wood	Rough wood, pine, tropical
Aluminum	Unalloyed/unwrought scrap
Machinery	Internal combustion engine parts, pumps, temperature control equipment, filters and purifiers, spray equipment, material handling equipment, earthmovers, weaving and knitting machines, rolling mills, metalworking and printing machinery, office machines, values, bearings, textile processing machinery.
Electric machinery	Generators, motors, transformers, rectifiers relays, radiotelephonic equipment, passive electrical components, switches, control panels, ICs, transistors, electronic devices
Optical, precision	Surveying and drawing instruments, temperature measurement and control instrumentation, medical instruments, X-ray analysis and control equipment

industrial products and technology have increased because of increased construction and changing policies.

New construction included the Honam Railroad, the Samchon Port, expansion of Kimpo Airport, telephone facilities, long-distance telephone systems, Hapchon Dam, Chusam Dam, Nakdong River Estuary Barrage, nuclear power plants, large unit agricultural developments, and construction of an art center. These occurred as Korean policies shifted toward high technology and quality improvements in traditional and new industries. U.S. suppliers found a market by exporting manufacturing equipment to accommodate these goals. Other exporters responded as Koreans began regional and social developments, as well as urban expansion. This process created demands for foreign equipment and technology. Still others met Korean needs to improve not only their telecommunication systems but also their water resources and postal services. Finally, others responded to the introduction of pollution controls, housing construction, and medical care.

Table 6.1 presents the best export prospects for U.S. firms. This particular list came from the U.S. Department of Commerce and the Foreign Service Branch in Seoul. It reflects how construction and policy, along with societal needs, changed. In the late 1970s, Korea's R&D capabilities were limited. To improve, the ROKG invested in science and technology projects; therefore, the demand for imports of sophisticated analytical equipment increased substantially. The same thing happened when the ROKG upgraded existing research institutes. The ROKG promoted private sector involvement in R&D and public education to train researchers and scientists.

AGRICULTURAL PRODUCTS

Korea imports $1.2 billion of U.S. agriculture. These figures make Korea the fifth in total dollars of U.S. agricultural exports. These figures should increase. Koreans consume more U.S. farm products in dollar amounts than Canadians do. The U.S. market shares (42.6 percent) in agriculture are quite large ($3 billion total market). The liberalization ratio for imported agriculture tends to remain high. That has created trade friction. Agricultural trade specialist Julian Heron, founding partner with Heron, Burchette, Ruckert & Rothwell, cites two reasons for exporting. Buying U.S. agricultural products makes the Koreans healthier, and it satisfies the outcries of unfair trading practices. Without fair reciprocity in agricultural trade, he believes that Koreans would "out-Japan" Japan.

While liberalization in agriculture has increased, Korea continues to protect farming families and the rural community from U.S. importers. Julian Heron believes the tact now is to use "the umbrella of food safety and phytosanitary problems." The ROKG has been reluctant to intervene in these restrictions of U.S. products. It is frustrating because expectations of open markets are shattered. Whether these are real issues or sidestepping measures to avoid U.S. agriculture products is debatable. Nevertheless, this sector will likely increase demand for processed foods, especially with increased standards of living.[3]

In 1986 nonagricultural U.S. exports to Korea totalled $4.95 billion versus agricultural exports of $1.29 billion. The Korean GNP was $94.1 billion; the per capita income was $2,371. Since then, Korea's economic growth has been significant. Duties on some imported foods still remain high (30–50 percent) because the government has a policy of food self-sufficiency. There are, however, major problems: limited space, changing consumption patterns, erratic climatic conditions, and a lack of effective production incentives.

Leading the high-value agricultural imports are milled rice, oilcakes, and meal; palm oil; undressed hides and skins; animal fats; and molasses. In 1989 the ROKG quota for imported beef increased to 39,000 tons. Other high-value imports include refined sugar, preserved fruit, macaroni, biscuits, mutton, eggs, edible nuts, fresh and preserved vegetables, cigarettes, and a variety of vegetable oils.

Table 6.2
Fastest Selling Agricultural and Wood Products

HS	Description	1987 Jan.-Dec.	1988 Jan.-Sep.	Percentage Change
0304	fish fillets	2,596	26,758	623.3
0306	crustaceans	6,786	18,728	234.4
2106	food preparation	3,292	8,977	243.4
2301	flours, meals,	7,726	10,966	109.8
2401	unmanufactured tobacco	6,239	23,961	392.5
2402	cigars, cigarettes	3,897	21,688	674.7
4102	raw skins sheep lambs	29,605	41,196	111.7
4409	wood continuously shaped	506	12,058	993.2
4412	plywood, veneered	10,923	64,806	856.4
4705	semi-chemical wood pulp	752	8,899	977.8

Source: Compiled by the Korean Foreign Trade Association, What To Sell
To Korea, 1988.
Note: Percentage change is a one year projection (1988) based on trends.

The restricted items have tended to be corn, wheat, soybeans, grain sorghum, soybean meal, pure-breeding cattle, beef, cottonseed oil, homogenized food, orange juice, feeds, onions, coffee creamer, and almonds. The ROKG has liberalized these markets. In 1989 the United States and ROKG reached an agreement on wine exports as well as cigarettes, despite strong resistance within the media and population, based partially on health issues. Tariffs have been reduced from an unweighed average (i.e., not dependent on number or dollar amount) of 23.7 percent (1984) to 18.3 (1988). Many of these items are less restricted than just a few years ago (see Table 6.2).

Korea still relies on agricultural imports, particularly corn, wheat, soybeans, beef, cotton, hides, and skins, to meet a variety of needs. The ROKG hopes to lower government deficits by reducing crop and fertilizer subsidies. If continued, that would further reduce agricultural incentives and crops. Domestic markets have expanded as salaries have increased. Koreans are spending more on fast foods and food preparations.

Although Korea limits wood materials for some building construction, the market is changing. Koreans have more money to spend on apartments so architects and builders use sophisticated designs and expensive materials.

Table 6.3 shows that the largest export dollars come from agriculture and wood products. Certain commodities continue to show high volumes. These include cereals such as wheat, meslin, and maize (corn)—$500 million worth. These grains represent about half of the low-value exports to Korea. Cotton continues to show high volume because of textiles. These volumes are followed by raw hides, which are twice the volume of wood pulp. Exporting hides is an active business for the cattle

Table 6.3
Largest Volume of Agricultural and Wood Products

(Unit: $1,000, %)

HS	Description	1987 Jan.-Dec.	1988 Jan.-Sep.	Percentage Change
1001	cereals			
	wheat and meslin	429,705	401,953	24.9
	maize (corn)	377,024	394,682	46.1
1201	soy beans	245,602	196,920	18.9
4101	raw hides	766,642	717,832	29.7
4702	wood pulp	364,195	373,272	58.9
5201	cotton	514,298	538,701	46.0

Source: Compiled by the Korean Foreign Trade Association, What To
Sell To Korea, 1988.
Note: Percentage change is a one year projection (1988) based on trends.

states of Texas, Oklahoma, and Montana. Korea buys these as low-value
purchases, then transforms them into expensive consumer items (brief-
cases, boots, shoes) and exports them to the United States, Japan, or
Europe.

Government policies have affected agriculture imports. These policies
include increased rice production, development of an infrastructure for
irrigation and land reclamation, diversification of crops toward high
value products, farm mechanization, expansion of livestock feeds, and
improvement of marketing and distribution systems. Koreans plan to
reduce dependence on imports by increasing production of food and
forage crops and by introducing import taxes on agricultural products.
Such taxes would finance programs and should increase domestic production and stabilize prices.

Demand for forest products has increased because of the rapid economic growth in the Pacific Rim. Economic prosperity in Korea places
increased demand for both hardwood and softwood. The southcentral
region of Alaska is ideally suited for capturing some of this market. The
facilities are there, "sawmills, pulp mills, logging camps, services and
manufacturers, transportation facilities services infrastructure and processing of by-products."[4]

Table 6.4 lists those wood products that are selling the fastest and in
the highest volumes. This table was constructed from information provided by the Korea Trade Promotion Corporation (KOTRA).

The list of Korean importers—Jinido Corporation, Eagon Industrial
Ltd., Ssang Ma Corporation, and Samil Kongsa—were all randomly
selected. The wood products they imported most are rough wood; pine;
tropical or continuously shaped wood; plywood, veneered; and semi-
chemical wood pulp. Exporters should make other contacts than these
to ensure the best possible arrangements.

Table 6.4
Best Selling Wood Products

HS	Description	List of Korean Importers
4409	wood continuously shaped	Jinido Corporation C.P.O. Box 242
4412	plywood, veneered	Eagon Industrial LTD. 825 Towha-dong, Nam-gu Inchon
4702	wood pulp	Ssang Ma Corporation 612-1 Igok-dong, Talso-gu Taegu
4705	semi-chem wood pulp	Samil Kongsa LTD. 656-283, Songsu-dong Seoul

In 1988 the U.S. exported $189 million worth of wood to Korea. This figure is 38 percent higher than the previous year. In 1989 figures were ahead of 1988's. The projections for 1995 could reach $500 million despite barriers, for Korea has strict standard sizes for framed construction. The use of wood products is discouraged due to the dominance of masonry products in the building industry and unfavorable building codes and regulatory policies.

Some agricultural products remain exempt from the policy of rapid import liberalization because a fourth of Korean families live on farms. Agricultural policy adversely affects them. Consequently, agricultural reform is balanced against social and political changes.

This sector is giving way to export demands. The ROKG is reluctantly opening farming from pressure of Section 301 and based on demographic shifts from urban to rural populations. Cities promise higher standards of living, better health-care facilities, and educational opportunities.

In 1988 the ROKG reduced tariffs on 691 items, averaging from 22 percent to 14 percent. Import duties on 300 consumer goods including chocolate, perfume, cosmetics, carpets, refrigerators, recorders, radios, and washing machines ranged from a high of 24.11 percent to a new low of 14.46 percent. The measure also applied to 391 items of raw material, including cotton yarn, ethylene, beef tallow, molasses, gold ingots, lumber, and electrograde bars.

THE FASTEST SELLING PRODUCTS

In 1958 exports of manufactured items accounted for 31 percent of export revenues. In 1988 it was about 90 percent. These U.S. exports to Korea have increased over the past two decades: electric and nonelectric machinery, industrial raw materials, high-technology scientific products, logs and lumber, grains, raw hides and skins, chemicals, pulp and paper,

Table 6.5
Chemicals, Cloth, Stone, Glass, and Metals

HS	Description	1987 Jan.-Dec.	1988 Jan.-Sep.	Percentage Change
2901	cyclic hydrocarbons	246,822	391,216	144.9
2905	acrylic alcohols	152,476	237,813	113.0
3402	organic surface agents	22,884	49,950	177.9
3504	dextrins, starches	2,887	13,231	532.0
3904	polymers vinyl chloride	37,696	59,725	104.4
4002	synthetic rubber	83,870	132,562	119.5
5007	silk fabrics, woven	73,589	112,929	128.5
5403	yam of artif. filament	26,675	51,203	143.2
5512	woven fabric	9,917	16,138	140.6
5601	wadding of textile matr.	6,343	14,286	294.1
5603	nonwoven	8,753	36,188	465.7
6802	monumental or bldg.stone	1,187	20,546	416.1
6910	ceramic sinks	2,110	13,825	865.6
7005	glass and glassware	15,612	29,453	134.2
7204	ferro-alloys	53,082	74,197	100.3
7401	cooper mattes	4,582	39,600	342.0
7403	cooper refined	153,294	254,397	143.9
7409	cooper plates	20,323	29,937	108.8
7601	aluminium, unwrought	298,489	408,213	106.9
7602	aluminium waste	15,943	22,536	128.4

Source: Compiled by the Korean Foreign Trade Association, What To Sell To Korea, 1988.
Note: Percentage change is a one year projection (1988) based on trends.

computers and peripherals, scrap iron, textile yarns and fabric, and commercial aircraft. The next two tables (Tables 6.5 and 6.6) show just the rates of increase for exports to Korea.

The left columns show the HS number for each commodity, followed by descriptions. The next two columns, the unit figures, are in $1,000 increments. Because 1988 figures were not completed, these are projected figures. The percentages are trends. Such information comes from a listing put out by the Korean Foreign Trade Association (KFTA); however, these tables combine the data to show high percentage changes (over 100 percent increases).

Petrochemicals and the refining industry are booming. In 1987 the total of petrochemical products accounted for $42.2 million in exports. The largest Korean firms produce refined petrochemicals, often with U.S. firms in some license agreement or as joint ventures. Since Korea imports 80 percent of its energy needs, the ROKG watches international prices closely and regulates this industry.

Table 6.4 includes inorganic and organic chemicals. The ROKG policies explain the rapid growth in plastic materials such as polymerization products, polyethylene, ethylene, and polystyrene, and in aluminum products.

Table 6.6
Fastest Selling Machines and Other Products

HS	Description	1987 Jan.-Dec.	1988 Jan.-Sep.	Percentage Change
8408	diesel engines	32,258	66,644	207.0
8429	bulldozer	16,661	26,546	131.2
8444	machines for drawing	22,638	27,271	111.9
8479	machines not specified	306,160	669,681	200.4
8502	electric generating	17,529	78,512	816.2
8512	lighting equipment	7,798	13,153	149.0
8514	Indust. elec. furnaces	62,448	83,690	125.6
8517	electric apparatus	70,661	138,622	155.1
8526	radar apparatus	26,374	52,454	156.6
8543	electric machines	32,153	52,267	128.7
8802	aircraft vehicles	304,474	701,499	143.9
8901	aircraft arrestor	2,933	17,858	519.9
8906	warships	5,954	13,027	622.7
9013	liquids laser diodes	15,690	18,100	100.5
9031	measuring instruments	77,894	168,884	256.5
9108	watches	32,131	52,621	136.4
9113	strap, bands, bracelets	1,442	11,628	862.3
9508	swings, galleries	22,743	42,254	548.8

Source: Compiled by the Korean Foreign Trade Association, What To
Sell To Korea, 1988.
Note: Percentage change is a one year projection (1988) based on trends.

Most increases go for infrastructure expansion. The ROKG supports the building of many highways, power plants, and roads. Construction accounts for many other products, such as equipment machines and parts.

EQUIPMENT MACHINES AND PARTS

The shipbuilding industry faces hard times. In 1989 the Hyundai strike in Ulsan resulted in antilabor violence, while the long-term strikes at Samsung shipyard and at Union Steel were finally settled. But that happened only after serious charges and counter charges interrupted productivity. The strike at Samsung heavy industries shipyard on Koje Island lasted much longer than most. Both promanagement workers and yard workers argued over the issue of representation.

Some people think the intransigent style of managers toward labor leads to strikes in this and related industries. In 1988 the largest plant of Poonsang Metal at Ankang, near Ulsan, recorded 3,600 striking workers. Those who normally manufacture ammunition and explosives stayed off work for several months. At one point 1,700 police surrounded the plant and arrested some 37 strikers.

Labor unions demand higher salaries and better working conditions. Despite labor unrest, the manufacturing industries thrive as seen by sales of equipment machines and parts. Table 6.5 provides information about the fastest selling machines in Korea.

These items were taken from Korean lists. Two other items are electric machinery—generators, motors, transformers, transistors, and electronic devices—and optical and precision machines including surveying and drawing instruments, temperature control instrumentation, medical instruments, and x ray equipment.

SEGMENTED MARKETS

The Republic of Korea, with a population of 42 million people, has a per capita income of $4,500 (1989), but should pass $5,000 by 1990 and $10,000 by 2000. Korea has sustained one of the highest real economic growth rates (12.2 percent) on record. Since the mid-sixties, GNP has increased 10 percent a year.

Location and demography help you identify Korean marketing areas by class and industry. About two-thirds of the population lives in cities greater than 50,000. Seoul, Pusan, and Taegu represent about 67 percent of the urban population. Of these three large cities, the metropolitan area of Seoul contains about 25 percent of the country's people and probably about 25 percent of the consumer markets. Just about all large Korean firms operate out of Seoul, the nation's capital and leading industrial center.

Other industrial cities are Pusan, Taegu, Inchon, Suwon, Masan, Ulsan, and Pohang. Many of these specialize in certain industries. Taegu is known for textile manufacturing; Pusan is important in food processing, shipbuilding, plywood, and rubber products; Ulsan is a center for the chemical and petrochemical industry and the site of the Hyundai shipyard. Seoul is prominent in the wearing apparel field and paper and printing; Masan is the site of a free export zone; Gumi is the site of an electronics complex; Changwon is the site of a machinery complex; and Yochun is the site of chemical and petrochemical industries.

Koreans have money to spend, but they save about 34 percent of their earnings. Urbanites buy Korean stocks speculatively, even taking out bank loans to purchase shares on the stock market. While economists worry about the practice of speculation on the stock markets, Koreans know that the 1989 Composite Stock Price Index is up seven times from the 1980 figures. As their incomes have increased, Koreans are taking more risks.

They are also buying more consumer goods. They want household appliances and hand tools for home repair. They are fashion-minded professionals, who are spending more on appearance, restaurants, and clothing. Both the cosmetics industries and fast-food restaurants do a lively business in Korea. Young Koreans, like those in America, also want certain brand names. "Experimenting with new products in the Korean market could potentially prove quite lucrative," says Ian Davis at the U.S. Department of Commerce.

These demographic and social changes spell profits for U.S. exporters who meet basic needs. Some exporters already know this, since U.S. exports to Korea increased by 27 percent (1987) and 40 percent (1988). Successful exporters know where these markets are and how to penetrate them. Successful companies include 3M, American Can International, American Express, Avis, Corning International, Dow Chemical, General Dynamics, General Foods, Hewlett-Packard, Hyatt, Eli Lilly, Monsanto, Motorola, Ralston Purina, Sherwin-Williams, Summit, U.S. Wheat Associates, Union Carbide, Westinghouse Electric, and Arthur Young & Co.

General Motors invested $221 million (1988) in various Korean partners, including Daewoo Precisions, Shinsunbg Tongsan, Hankook Tire, Korean Steel Chemical, and Samlip. Cal Tex invested $63 million in Honam Oil, while Ford Motors put $61.3 million in Kia Industries and Mando Machinery. Other big investors were IBM, $28.97 billion; Arco (Yukong) $25 billion; Autec (Kwak Oh Whyang and Han Bok) $23.39 billion; Carrier (Daewoo) $22.47 billion.

Problems do exist. The major ones are the management control/equity ratio, personnel and labor relations, and control of intellectual property rights. Most U.S. exporters successfully work these out. But these disputes are expected, as U.S. exporters enter into some joint venture or investment arrangement.

RECOMMENDATIONS AND CONCLUSIONS

Korea is the world's leader in electronic household appliances, including microwave oven production, color televisions, and VCRs. Koreans build 9 million microwave ovens (40.5 percent of the world market). TV production numbers 11 million (14.1 percent). Koreans manufacture 8 million units of VCRs (about 25.4 percent of world demand). For them to export these products, they must import as well.

U.S. suppliers should adapt to Korean's markets. It helps to strip down U.S. products to the basic production unit, including the parts. U.S. exporters must quote prices based on repeat business generated by demand for spare parts, components, and auxiliary equipment. Emphasize and sell the idea of superior quality, which results in lower replacement parts and longer product use. Finally, investigate possible warehousing arrangements in Korea that would allow for larger shipments and cheaper freight rates on transpacific voyages.

As marketing strategies change, so must the monitoring. Ron Gilbrich, Vice President for Wrangell Forest Product (Ketchikan, Alaska), summarized it this way: "We add as much value as we can to our products before they are shipped. We try to provide our customers with products that meet their needs rather than try to convince them they should use products that are handy for us to produce." The top value of agricultural imports are in horticultural products such as fruits, nuts, and vegetables. The worth of those imports for 1988 was about $3.7 billion.

Korea has evolved from largely an agricultural, subsistence economy into an industrial one and is edging up the technological ladder. Koreans sell high-value products, which account for much of the fastest and largest export volumes.

Their economic base is rooted in government policies. The ROKG builds a diversified and strong industry which, in turn, promotes Korean exports. U.S. suppliers with product demand and know-how could benefit from Korea's emphasis on higher technology and upgrading quality (competitiveness) of its manufactured goods.

Koreans remain vulnerable to worldwide events. The recession and soaring costs of oil imports put them on the economic skids. All of that is behind them now as they lead the world in exporting household electronic appliances. They have increased agricultural production and even have built deluxe hotels.

NOTES

1. "Promoting Trade Through Academia," *Business Korea*, January 1989, 56.
2. "More than Oranges and Beaches," *Business Korea*, March 1989, 62.
3. Stephen Lande and Hellis Crigier, "Getting to the Root of Trade Disputes," *Business Korea*, December 1989, 64–66.
4. Becky Bear and Frank Seymour, "Market for Southcentral Timber Is the Orient," *Alaska Journal of Commerce*, May 3, 1988, 24.

7

Korean Economy and U.S. Trade

The World Affairs Council spent one year studying the growing importance of South Korea to the United States. The study presented some new thinking about the economic and political issues between the two countries. Basically the study gave priority to economic issues for several reasons. Economic strength translates into national power. That is why U.S. exporters frustrated about the Asian trade challenge would welcome a Japanese and Korean policy review. Appropriate policy would begin to alleviate some pressure, but other alternatives would also need to be pursued.

From the Koreans' perspective, an American lobby effort might help. From the Americans' perspective, a better understanding of South Korean economic policy would certainly be useful. These strategies would strengthen both the independence of each country, while at the same time they would establish significant trade linkages. It is in everybody's interest to encourage Korean democratic pluralism, with appropriate modifications. Korea will not likely adopt a U.S. style of democracy at all levels and in all situations.[1]

The economist Rudiger Dornbusch describes the Pacific Rim as the place where we battle for our standard of living. The annualized trade deficit with Japan increased from $10 billion in 1980 to $46.6 billion in 1988. In 1989 it equalled $45.5 billion. For the twelve Pacific Rim countries the total trade deficit exceeds $76.5 billion.[2]

Business interest and policy strategists are frustrated about these figures. Because of these figures and reverse investments, Congress is considering possible restrictions on foreign investment in the United States. Furthermore, some in Congress have an interest in negotiating trade agreements with Japan, Taiwan, and other East Asian countries. Additionally, Congress is worried about the European Community plans to integrate its market by 1992. Members worry about protectionism in a "fortress Europe."

To assist its 180,000 businesses and several thousand organizations, the International Division of the U.S. Chamber of Commerce published an evaluation of that bill. According to their assessment, the 1988 U.S. Omnibus Trade and Competitiveness Act is not "purely protectionist, it's a procedural protectionist." Section 301 and "Super 301," regarding unfair foreign trade practices, are invoked only if bilateral trade is lacking. The Chamber of Commerce does not think the bill is a "massive erosion of the President's discretion in administering trade policy." And finally, they do not think the bill "represents a major retreat from the historical emphasis of the United States on multilateral trade agreements in trade policy."[3]

They applaud the passage of the bill for three reasons: (1) it promotes market access with mandates for violators; (2) it allows for export expansion (for small business and agriculture); and (3) it provides for import relief (antidumping and countervailing duty laws, intellectual property protection). Congress and the Chamber of Commerce aren't the only ones who advocate positive changes.

In a series of articles in the *Harvard Business Review*, twenty-three leaders speak out on the larger problem of international trade. These leaders think that the United States must face the painful facts about why its standard of living is decreasing. As a nation, they believe that the United States must adjust to economic shifts. They believe the United States has the "British disease," because of "flabby management." By "British disease" is meant (1) that the U.S. labor force does menial jobs, (2) that education is failing, (3) that executives shuffle paper, and (4) that quality is lacking. Industrial leaders should, therefore, realize their role and take possible remedies that will make U.S. products more competitive.[4]

U.S. products are often not competitive, yet this country's economic hegemony is not yet over. As changes in the business world accelerate and as trading partners in the world multiply, it becomes increasingly difficult for executives to keep up with what's going on. Both their sources of information and discretionary time for reading are limited. Aside from knowing about student unrest and labor disputes, most Americans don't know enough about an important ally and trading partner—Korea. Ironically our limited exposure and blurred TV images come precisely at the time that our global village puts us closer together.

There is no quick fix for getting a focused picture of what to do, but one fact is obvious. That fact remains indelibly imprinted on our minds. Executives know firsthand that the United States is a debtor nation now, with serious trade imbalances. They recognize economic changes more than most, especially as they travel to Korea or Japan. That unrelenting velocity of change seems greater now than in former days of black and white RCA TVs and record players.

Yet even they may not know much about Tongyang Nylon or Samsung. Tongyang Nylon, a major Korean computer company, is gearing up to make hard disk drives. Their affiliate, Hyonsung Computer Corporation, recently signed an agreement with Brand Technologies of Woodland Hills (California) to sell Brand-designed hard disk drives in the Far East. Conversely, Tongyang produces the computers at its Korean Gumi plants. Already in the component side—terminals, minicomputers, and IBMPC XT and AT compatibles—this would further expand its exports to the United States.[5] Korean Samsung already makes a supermicro computer. Fortune Inc. produces the Korean SPC–3000, which can link twenty-eight users on a system for up to sixty-four megabytes.

To understand the Koreans and our trade imbalance let's look at their past and our involvement with them. If we are to avoid repeating the same old mistakes of the past, we should begin analyzing the results of our engagements in international development, especially in matters of Korean trade.

No one debates that trade is the driving force of Korea's sudden leap into international prominence. The Koreans have witnessed two decades of prolonged economic growth. Excluding 1980, yearly GNP growth has been 5 percent or higher. Within two decades the per capita income has steadily risen: $103 (1964), $2,296 (1986), $4,500 (1989). How have Koreans accomplished so much? What role has the United States played? What are major factors behind product choices for exporting? Behind this obvious process of match making are the deeper international issues of trade imbalance and foreign policy. That is why the best place to begin is with the development of the Korean economy and U.S. trade. If that assumption is valid, then the next question becomes: Did early bilateral relations between the U.S. and Korea begin both Korea's export success and U.S. exporters' opportunities for expanded exports to Korean?

Table 7.1
Foreign Trade Trend

Year	Export	Import	($ bil.) Balance
1981	20.7	24.3	-3.6
1982	20.9	23.5	-2.6
1983	23.2	24.9	-1.7
1984	26.3	27.4	-1.1
1985	26.44	26.46	-0.02
1986	33.9	29.7	4.2
1987	46.2	38.5	7.7

PRODUCTION OF WEALTH

Production leads to wealth. But that does not answer this question: "What factors in Korea lead to increased production?" Generally speaking, any sustained development results from hard work, timely decisions, and alignment of national economic goals to business interests. These factors are found in the case of Korean trade. The government also capitalized on the Confucian tradition of order and hierarchical authority. Most analysts point to the influence of religious traditions on trade, but only as they were accompanied by an increased literacy. Skilled laborers, educated executives, and sophisticated government officials pushed the latest Five Year Economic Plan, which resulted in an average of 7.6 percent (12.5 percent, 1986) GNP growth rates. Other contingent factors contributed to the 1986 high year—low oil prices, low dollar/yen exchange rates, low domestic prices.

The ROKG shifted its earlier policies of import substitution to ones of export promotion. By design, exports have been the driving force behind Korea's economic success. For the 1962–87 period, export volumes rose 841 times (from $55 million to $46.2 billion), averaging 31.6 percent. While not as high, imports are increased. During this time, imports increased 90 times—from $42 million to $37.8 billion. Yet Korea's emphasis on trade, favoring exports, doesn't tell the full story.

Korea lacks natural resources. That fact certainly accounts for the necessity of trade. Without it, its economy would wane; by it, it thrives. The specific amounts of foreign trade are listed in Table 7.1 by exports and imports for seven years. Korea only recently reaped the benefits of these government policies. Until 1986 imports exceeded exports by variable decreasing amounts.

In 1986 Korea recorded its first annual trade surplus. That pattern has continued. Using capital investment, the Koreans built their economy around the trade machine. In 1981 the export equation was in the red by $3.6 billion. Korean imports exceeded exports through 1985. After

Table 7.2
Korean Trade Trend with United States

Year	Export	Dependency	Import	Dependency	($mil.) Balance
1981	5,651	30.0	6,050	23.2	-399
1982	6,119	28.3	5,956	24.6	163
1983	8,128	33.6	6,273	24.0	1,855
1984	10,479	39.8	6,875	22.4	3,604
1985	10,754	35.5	6,489	20.8	4,265
1986	13,880	40.0	6,545	21.0	7,335
1987	18,311	38.7	8,758	21.4	9,553

1986 note a shift (1986, surplus $4.2 billion) in volume (1981, deficit $3.6 billion).

U.S. TRADE

Table 7.2 specifies the relations between Korean trade with the U.S. by year (1981–87), for both the export figure and dependency ratio. The dependency figure (exports and imports) is the ratio of Korean trade with the United States over the total volume for all other countries. For example, in 1981 the Koreans exported items to the U.S. worth $5.65 billion. That figure represented a third of the total volume for all Korean exports and a 30.0 dependency ratio as well.

This procedure allows for comparisons not only between the countries but also for all other countries. The trends in Table 7.2 present at least two problems. First, over time (1981–87) Korea has become overly dependent on exports to the United States. Like the previous table, this one shows how that pattern has changed. While Korea's dependency has moved upward through 1987, imports from the United States dipped lower from a high of 1982. The Koreans hope to reduce their U.S. dependency on exports while increasing their imports of U.S. products.

The second problem is related to the first. The ROKG wants U.S. suppliers to have more of the Korean market share. The reason for this imbalance is obvious—the volume of exports from Korea to the U.S. has drastically increased, but it is not reciprocated. In 1987 the total volume of trade between the two countries reached $27,069 million, which ranked Korea seventh in trade partnership with America. Korean exports to the U.S. reached $18.3 billion. Imports from the United States were only $8.75 billion. Such heavy dependency results in Korean surpluses and government desires to narrow the gap.

Table 7.3
Korea's Trade with Major Partners

		U.S.		E C		Japan ($ mil. %)	
	Year	Amts	% Ttl	Amts	% Ttl	Amts	% Ttl
Exports	1981	5,611	30.0	2,686	12.8	3,444	16.4
	1982	6,119	28.3	2,826	13.1	3,314	15.3
	1983	8,128	33.6	3,025	12.5	3,358	13.9
	1984	10,479	35.8	3,217	11.0	4,602	15.7
	1985	10,754	35.5	3,160	10.4	4,543	15.0
	1986	13,880	40.0	4,305	12.4	5,426	15.6
	1987	18,311	38.7	6,597	14.0	8,537	17.8
Imports	1981	6,050	23.2	1,925	7.4	6,374	24.4
	1982	5,956	24.6	1,732	7.1	5,305	21.9
	1983	6,273	24.0	2,151	8.2	6,238	23.8
	1984	6,875	22.4	2,713	8.9	7,640	24.9
	1985	6,489	20.8	2,991	9.6	7,560	24.3
	1986	6,545	21.0	3,215	10.2	10,869	34.4
	1987	8,758	21.4	4,613	11.2	13,657	33.3

OTHER TRADING PARTNERS

By comparing these volumes with the European Community and Japan, readers can interpret international trends (Table 7.3), a process that is necessary before any application is made. The two rows are exports and imports by year, from 1981 through 1987. Column figures show three country areas—the United States, the European Community, and Japan. The comparisons elaborate the dependency ratio. The U.S. is the prime receiver of Korean goods. Beginning in 1981 the amount of money spent on U.S. imports from Korea is greater than the combined imports of both the European Community and Japan (1982, U.S. $6.2 billion versus EC $2.83 billion plus Japan $3.31 billion). That differential continues throughout the years 1983 to 1987, with the figures after 1984 showing an average of over $3 million difference.

In the case of imports into Korea, the figures are reversed in two ways. Not only do Americans export less to Korea than the EC and Japan combined, they also have a ratio (U.S. goods exported) that is proportionally less than the figure for Japan. The water shed date of 1983 is that time from which imports from Japan to Korea accelerate. In 1986 and 1987, the Japanese show the highest amounts ($10,869 million and $13,657 million). Japan exported more to Korea in 1987 than they imported from them ($13,657 million versus $8,537 million). For both the United States and Europe, Korea exported more (U.S., $18,311 million; EC, $6,597 million) products than were imported (U.S., $8,758 million;

Table 7.4
Import Trends from the United States and Japan

Imports by Country	1986	1987	1988 Jan.-Mar.
From U.S.	6,545 (20.7)	8,758 (21.3)	2,568 (22.5)
From Japan	10,869 (34.4)	13,656 (33.3)	3,582 (31.4)
Total Imports	31,584 (100)	41,020 (100)	11,407 (100)

Source: Data from the Korea Foreign Trade Association, Korea's Policies to Increase Imports, May 1988, p. 32.

EC, $4,613 million). The ROKG put some policies in place, but are these enough to bring about balanced trade?

IMPORT TRANSFERRABLE ITEMS FROM JAPAN TO THE UNITED STATES

People know Korea's reputation in exporting, but they know less about the trade deficit. Until 1986, Korea encountered deficits every year. After that time, the ROKG wanted less dependence upon supplier countries. In order to correct an imbalance and avoid dependency, the ROKG and private businesses made an effort to diversify their import sources.[6] Some 335 items were selected by the government and by two major trade organizations. These items are recommended to importers because, in part, this policy shifts buying sources from Japan to America. As of December 1987, a total of $3.7 billion of imported goods, usually supplied by the Japanese, was listed for diversification. By 1989 that figure increased substantially.

Two associations, numbering 13,000 and 4,000 members, respectively, identified these 335 items as potential items for importation. In fact, an Import Diversification Promotion Committee, comprised of Korea's fifty leading business groups, was established specifically to deal with the problem of U.S. access. The results of that committee are revealed by statistics.[7]

Korean policy toward the United States and Japan began to show gradual effects several years ago (see Table 7.4). It was accomplished through buying missions, promotions at international trade shows, and increased U.S. media coverage. Favorable U.S. statistics suggest some impact of the ROKG's policy. This policy did affect public and private trade initiatives. Such an implementation strategy shows how Korea's economy can turn on a dime.

While U.S. imports into Korea steadily increased during this two and a quarter year period, those same percentages decreased for Japan. These figures reveal that the efforts of Korea to shift its import sources to the United States are gradually succeeding. U.S. suppliers should recognize Korea's efforts. More importantly, they should evaluate their potential to export these 335 selected items. Since these 335 items are mostly raw materials and capital goods, Korean importers want stable suppliers. The growth in these items parallels economic trade expansions.

IMPORT LIBERALIZATION ITEMS

Korea has only recently modified its policy of restricting household consumer goods. Concomitantly, domestic industries have only recently been able to compete with foreign competition. Since 1980, the ROKG policy has moved forward, toward greater market openings. That means that there are more items for which U.S. exporters can get automatic approval. Today nearly all manufactured items are automatically approved (99.5 percent).[8] In calculating all items, we find the ratio is 94.7 percent. In fact, of the 10,241 items, only 547 cannot be automatically approved.

Thus Korea's policies and import liberalization should lead to increased U.S. export opportunities, partly because of pressure from U.S. trade negotiators. U.S. representatives request, even demand, reductions in the following sectors: manufactured goods average 8.8 percent, primary goods average 3.2 percent. Korea's tariff rates on imports average 16.8 percent for manufactured goods and 25.1 percent for primary goods.

U.S. negotiators continue to make headway. Liberalization is taking place, however, its pace and scope are questioned. These negotiations either take the form of a product specific approach or a generic one. More recently the ROKG announced plans for some special laws to "reduce nontariff import barriers, removal of restrictions on overseas travel and related currency control measures, and the easing of restrictions on foreign participation in trading company activities."[9]

FAIR TRADE AND GOOD COMMUNICATION

U.S. Congressman Don Bonker argues that the United States should develop policies for tracking trade patterns, before they become international crises that affect our standard of living.[10] His feelings are that most Americans don't know enough about the perils of protectionism, or international competition, even how local business can respond favorably to our export opportunities. Literacy, he believes, is the first step to improve trade imbalances. But perhaps more importantly than knowledge is policy. He thinks the U.S. needs a national trade policy on exports.

To summarize, the Korean economy, like Japan's, is heavily dependent upon U.S. trade. If Korea continues along this path, protectionists will be clamoring for restrictions. Already the European Community is restricting Korean imports. By contrast somewhat with the Japanese business community, it seems that the Koreans have taken more initiative.

Yet surprisingly, in 1989 Korea was not listed on the "301" mandatory negotiations while Japan was. Korea has initiated the open-door policy (the tariff reductions, the foreign investment liberalization), import source diversification (restrict imbalance of Japanese products, provide incentives for imports from U.S.), and the favorable currency situation (high yen, strong won, low dollar).

Going from rubble to riches, evidently Koreans have gained new confidence as risk takers. Whatever their many motives, tangible results are evident. Foreign firms can obtain trading licenses. Laws now guarantee the protection of intellectual property rights (total enforcement will come). Foreign banks in Seoul and Pusan can establish multiple branches. Life insurance specialists can now conduct business there. Even foreign-owned joint ventures are possible. The international travel agencies in Seoul resounds with a plethora of ticket requests. Their automobile market is no cul de sac; it is open to foreign dealers. Finally, Koreans have become connoisseurs of cheaper imported wines, cigarettes, and agricultural products.

According to U.S. Chamber of Commerce members in Korea, the opening of Korea's economy to U.S. trade is significant. "Due recognition of the ROKG's market opening should be given. But there is some distance left to go."[11] These developments increased not only U.S. exports but also U.S confidence that Koreans are responsive and responsible trade partners. But this latter view is often debated.

From 1963 to 1988 increased Korean exports volume (and corollary growth rates, averaging 31.6 percent) have tended to push U.S. imports upward as well (increased 90 times; $0.42 billion to $37.8 billion). It is a reciprocal, bilateral relation. Trade between Korea and the U.S. should continue its steady upward spiral (Korea ranked seventh for U.S. exports).

Will Korean exports ($18.31 billion) and imports ($8.76 billion) continue to leave significant surpluses ($9.5 billion)? Perhaps. But Korea won't skirt this issue. The Koreans increased American exports to Korea by 32.7 percent (1987).

NOTES

1. Edward A. Olsen, "U.S.-ROKG Relations: Common Issues and Uncommon Perceptions," *Korea and World Affairs* 13 (Spring 1989): 25–26.

2. Amy Albertson Tuncel, "Doing Business in the Pacific Rim," National University Teleconference Network, February 8, 1990.

3. International Division, U.S. Chamber of Commerce, *The Omnibus Trade and Competitiveness Act of 1988* (Washington, DC: U.S. Chamber of Commerce, 1988).

4. President and Fellows, "Competitiveness: 23 Leaders Speak Out," *The Harvard Business Review* (July-August 1987):106–23.

5. Christopher Mead, "Tongyang Nylong Enters Hard Disk Drive Market," *Korea High Tech Review* (August 1987):3. Mead puts out an excellent newsletter. Write Mead Ventures, P.O. Box 44952, Phoenix, Arizona 85064.

6. Korea Foreign Trade Association, *New Opportunities for Exporting to Korea* (Seoul: KFTA, 1989). KFTA, World Trade Center, 159–1 Samsung-dong, Kangnam-ku, Seoul, Korea. The book lists the items by industrial sector, including the volume amount and the percentage controlled by Japan. It is divided into machinery and mechanical appliances (chapter 1); electrical machinery and equipment (chapter 2); precious stones, iron, and steel (chapter 3); chemical and allied industries (chapter 4); textiles (chapter 5); and an appendix. Within each of these sections, there is a column which lists Korean importers or end users and their addresses. Exporters can contact these Korean firms.

7. Korea Foreign Trade Association, *Korea's Policies to Increase Imports* (Seoul: KFTA, 1988), 4.

8. Seung-Soo Han, *Responsive & Responsible: Korea's Trade Partnership with the United States* (New York: Reid and Priest, 1989), 4–5. For information, write: Reid and Priest, 111 19th Street, N.W., Washington, DC 10036.

9. U.S. Chamber of Commerce, *United States-Korean Trade Issues* (Seoul: American Chamber of Commerce in Korea, 1989), 1.

10. Don Bonker, *America's Trade Crisis: The Making of the U.S. Trade Deficit* (New York: Houghton, 1988).

11. U.S. Chamber of Commerce, *United States-Korean Trade Issues*, 8.

8

Priority Items

Knowing Korea's industrial priorities sheds new light on what U.S. priorities for export items should be. Chapter 6 identified the best overall export items. It also explored specific examples of those export items that show the largest percentage of increases. Those included agriculture, wood products, chemicals, and machines. As used in this chapter, priority items are just some of those long-term, high-volume industrial items that should attract interest from U.S. firms that export to Korea.

From the Koreans' viewpoint, they select those priority import items that allow them to achieve certain economic goals. What drives the Koreans toward these priority items? Some scholars say it's the same collective energy that motivates them to make the transition toward democracy, toward political readjustments, and toward the restructuring of their economy.[1] Other scholars believe the criteria for success begins with their neighbor, Japan. The death of Hirohito, Emperor of Japan, occasioned widespread but peaceful expression of anti-Japanese sentiment. Coming into economic maturity, the Korean sentiment is to out shine Japan, the "Rising Sun" of East Asia. That is one reason that they now export office equipment—desktop photocopiers, facsimile machines, and dot-matrix and laser printers. Two Korean beams that shine bright are electronics and manufacturing. As the Asian competition intensifies, family-run conglomerates (chaebols) in these two industries illuminate the Eastern horizon. The Koreans are competing with the Japanese in these high volume markets.

For them to do that requires that they develop self-sufficiency in manufacturing parts and designing their own technology—importing test equipment is a high priority for Koreans.[2] That explains why their electronics equipment ranks so high. They are importing these items in high quantities—cold cathodes, diodes, transistors, rectifiers, relays, electrical components, switches, control panels, transistors, and electronic devices.[3]

Electronic products account for 7 percent of world trade: computers (30 percent), telecommunications equipment (20 percent), consumer electronics (20 percent), parts (20 percent), and business electronics (10 percent). While the United States is still the leader in computers, Japan leads in consumer electronics and telecommunications equipment. From 1983 to 1988 Korea doubled its export profit ($3 billion to $6 billion); their imports also doubled ($2 billion to $4 billion). Surprisingly twenty-five companies account for 50 percent of the market, while eighty account for 80 percent of the world's market.[4]

Both Korea and Japan developed electronics policies—export promotion, balance-of-payment, international competition—to reach economic, not political, goals. The Koreans use trade policy and domestic electronics policy to achieve high volumes. The former classification included customs tariffs, export subsidies, and market access arrangements. The latter has included military R&D, general subsidies, public sector procurement, government guidelines, and restrictions on foreign investments.[5]

BEST PRODUCTS FOR CHEMICAL AND RAW PRODUCTS

Veteran exporters instinctively know the export priority items. To learn these priority items, try classifying the Korean economy into three stages of restructuring and development: (1) the economic changes occurring until 1973, in which Korea basically shifted from an agrarian economy to an urban-centered labor intense manufacturing one; (2) changes through 1979, whereby Korea recorded heavy capital investment in heavy and chemical industry; and (3) changes since 1980, which launched Korea into higher industrial orbits such as those found in high tech consumer goods and service industries.[6]

These changes reveal something about market expansion, but they

Table 8.1
Largest Volume of Chemical Products

			Units: $=1,000, %	
HS	Description	1987	1988	Percentage
		Jan.-Dec.	Jan.-Sep.	Change
2601	iron ores	393,964	316,118	4.1
2701	mineral fuels, oils	976,372	828,474	19.9
2709	petroleum oils	3,702,088	2,943,855	18.2
2710	petro oils bitumius	817,449	416,472	-25.6
2711	petro gases	405,061	389,899	39.5
2933	heterocyclic compound	279,783	266,283	30.1

Source: Compiled by the Korean Foreign Trade Association, What To
Sell To Korea, 1988.
Note: Percentage change is a one year projection (1988) based on trends.

also provide something else—an insight into why certain products are in high demand. The divisions of this chapter reflect these three levels of economic development—extractive, industrial, and service.

Table 8.1 shows the largest volumes of extractive products that the Koreans currently import. The numbers in the HS (harmonized system, the international classification for identifying products) column designate the description given in column two. These numbers are both a part of the Shipper's Export Declaration (SED) and the U.S. export classification system (8,000 commodity classes), giving all quantitative data requirements for commodities in the metric system of weights and measures.

This table reveals an increase in all items except petroleum oils bitumius, which recorded a 25.6 percent decrease between the two years. The information recorded in this table also correlates with other sources of information, showing high volume imports for: (1) fuels/distillates (petroleum and bituminous products); (2) inorganic chemicals (aluminum, chromium, and titanium oxides; phosphates and phosphate borates; silicon carbide); (3) organic chemicals (styrene, hydrocarbon halogenated derivatives, ethylene products, propylene, cerephalic acid, acrylonitrile, heterocyclic compounds and nucleic acids, epoxides, ketones, saturated polyesters); (4) plastic materials (polymerization products, polyethylene, ethylene, copolymers, polystyrene); and (5) aluminum (unalloyed/unwrought scrap). Table 8.2 is another example of the raw products that are imported.

BEST PROSPECTS FOR MACHINERY AND PARTS

The best prospects for exporting to Korea are found in Table 8.3. All items but one—machines for textiles—show an increase in volume.

Other items not listed in Table 8.3 comprise the electric machinery: generators, motors, transformers, rectifier relays, radiotelephonic equip-

Table 8.2
Largest Volume of Raw Products

		Units: $=1,000, %		
HS	Description	1987 Jan.-Dec.	1988 Jan.-Sep.	Percentage Change
7204	scrap iron	382,297	420,527	61.4
7208	iron flat rolled	407,896	253,142	-15.1
7219	stainless steel	336,374	364,776	49.1
7601	aluminium, unwrought	298,489	408,213	106.9

Source: Compiled by the Korean Foreign Trade Association, What To
Sell To Korea, 1988.
Note: Percentage change is a one year projection (1988) based on trends.

Table 8.3
Largest Volume of Machines and Parts

		Units: $=1,000, %		
HS	Description	1987 Jan.-Dec.	1988 Jan.-Sep.	Percentage Change
8445	machines for textiles	345,971	224,891	-11.1
8471	data process machines	469,315	555,433	80.6
8473	parts # 84.69-84.72	316,808	407,525	88.9
8479	machines not elsewhere	306,166	699,681	200.4
8522	parts #85.19-85.21	267,190	253,763	31.0
8529	parts #85.25-85.28	339,934	256,525	1.2
8356	switching apparatus	230,848	264,984	54.7
8540	cold cathode	332,042	310,585	28.4
8541	diodes transistors	423,440	353,624	10.9
8542	integrated circuits	1,791,061	1,740,273	37.9
8708	parts motor	511,862	404,737	5.5
8802	aircraft vehicles	304,474	701,499	143.9

Source: Compiled by the Korean Foreign Trade Association, What To
Sell To Korea, 1988.
Note: Percentage change is a one year projection (1988) based on trends.

ment, passive electrical components, and switches, not to mention control panels, transistors, and electronic devices.

A fuller list includes internal combustion engine parts, pumps, temperature control equipment, filters and purifiers, and spray equipment as well as general machinery for handling equipment, earthmovers, weaving and knitting machines, rolling mills, metalworking and printing machinery, office machines, valves, bearings, and textile processing machinery.

The best prospects for exporting are optical and precision machinery, surveying and drawing instruments, temperature measurement and control instrumentation, medical instruments, x-ray analysis, and various types of control equipment.

Other listings include electronics and accessories, computers and peripherals, electronic industry production and test equipment, medical equipment and supplies, scientific and analytical instruments, telecommunications equipment, and pollution control. The need for Koreans to import these products reflects just how much the Korean economy has developed over the past few years.

ELECTRONICS AND ACCESSORIES

The Sixth Economic Plan, and latest Five-Year Economic Development Plan (1987–1991), once again places high priority on both the production of electronics products and the fostering of indigenous technology. The government views the electronics industry as the driving force behind Korea's industrial achievements. Because of ROKG's commitment, this industry should flourish as a strategic export industry. By means of the Industrial Development Law the ROKG has officially established this industrial sector as a priority area.

Another factor making these priority items so attractive comes from outside Korea. World markets, as an external force, are responding to rising demand for sophisticated electronics consumer and industrial products. As a result of these trends, the electronics and accessories products should steadily expand through the 1990s. Look for Korea's export-oriented electronics industry to generate more U.S. exports.

The 1987 total volume dollars of imported goods into Korea was $17.4 billion, consisting of $6.9 billion for consumer electronics, $3.2 billion for industrial electronics, and $7.3 billion for components and parts. Korea's electronics exports grew at an average annual rate of 28 percent (1980–1987), accounting for 10 percent for all exports. From 1986 to 1988 that percentage increased to over a fifth of all exports. But Korea is not only a major producer and exporter of electronic products, it is also a major importer. Korean imports of electronic parts and components, including integrated circuits and semiconductors, grew at an annual average growth rate of 30.0 percent (from $1.2 billion in 1982 to $5.9 billion in 1987). That is a fivefold increase. Imports in this one area alone represent about 77 percent of total imports in 1987 and over 80 percent in 1988. Consumer and industrial electronic equipment manufacturers (about 560 firms) both produce and buy electronic components. They produce radio receivers, televisions, video cassette recorders, musical instruments, electronic watches, microwave ovens, speaker systems, computers, peripherals, electronic calculators, data communications systems, and photocopying machines. To continue this rapid production of goods, the government supports new plant constructions, modernization and expansion of existing production facilities, and more expenditures on R&D operations. Their exports go to world markets, with computers, VCRs, magnetic tapes, telephone sets, and semiconductors leading the list.

COMPUTERS AND PERIPHERALS

Besides electronics and accessories, Korea displays other examples of high technology developments. Although high tech takes several forms of specific product development, new applications of computers and related equipment rank high on the priority lists. More important than that, the Koreans persuade us of their increasing sophistication in using this technology. Both the number and scale of their commercial activities are impressive. As with other priority lists, the growth in this sector comes, in part, from the ROKG initiatives and funding. The Korean government formulated a strategic master plan. The ROKG plans to install a National Computer Network (NCN) by the year 2001. To accomplish this, computer experts will link five computer subnetworks into one national system. Their plans are twofold: to complete the task by the year 2001 and to spend approximately $474 million in development and equipment costs.

ROKG has additional plans for new applications of high tech. The Korean government plans to develop basic computer programs for their industries. As in other projects, the ROKG will probably buy equipment and software from outside sources. Because of these initiatives, look for ripple effects. The government's lead on computer networking and decentralization should also impact advanced private-sector computer users. This, in turn, should spark significant demand for other types of computers and peripherals. Look for a wide range of applications, particularly in the business and commercial fields.

Still another example of Korean high-tech development is found in communications fields. The ROKG gradually plans to open public telecommunications facilities for commercial data communications services. U.S. exporters should anticipate substantial sales of various computer sizes. Both computers and peripherals serve as main host computers for networking. Since these are network systems, project directors also need distributed data processing, database formation, and attachments to the main system.

Korea's increasing sophistication in computers and peripherals has direct implications for U.S. exports. Such major expansions, though, attract competitors. Already the Japanese have extensively penetrated this market. Since the design and manufacturing of so much of the Korean computer output comes from Japan, American suppliers need to offer more. Japanese manufacturers, because of geographic proximity, have an inside track in selling to Koreans. Based on government and financial reports, we know this Asian neighbor goes after these markets. The strategy is confidential, but from Korean customers, brochures, and advertisements the pattern is clear. Japanese sales forces accommodate the Korean buyers; therefore, American strategies must counter the Japanese offers. U.S. suppliers should offer sophisticated technical assistance and the encouragement of sales engineers. Once Koreans specify American components, that should mean that U.S. importers can gain a competitive edge.

At the Olympic Games, Koreans used a combination of interlinked systems, IBM, and AT&T, along with Goldstar-built AT&T monitors and Olivetti PC24s to compile results of the events. IBM 4381s and 36s combined with AT&T 3820s provided the hardware, while Koreans from the Advanced Institute of Science and Technology (AIST) developed the software. Besides these efforts, the AIST has had other computer projects.[7]

The Ministry of Science and Technology projects that the population of imported computers should double between 1990 and 1994. Computer installations will increase at an average annual rate of 17 percent for small/medium and large-scale computers. Those projects include a 27 percent annual rate increase for minis and special purpose mini-level computers. This reflects the accelerating shift to mini- and microcomputers that began in the early 1980s. The IBM XT and AT compatibles perform functions formerly done by small and medium computers. The demand for computers and related equipment should remain heavy and even increase at least 10 percent during the next few years.

The principal importers will be government agencies and public organizations. U.S. suppliers should respond to anticipated increased demands created by the project formation of the National Computer Network (NCN, including the Administrative Computer Network). Very large computers, super computers, and peripheral equipment represent the best market for U.S. suppliers. Imports, valued at $469.3 million in 1987, are projected to increase at an average annual growth rate of 10 percent through 1991.

The Ministry of Government Administration formulated a master plan for the installation of the NCN by 2001. The NCN consists of five computer subnetworks to be established and integrated into one nationwide Integrated Services Digital Network (ISDN) by the year 2001. This includes networks for (1) administration, (2) education and research, (3) banking and finance, (4) national defense, and (5) public security. The first subnetwork, the administrative computer network, is to computerize the functions related to resident registration, real estate management, economic statistics, export-import customs administration, employment management, and automobile management. Of particular interest to computer suppliers are the first three computer subnetworks being rapidly developed.

While Samsung Electronics, Goldstar, Daewoo Telecom, and Hyundai Electronics are gearing up for the plan, U.S. exporters could, too. U.S. suppliers could export computers for networking, distributed data processing, database formation, or for attachment to the NCN and the ISDN. The present U.S. share, an average annual rate of 10 percent through 1990, could reach $240.67 million by 1990. That figure could increase significantly for two reasons. First is the local awareness of technical leadership of American firms. Second, ROKG policy encourages imports from non-Japanese sources. Major suppliers to Korea are IBM, UNISYS, CDC, Prime, DEC, NCR, Hewlett-Packard, Honeywell, DG, and Wang.

ELECTRONIC INDUSTRY PRODUCTION AND TEST EQUIPMENT

Koreans see the growth of the electronics industry as one major component of their economic development plan. Both the ROKG and the private sector are committed to expansion and modernization of this industry. They are convinced that the Korean electronics industry can maximize value, quality, and sophistication. Already their finished industrial and consumer goods support this belief. Sophisticated Korean products continue to attract significant new capital investments. This, in turn, creates good opportunities for sales of U.S. production and test equipment.

Long-range plans call for automation of every sector within the industry. Koreans believe that electronics innovations keep costs down, while at the same time such strategies increase quality. However, to upgrade their product quality, they must modernize not only the electronics industry but also the technical reliability and sensitivity of their equipment. This is essential if they are to compete in export world markets with the Japanese and Americans. As a result of these plans, potential U.S. exporters of automatic production and test equipment should develop definite market strategies of their own. Look for specialty and emerging areas on the horizons. Increasing demand and exports should come from microelectronics. Korean markets for electronics industry production and test equipment continue their patterns of growth.

Through promotion, U.S. suppliers could strengthen demand. With proper promotion strategies, they could increase responsiveness not only to the products but also to the prices. How? By sales promotions and advertising campaigns, or through Korean sales representatives or some form of media. Most of the sales and marketing of components come from promotion. Based on U.S. Chamber of Commerce data this promotion centers around five activities: (1) advertising in trade journals, (2) listings in product catalogs, (3) participation in trade shows, (4) direct contacts through sales staff, and (5) promotion. The fifth activity of promotion evolves from good, established relations with trading firms. As a means for distributing products, suppliers know that this is especially effective in Korea. Here good relations and an understanding of the market are vital to the supplier's success.

MEDICAL EQUIPMENT AND SUPPLIES

Various factors contribute to the increased medical outlays in Korea. Some of these are (1) the vastly increasing number of eligible welfare patients and insurance subscribers under the national health insurance program; (2) the rapidly rising standard of living that allows more people to obtain better health care; (3) changes in medical treatment due to technical innovations; and (4) the general rise in health patients. The sixth Five-Year Economic Development Plan calls for an increase in the number of insurance subscribers, which numbers 23.4 million (56.3 percent of the total population). To care for increased numbers of eligible welfare patients and insurance subscribers, plans have been instituted to expand service and construct public and private hospitals.

Despite these local developments, few medical items currently produced in Korea are considered top quality products as measured by international performance and quality standards. Korea is unable to meet the increasing requirements of renovating facilities and upgrading their medical programs. Even as current ROKG plans are being implemented, experts agree that Koreans should continue relying on foreign suppliers to meet medical equipment needs for many years to come.

In the medical equipment and supplies area, proper promotion is the key to sales. You need to determine your promotional objectives. Do you hope to increase sales or establish some networks of potential customers? The former is direct, but the latter may pay greater dividends. The Korean network, in all its complexities, promises long-term success. Getting to the right decision makers in hospitals or outlets is crucial. A strong service component is also necessary. Remember that Koreans like service. You might think about linking service to promotion. But perhaps the most important factor is to find Korean representatives who know the key decision makers. Find out buying cycles and who to contact. Where do they buy the products now? How will you help them? Once you start your campaign, try to determine how effective your promotional strategies are. You probably will need to finetune them along the way.

SCIENTIFIC AND ANALYTICAL INSTRUMENTS

Koreans weren't the first to use "technopolises" to combine the concepts of technology and city-state (*polis*). This idea actually refers to government strategies found in both Korea and Japan to import scientific analytical instruments.

The ROKG is not merely developing the city of Taedok into a technopolis; it is also moving all of the thirteen state-run research institutes there. The total cost is $287.5 million. By contrast, Japan selected nineteen technopolises from their forty-seven applicants. The Japanese have scattered these technopolises throughout their prefectures.

The ROKG envisions these R&D centers as private research institutes (focused in high-tech areas) much like those of the Japanese. Such policies promote sales, especially for high quality scientific and analytical instruments.

The ROKG intends to invest $14.3 billion in science and technology projects between 1987 and 1991, with an annual growth rate of 15.7 percent (from $2,080 million in 1987 to $3,721 million in 1991). The funds will be used to upgrade existing research institutes from 2.0 percent of the GNP (1986) to 2.5 percent (1991). The ROKG will not simply buy scientific and analytical instruments, they will also provide services for an increasing number of researchers, from 9 per 10,000 population (1986) to 18 (1991). This is specified in the sixth Five Year Economic Development Plan (1987–1991). Very few of these necessary instruments are available from local sources.

TELECOMMUNICATIONS EQUIPMENT

In Korea you can readily find telex and fax services, photo-telegraphic facilities, even cable services. The ROKG plans to expand these services. The Korean government wants to update its communications facilities. Although they have improved dramatically in recent years, the Korean telecommunications infrastructures remain inadequate to meet future needs. For now, however, most hotels have good communication links with the outside world.

Direct dialing is possible from Seoul. You can call major provincial cities in Korea. However, in order to meet emerging needs, several projects are already underway: (1) Direct dialing systems are being installed in Korean communities around the nation. (2) Electronic switching systems (ESS) are replacing existing mechanical exchange systems as fast as they can be installed. (3) One million ESS lines will be introduced each year through 2001. The cost is $29.1 billion. (4) Current plans call for developing digital communications networks and improving services to meet the needs of an emerging information-oriented society. (5) Korea is expanding and modernizing its broadcasting facilities to meet the increasing demand for domestic and international communications. The 1988 Olympics accelerated this whole process.

Two dominant factors are pushing the sales of telecommunications equipment: (1) significant expansions of telephone switching systems and (2) diversifications in other Korean telecommunications networks.

POLLUTION CONTROL

Industrialization is a double-edged sword for any society. It results in a higher standard of living and affects quality of life. Yet its benefits can be tainted by severe pollution in the industrial and urban areas. To combat this negating trend, the ROKG is enforcing stricter government controls through legislation. At the same time, they are providing more money to solve the problem.

The market for pollution control equipment has grown from $300 million in 1985 to $442 million in 1988. Approximately 470 Korean manufacturing firms, mostly small and medium companies, produce pollution control equipment. However, given the way the implementation strategies are organized, American firms should work with these Korean firms for part of this market.

The benefits are worth it. The Korean firms get discounts and low-interest loans, while Americans are assured of market positions. Joint ventures with Korean companies are the trend. Already the volume of U.S. imports as part of a joint venture totalled $130 million (1986). Some analysts project an annual real growth of 12.6 percent until 1990, when the imports should be $208 million.

With the passage of new legislation—the Environmental Preservation Law—all Korean firms are potential buyers. Those engaged in industrial pollution are required to install control equipment. Until 1987 the government only monitored the problems; now they evaluate them. Because of industrial violations and subsequent penalties, pollution control as a desirable policy and the need for pollution control equipment as implementation strategies of that policy make this a high import priority.

This area may be particularly attractive to U.S. exporters for two reasons. First, the government provides limited customs-duty exemptions on certain pollution control equipment that is approved in advance. Second, U.S. exporters to Korea have a special designation. Before diversification, about 80 percent of the early pollution equipment (1986) came from Japan. After diversification, sales are shifting toward U.S. suppliers.

Since this is a specialty item, U.S. exporters must be creative in establishing their contacts. One of the best ways to secure contacts would be through trade shows, a place which also allows exporters to conduct technical seminars. In either late April or early May the Korea Environmental Preservation Association sponsors (in Seoul) its international exhibition for pollution control equipment. The event for 1989, International Exhibition for Korean Environmental Pollution Control, was held April 24–28. If you are interested write the sponsoring organization, KEPA, 45, 40Ka, Namdaemun-ro, Chung-gu, Seoul.

Those companies with certain types of equipment have the best prospects of selling their products. These include, but are not limited to, multicyclone separators, packed towers, bag filters, chemical balances, atomic absorption spectrometers, dissolved oxygen meters, liquid chromatography equipment, gas chromatography equipment, submersible aerators, and surface aerators.

Firms with these products are advised to use Korean sales agents, since sales volumes depend upon contacts. Korean agents could distribute information and demonstrate equipment performance. Oregon hired its own Korean agent to establish export outlets.

KOREANS IN OREGON

In May 1989 a Korean delegation—Foreign Trading Agents in Korea—visited Oregon. This association of 4,700 members, known as AFTAK, serves an intermediary capacity. Its members, serving a crucial need for most exporters, import trade items into Korea. Every trader knows that finding Korean importers can be difficult, if not altogether frustrating. That is why Dae-Jung Kim wanted to bring a Korean trade mission to Oregon. Mr. Kim invited buying agents (representing overseas suppliers and manufacturers) to meet with Oregon exporters. The Korean agents came looking for priority items—those trade offerings that rank high on government, business, consumer, and industrial lists. Because of present demands, certain items take precedence over other commodities, whether Korean agents are buying, importing, or selling.[8]

These Koreans went to Oregon looking for priority items not found in other states. On that particular trade mission to Oregon, the Koreans wanted a variety of agricultural products—corn, sorghum, soybean—and some industrial equipment (tools, supplies). Some products were low-value items—wood products, draft linerboard, and secondary fibers. Others were high value, sophisticated technological items—medical and testing equipment.

In 1882, the United States and Korea signed a bilateral Treaty of Commerce and Navigation. Today Korea has bilateral agreements with ten other countries: West Germany, Switzerland, the Netherlands, Belgium, Tunisia, the U.K., France, Sri Lanka, Senegal, and Bangladesh. These strong diplomatic-business ties suggest an international, even strategic, importance to Korea's priority items of trade.

NOTES

1. Danny M. Leipziger, ed., *Korea: Transition to Maturity* (New York: Pergamon Press, 1988).

2. Marc Brien, "Outshining the Rising Sun: the Korean Electronics Industry Circumvents Japanese Dominance," *High Technology Business* (February 1989):13.

3. The best prospect list was taken from a list developed by both the U.S. Department of Commerce and Korea Foreign Trade Association. See the KFTA monograph: *What To Sell To Korea* (December 1988).

4. Michael M. Kostecki, "Electronics Trade Policies in the 1980s," *Journal of World Trade* 23 (1989):17.

5. Kostecki, p. 18.

6. Ung-Soo Kim, "Comments on Economic Development in South Korea," in *Development and Cultural Change: Cross-Cultural Perspectives*, ed. Ilpyong-J. Kim (New York: Paragon House, 1986), 65.

7. Oles Gadacz, "The Systems Behind the Scoring at the Olympics in Seoul," *Datamation*, September 15, 1988, 26.

8. Patty McWayne, "Oregon's Korean Connection," *Oregon Business*, May 1989, 50.

_____ **III**

Know This People

9

Korea and U.S. Origins

Even though countries sign bilateral agreements, they nevertheless disagree. "The best laid political plans can actually make it more difficult for us to remain a foothold," said one U.S. exporter about Korea. "U.S. trade bullying fans the flames of anti-Americanism here, and American business pays for that." Complaints over closed markets seem legitimate. But there are times when a step forward and a step backward could prove equally disastrous. As this exporter said, "Koreans feel that they're being pushed around and that the U.S. doesn't recognize the great strides they have made."[1]

Korean laws require firms who trade with U.S. firms to get approval before they either endorse types of agreements or evaluate how they fit into current policies. Agreements with Korean firms are not finalized by the parties involved. Korean business transactions differ, somewhat, from those in the United States. That difference is both a function of law and government. These differences have direct implications on business deals and profits.

In contrast with the United States, Korea has civil laws, not common laws. Common laws are based on custom, tradition, and judicial decisions, while civil laws pertain to private rights for each institution. The former is general and is applied in all cases; the latter is specifically applied in each case. Therefore, the Korean civil laws apply to each case of interpretation by the minister in charge of that institution. From a business perspective, that means that without direct government approval no legal basis exists for business deals. To understand Korean law is to know this people and how to conduct business deals better.

"Under the Korean legal system, statutes serve only as general statements of principles and considerations which should be applied by the competent ministry in regulating the relevant transaction or conduct."[2] Through this procedure, authority remains clearly at the top. This means each government agency interprets business deals. Therefore lawyers look not to the courts and decisions made there as a precedent but to both the relevant ministry and what seems to be already working. To avoid difficulties, involve those "familiar with the cultural, political and legal considerations relevant in negotiating an agreement in Korea." Without following these guidelines, "the U.S. business is not likely to be in a position to realize fully the financial benefits it expects to achieve from the business transaction."[3]

As we learn more about Koreans, we come to appreciate not simply their laws but certainly their cultural uniqueness in Asia. In Hong Kong and Singapore business is conducted in English, simply because these locales were, at one time, Western colonies. Not so in Korea. In Korea you can conduct some business deals in English, but usually you'll need interpreters. On the other hand, the Korean language is easier to learn than, say, Japanese. Korean religious traditions differ from the Japanese as well. "Japan has a stronger Buddhist influence, and Korea has a stronger Confucian and Christian influence."[4]

Koreans work long hours, quickly. They work not just long hours, but with great speed. Koreans are unrelenting workers, averaging over 2,833 hours per year. That figure is greater than for workers in the United States (1,898 hours) or Japan (2,168 hours). Sometimes they work too fast. In their eagerness to get things moving, they could lose quality control. Fortunately that is not the case. They control quality on site. Many Korean factories recycle products before they go out. To do that they designate locations as "rework areas." This way they ensure quality control for work quickly done. Until now, long hours and fast turn around worked; it paid great dividends for Koreans.

But now their industrial base is changing. So too must their labor segment. Industrially speaking, the Korean economy is moving from one based on basic technology assembled products to one propelled by higher technology (semiconductors). Admittedly, Korea's labor force is both prepared for and the primary cause of its economic transformation. Skilled blue-collar workers now demand higher wages, as do the highly motivated scientists and engineers. Both labor segments are becoming even more highly trained and technologically sophisticated. Under these circumstances, the trend toward higher labor costs has pushed Koreans further away from their total dependence on labor-intensive, low-value-added industries (apparels). These types of industries (basic electronic assembly) employ cheaper labor forces now found in other Southeast Asian countries.

This has resulted in the Koreans both moving their exports upward in value and promoting their segmented markets better, obviously clothing and certainly consumer electronics. These changes, in turn, could definitely improve U.S. export potentials.

PATRON TO PARTNER

Over 100 years ago (1882) Korea was an underdeveloped "Hermit Nation." Naturally, in bilateral relations, the U.S. dominated in size, military power, and political influence. Today the United States is no longer the undisputed patron. Politicians and business executives must adjust their views to understand Korea's new international role. We are equal partners. Any assessment should factor in the rapid changes in Korea and in trade policies. Opinions vary depending on the kind of relationship that is emerging. U.S. Assistant Secretary of State Gaston Sigur believes that "the fundamental relationship between the United States and the Republic of Korea is sound. The underlying elements which have made us close military allies and active trading partners have not changed."[5] Secretary Sigur assumes that the underlying elements have not changed. That assumption, however, is not shared by everyone. Some scholars believe that "the world has changed, but America has not." John Steinbruner, director of the Foreign Policy Studies Program at the Brookings Institute, worries about trends. "Can we face our challenges from a position of strength, in full command of our extraordinary resources, or will we ignore them until forced into full retreat, in crisis, with our strength diminished?"[6]

As for East Asia, foreign policy analysts Harry Harding and Edward J. Lincoln argue that "American economic hegemony and strategic bipolarity seem to be ending first in Asia."[7] Three economic and political pressures are building in East Asia. First and foremost, Asia is becoming an economic power with greater interdependence, one country with another. Politically speaking, these countries prefer freedom from outside influence, particularly with regard to economic expansion. The second pressure point is political liberalization. The third is political participation. Citizens here want to participate in international politics.

•

These Asian countries favor equal treatment from Moscow and Washington. Since these are the same countries—South Korea, Taiwan, Hong Kong, Singapore—that account for 60 percent of the U.S. trade deficit, we must realistically assess the pull toward new political centers here.

From a historical perspective, political scientist Karl Moskowitz assumes a positive attitude about Korea-U.S. diplomacy. He described the mutual benefits. After the Korean War, American military and civilian programs provided Korea with (1) reconstruction programs for war damage, (2) resources for military training and defense, (3) basic commodities and raw materials, (4) foreign exchange, and (5) technical and institutional assistance.[8] Korea gained much, but so did the United States.

The historian Fred Harvey Harrington develops a different argument, one more negative. In analyzing the relations between 1882 and 1905, this writer describes how frustrated American diplomats were with Korea. Because of them, the Korean government was undermined.[9]

Finally, Robert A. Scalapino and Sung-Joo Han are futurists. In making their comments, they are guardedly optimistic. "South Korea will be more assertive and, in some respects, more independent in its relations with the United States as time passes, betokening the movement from client to partner."[10] The bilateral relations were once asymmetrical, skewed toward U.S. demand. This is no longer so, as Korea assumes greater responsibility for its economic and military future.

The United States has decreased its direct military aid to South Korea, despite continued military buildups in North Korea. Now the ROKG pays for about 40 percent of its investment in defense, of which about 85 percent comes from the United States. Seoul pays over $1.9 billion for the support of 43,000 American troops. Incidentally, the U.S. 8th Army is moving outside Seoul's prime real estate area. But the real issue is command. Younger Korean generals want greater control over the combined U.S.-Korean forces.

The Koreans also want to build their own weapons, including more than K–2 rifles. They prefer these: surface-to-surface missiles, multiple rocket launchers, armored vehicles, tanks, destroyers, patrol vessels, and sophisticated aircraft. According to General Ryu-Joon Hyung, they want "precision products such as aircraft, guided missiles, telecommunications equipment, and automatic weaponry" built by Koreans in local industries.[11] The U.S. government views these developments negatively for four reasons: (1) Such a practice would further contribute to the trade imbalance. (2) Already some provisions are made to offset trade in the smaller weapon systems, and this is enough participation. (3) If these policies were implemented, who would guarantee protection of the intellectual property rights? (4) There is the potential that some weapon sales could eventually end up in Third World countries.

Historically speaking, military, political, and economic matters seem to go together. Military, diplomatic, and economic issues are not new to this region.

History records ironic notes. It was Japan, not America, that began the westernization and modernization of Korea. Although not intended, Japan's policies forever changed Korea's economy. The Japanese wanted an expanding, agriculturally based Korean economy. Yet, in fact, they achieved much more. Their unsuccessful strategy began in 1876, when Korea signed the Kangwha Treaty with Japan, giving her trade advantages and direct influence. The treaty was short-lived, because China resented the Japanese presence. At the urging of China, Korea signed the 1882 U.S. treaty. That treaty ended earlier U.S. confrontations of "gunboat diplomacy" (1871 American incursion). King Kojong, then ruler of Korea, also modernized his army and the country's economy in response to these intrusions.

In 1883 Lucius H. Foote, a career diplomat, and Dr. Horace N. Allen, a missionary doctor, gained the confidence of King Kojong. Horace Grant Underwood, an educator and translator, advised the king. The first American businessman to establish a trading company at Inchon in 1884 was Walter Townsend. By 1889 executives established joint ventures with Koreans. They built the first electric power plant, installed the water works, built tram cars, and began the first telephone system. Americans exported everything from Coca-Cola to bibles. U.S. foreign aid and business investments made an economic impact, while the infusion of Christianity resulted in social changes. The missionary influence records these changes: the liberal arts education system, greater education for women, social programs, and more hospitals, schools, churches.

The year 1982 marked the centennial of the Treaty of Peace, Amity, Commerce, and Navigation. From that beginning until now, Korea has time and again decided that the United States would be its trading partner. From the first encounter in 1882 until now, Korean relationships have gradually changed.

REGIONAL POWERS

The Japanese initiated modernization through their expansionist policies. They entered Korea in 1905 to formalize their control, while President Theodore Roosevelt acquiesced. In 1910 Japan annexed Korea, gaining full control at King Kojong's death. Japan ruthlessly controlled Korea. Yet President Woodrow Wilson, like his predecessor, accepted a status quo foreign policy toward Japan. Ironically Japan, who now worries about Korean industries, developed the Korean economy.

Nahm believes Japanese economic development and modernization actually occurred after 1931.[12] Inadvertently, Japan aided Korea's economic development by bringing the needed capital, a coinage system, financial and commercial institutions, and industry. Moreover, the Japanese also expanded the railroads and highways, improved harbors, and transferred modern technology.

Following the thirty-five years of Japanese occupancy, people of the world responded sympathetically to Korea's plight. Nevertheless after World War II, Russia and the United States divided Korea as a temporary measure. The Russians wanted warmer ports for their vessels and the industrial area. Americans settled for the agrarian south. Original plans for reuniting the two halves through free elections never materialized as Pyongyang and Seoul established rival governments.

The first and only leader of North Korea has been Il-Sung Kim. As head of the Democratic People's Republic of Korea (1948), he aggressively took charge. By 1950 Kim revealed his own plans of reunification. The Soviet-backed North Korean army launched a full scale invasion of South Korea. For three years this Soviet-backed regime, sometimes with the aid of Chinese forces, fought the U.S.-led United Nations divisions. The conflict ended with a truce signed at Panmunjom in 1953, a peace accord that stands today. Yet U.S. sentiments for South Korea remained high.

During the Korean War some 54,000 Americans and 2 million Koreans died. This war both forcibly dislodged 10 million Korean families and virtually destroyed Seoul. After the war and at a 1951 speech before the U.S. Congress, General Douglas MacArthur summed up the feelings of many Americans with these words: "The magnificence of the courage and fortitude of the Korean people defies description." Even with the peace accord, tensions remained.

Somehow through all of this the leader of North Korea, Il-Sung Kim survived. Some think he survived because of the diverted tensions and political maneuvering between the Chinese and Soviets. Kim has remained in power for forty years, becoming something of a cult figure, claiming to be The Great Leader of Korea in an almost semideified fashion. His claim to greatness is overshadowed by his government's abysmal economic failures. The economic race between the two Koreas is no real contest. While North Korea has the natural resources, South Korea's economy has safely outdistanced its neighbor. In fact, North Korea has a larger foreign debt than China.

From the beginning Pyongyang chose the *juche* policy (self-reliance). Since 1951 that idea has guided the North Koreans through the de-Stalinization campaign of Khrushchev and the subsequent drift in Sino-Soviet relations. But neither these Russian models (1950s) nor the Chinese economic ones (1980s) seemed to work as well as those chosen by Seoul (capitalism). The recent influence of China in the early 1980s with the great leap forward was short-lived. Pyongyang realized more quickly than the People's Republic of China (PRC) that these models, which were designed to exclude capitalist's taintings, don't work either. China has drastically cut back on its own commitment to capital imports. Now Pyongyang has once again moved closer to Moscow, as evidenced by the recent bilateral relations.

Discouraged by low economic production, Pyongyang has alternated its major playing partner. In 1986 the Prime Minister of North Korea visited Moscow to enter into long-range economic agreements. Both countries signed an accord for economic cooperation (1986–1990). Through these agreements, the Soviets provided the following technical and economic assistance: the construction of a nuclear power plant, the planning of maritime economic zones, and the exchange of modern technology via increased bilateral trade and travel. As Chinese leader Deng Xiao Ping relinquishes his rule to Jiang Zemin (who is clearly identified with a policy of economic openness to the West), China's relations with the Koreans could change. Geopolitical factors directly affect international security and economic trade.

CHANGES AND NEW CHALLENGES

The challenge for U.S. exporters is to take advantage of these political developments. U.S. business plans could include in them strategies on how to play this economic game. That entails an understanding of the major world powers. Changes and possibly new challenges exist here for U.S. exporters, but this region could become quite unstable, as it has before. For that reason exporters should evaluate their investments accordingly. While traveling or working in Seoul, business executives notice many more military soldiers (629,000 on active duty and 4,840,000 in reserves) than expected; they also don't expect to hear alert sirens.

Historically, the south was agricultural; now it's also industrial. South Koreans have put their international trade machine into operation and, by comparison, they have overshadowed the accomplishments of the north. In the mid-eighties total exports for South Korea ($31.5 billion, 1986) exceeded those for North Korea ($1.3 billion, 1985) by almost 30 percent. The same was true for respective imports ($35 billion versus $1.7 billion).

Few governments have taken each other by the throat as have these two. But why? Some say it's because of the volatile Korean temperament; others point to geographical locale—agricultural versus industrial concerns, much like in the U.S. Civil War. But the best explanation comes from a different perspective. These two governments of Korea, with their distrust and haggling, actually mirror the broader conflicts between Moscow and Washington. These broader differences—ideology, strategies of economic development, life styles—permeate the regional ones in two ways. Overall political differences find expression not only in inter-Korean relations but also, and more important for our concerns, in how their respective leaders develop their infrastructure and open their ports.

NORTH KOREA

The triangular relationship among North Korea, the Soviets, and China remains crucial to trade because of the potential for war. Both figuratively and economically, the threat of war affects not just the Seoul-Washington political link, but also the Anchorage-Inchon pipeline.

Two years ago a North Korean physician and ten family members defected. First they went to Japan because they feared what might happen to them in South Korea. Evidently, North Korean propaganda about the dangers in the South was effective. It took five days in Japan before the doctor began to unravel fact from fiction. This isolated experience illustrates the hostility. The tensions between the two Koreas run hot as well as cold.[13]

The South became quite anxious when North Korean leader Il-Sung Kim announced his desire for bilateral talks on military and political issues. This came at the same time that North Koreans filed some 44,000 alleged violations (June 1986–July 1987) at the Demilitarized Zone (DMZ) 439th Military Armistice Commission meetings. In August 1987 they filed some 12,300 violations alone. Even though China and Russia fielded Olympic teams, North Korea did not participate in the Olympics. And in the fall of 1987, North Korean gunboats attacked and killed eleven crewmen of a South Korean fishing boat, claiming the boat provoked the attack.

North Korea sides with Eastern Bloc countries; the South with the West. North Koreans import petroleum, grains and cereals, machinery and capital equipment, and cooking coal from Eastern Bloc countries. No one enters the country without an invitation by host organizations. International flights connect travel between North Korea, China, and the Soviet Union.

South Korea lists trade with more than 128 countries, about 26 more than North Korea. Since North Korea trades with Eastern Bloc countries, it and its allies are struggling economically. By contrast, South Korea's relations with the United States and its economy remain strong. The strength of this commitment was recently reaffirmed by the U.S. Senate. The U.S. Foreign Affairs Subcommittee set forth a resolution on Asian and Pacific Affairs which reads:

The Congress (1) reaffirms the commitment of the American people to the security of the Republic of Korea and the development of genuine democracy for the Korean people; (2) believes the North Korean government should cease its clandestine and reckless attempts to subvert the Republic of Korea; and (3) believes the North Korean government should agree to measures that will reduce tensions on the Korean peninsula. This includes more cooperative approach to the dialogue between the north and south, the genuine demilitarization of the Demilitarized Zone, the mutual and equitable reduction of military forces, family visitation and family reunification, and trade.[14]

Military buildups continue for both sides. The Korea-U.S. Combined Forces Command (CFC) began in 1978 as a strategic force. Joint plans include improved weapon systems: 28 Hawks, 133 Stinger SAM (599 reloads), 5 Sui Kiang FAC with 14 more planned (aircraft), 4 Ulson frigates, 2 Jupiters 88mm, and 2 (850-ton) patrol vessels. In comparison, North Korea has 100,000 commando forces equipped with 280 AN–2 low-flying transports, which are not detectable by radar. They also have 876 helicopters very similar to those used in South Korea. North Korea has 800,000 regular forces (1.2 times the force of South Korea), 3,500 tanks (2.7 times), 7,400 field artillery (2 times) and 1,500 aircraft (1.4 times). To counter these odds, the South recently purchased new planes and gained more air power. They now fly the new F–16 "Fighting Falcon," built by General Dynamics of Ft. Worth. If necessary, they can call on the 7th U.S. Air Force (Korea), formerly attached to 5th Air Force (Japan).

CONCLUSION

To conclude, bilateral relations between Korea and the U.S. have changed over the past 100 years, but especially in recent years. Americans disagree over just how much this region is undergoing drastic economic and political changes. Regardless of their interpretations, most scholars agree that South Korea will be more assertive and independent in its relations with the United States. These developments are, in some ways, as dramatic as the conflicts in Korea themselves. What began as patron relations continue, but Koreans are now equal partners. Korea is America's third largest partner in East Asia, behind Japan and Taiwan.

Export opportunities are there. That's obvious. How to size up other regional powers—Japan, Russia, China—is far less obvious. Exporters could exploit political developments with potential for explosiveness. Each side of the Korean peninsula represents a different life style. Economics play a big part. What is happening in the People's Republic of China (PRC) and Eastern European countries is happening in North Korea. South Korea's trade and economy are much stronger than the north, even though their armed forces are not.

Perhaps even unknowingly, Korea adopted several procedures of the

Foreign Affairs Subcommittee Resolution on Asia. (1) Korea did institute greater freedom of expression in newspapers and on television and radio. (2) The ROKG recognized political parties and their right to organize and participate in the political process. (3) The government established an independent judiciary, thereby respecting due process under the law and curtailing torture. (4) The government allowed citizens greater political participation. These steps should facilitate open dialogues, trust, and democracy. Changes in Korean domestic politics are also affecting bilateral trade issues.

NOTES

1. Daryl M. Plunk, "U.S.-Korean Relations: An American Perspective," *Korea and World Affairs* 13 (Spring 1989):8.

2. Trenholme Griffin, "Negotiating Agreements With Korean Business," *Korea's Economy* 2 (May 1986):11.

3. Griffin, 11.

4. T. W. Kang, *Is Korea the Next Japan?* (New York: Free Press, 1989), 9.

5. Senate Foreign Relations Subcommittee, *East Asian and Pacific Affairs*, Washington, DC: Senate Hearing, March 27, 1987, 23.

6. John D. Steinbruner, *Restructuring American Foreign Policy* (Washington, DC: Brookings Institution, 1989), 7.

7. Steinbruner, 6.

8. Karl Moskowitz, *From Patron to Partner* (Lexington, Mass.: D. C. Heath, 1984), 4.

9. Fred Harvey Harrington, "An American View of Korean-American Relations, 1882–1905," in *One Hundred Years of Korean-American Relations, 1882–1982*, eds. Yur-Bok Lee and Wayne Patterson (University, Ala.: The University of Alabama Press, 1986).

10. Robert A. Scalapino and Sung-Joo Han, *United States and Korean Relations* (Berkeley: University of California, Institute of East Asian Studies, 1986), 226.

11. Ryu-Joon Hyung, "Korea-U.S. Ties: Sitting on Defense," *Korea Business World*, May 1989, 10–11.

12. Andrew Nahm, "Modernization Process in Korea: A Historical Perspective," in *Modernization of Korea and the Impact of the West*, ed. Chang-Soo Lee (Los Angeles: University of California, East Asian Studies, 1981), 25–68.

13. Robert A. Scalapino and Hong-Koo Lee, *North Korea in a Regional and Global Context* (Berkeley: University of California, Institute of East Asian Studies, 1985).

14. Senate Foreign Relations Subcommittee, *East Asian and Pacific Affairs*, 25.

10

Korean Trade Policies

"It is time . . . to cope with new problems and new opportunities," said President Kennedy in his presidential inaugural address.[1] That same statement could be used to define Korea's trade dilemma. Korea's new problems are its need to spend trade surplus; its opportunities are found in open trade markets. It is painful, though, even for the ROKG. To have surplus money from exports means that many U.S. exporters and other groups interested in Korea want that money spent on them and their own purposes. Koreans hopefully intend to moderate current account surpluses. That won't be easy for both internal and external reasons.

From an internal view, pressures are mounting. Korea's real GNP is dropping from double digit figures to single digit ones. Besides that, troubles are coming from domestic prices, which, along with inflation, are going up. The ROKG hopes to keep the lid on wholesale and consumer prices. But these indexes are showing significant increases.

External pressures also contribute to this double bind. Korea needs to export to keep its economy strong, but receiving countries are already weary of Japanese and Korean products. The United States, Europe, and Canada continue to put restrictions on Korea's exporting machine. Trade with Korea is a volatile issue as Koreans continue to export a surplus.

That leads to trade tensions, foreign attempts to reevaluate the won, and possibly the stagnation of Korean trade policies. The Koreans also want to avoid stimulating rapid appreciation of the won. But how do they best stabilize the won's real value and exchange rate? Some suggest that the exchange system should be more flexible, more responsive to exchange rates of industrialized countries.

Koreans must also deal with the cultural ignorance and language illiteracy found among American business leaders. U.S. suppliers, according to Arthur Whitehill, don't understand the Koreans. "Americans are not noted for their competence in foreign languages. Only a handful of mature executives who are at a decision making level are fluent, or even reasonably coherent, in a second language—particularly those of Asian countries."[2] Furthermore, U.S. investors either take the short-term strategy or lack any strong commitment to international trade at all.

While most Americans have forgotten about Koreagate, some have not. Through Koreagate President Park gained direct influence to powerful U.S. legislators and diplomatic staff. To gain favorable status and treatment in bilateral relations, the Korean government mounted a strategy of payoffs. Between 1971 and 1975, $1 million was paid for creating a favorable Korean climate in Congress. Once exposed the ROKG lost face because of influence peddling.[3]

The politics of trade are just that—politics. Bad politics can taint the image of any country. Moon believes that Korea's image has been tainted. He cites evidence for his belief. First there was Koreagate, then the Unification church scandal. That was followed by the authoritarian and corrupt regimes of former Korean presidents. Now there is the charge that Korea is the second Japan. Moon isn't the only Korean worried about this label. Another concerned Korean is T. W. Kang. He lives in Japan, but works for Intel (a U.S. supplier of semiconductor devices).[4]

According to Kang, Korea has achieved prominence because of its policies of trade. Yet it was a hard fought battle, one which is not over. Because of its size, Korea is still vulnerable for several reasons. Korea is suffering a "brain drain." Many Koreans studying abroad or living outside Korea don't return home. They prefer the higher standards of living, as well as the better organizational climates found in other companies and countries. The ROKG is authoritarian, as are Korean businesses. Professionals would rather leave than be squeezed into that system.

Kang also takes a positive view. After all, his country has come a long way, mostly because of trade policies. This former "hermit nation" effectively competes with other industrial giants. Perhaps, he says, it is because Koreans are more flexible in negotiations than are the Japanese. The verdict on that point, however, is still out. Korea has yet to demonstrate that it can sustain this trade-reliant economy. Yet Kang is optimistic because of Korea's ties to Washington and Tokyo and because Korea is both a political and an economic ally of the United States. That assures Korea's future.

The image of Korea as a second Japan could be harmful. Most Koreans don't like it. But as the U.S. economy and standard of living decline, Japan and Korea could become the scapegoats. Koreans do point out that they are more flexible in negotiating their differences than the Japanese are. They point to trade missions. Then, they talk about the size of Korea compared to Japan. The Koreans say there are too many differences between them and the Japanese. They believe Korea's image as the second Japan could severely restrict "Korea's diplomatic maneuverability."[5]

Just about everyone agrees that Korea's policies on trade gave it a competitive edge. Exports initially propelled the rapid economic growth and built up such a momentum that the Korean Development Institute estimates it will continue.[6] The potential for economic growth should be realized through an annual 7–8 percent increase through the year 2000. The Korean Development Institute estimates exports would average about $173 billion per year, while imports would be $168 billion. Claims that Korean exports are not diversified may no longer be justified. Peter Petri found their exports as diverse as the United States's and more diverse than Japan's. Now Korea competes with products from the leading industrialized countries of the world.

Where did Koreans get their ideas about trade policies? Petri says from the Japanese. Koreans already knew the Japanese language, which made the assimilation of the Japanese industrial concepts and advanced technology much easier. Firms bought the technology they didn't have and copied it. Petri says, "They replicated another country's success policies. Japanese laws and policy papers are ubiquitous on the desks of Korean bureaucrats, and there are many specific examples of policy borrowing."[7]

Quality became increasingly important for the Japanese and Koreans. Their policies of quality control have paid off. But the Korean programs of importing technology from Japan now have the Japanese worried. They even discuss the "boomerang effect." They use this term to describe how their products go through Korea back out to export markets similar to Japan's.

Living close to Japan, Koreans have also been able to capitalize on those international barriers affecting the Japanese. As trade barriers extend to the Japanese, the Koreans move in with their exports. Whenever the United States limited the number of Japanese imports on TVs, the Koreans produced ten times the imports. The same was true for automobiles. The Japanese tested markets in Canada and the United States, only to be restricted from full exploitation. Once again the Koreans brought in their own models.

Korean politicians have guided the trade policies from the beginning—but with help from young industrial workers better educated than their counterparts in other East and Southeast Asian countries. Productivity is extremely high and increasing.

International success brings its own problems. It's painful to have money, for there are demands for economic and social reform. Economically speaking, Korean products (exported to U.S. markets) account for 40 percent of the export volume.

NEW POLICY DEMANDS

There are demands for new policies in Korea. As demands change, so do policies. Koreans have more than demonstrated their ability to direct their economy. Koreans have responded to mounting international pressures by developing new fair trade policies that are essential for profitable exporting. If policies get in the way of exporters, they either struggle by going over rules or crash while landing on top of them. Recently Onkvisit and Shaw showed just how much bother trade policies can be. "Japan requires six volumes of standards for each automobile. Without proper documentation, goods may not be cleared through customs. At the very least, complicated and lengthy documents slow down products."[8] These hurdles cause exporters to expend an excessive amount of energy while running straight for the profits.

Trade policies are partly hidden barriers between success and failure of international markets. And they come in the form of tariffs and nontariff barriers. Some are tariff barriers—import, export, protective, revenue, surcharge, countervailing duties, ad valorem duties, value-added, and excise. Others are nontariff barriers: subsidies, procurement, classification, documentation, license, inspection, standards, testing, exchange rates, credit restrictions, and performance requirements. Both are real constraints.

The ROKG has a policy of control. Ironically this country's competitive economy needs closer government supervision just when Korea's industries can compete internationally. Korea needs government finesse and diplomacy to steer it safely through troubled seas. Unexpectedly, trade policy becomes all the more necessary for three reasons.

First, most people in the world community expect some reciprocity in trade. That is what GATT is all about. With Korea's successes have come closer scrutinies of what the Koreans have done and are doing. Because trade affects U.S. living standards, Americans often think of Koreans as unfair traders. After all, tariff rates on all imports are still high, around 16 percent. These rates are, however, lower than the 24 percent average that they were, say, in 1983.

Second, the decision-making process is more politicized. There are questions of equity between rural farmers and urban consumers, men and women, white and blue collar workers. Then labor issues have taken a front seat, with even teachers on strike demanding higher salaries. Some want unionization everywhere, even in the public domain of education.

Third, the new government is weaker, more conciliatory. There are certain evidences of centralized and decentralized tendencies. While the unique roles of the chaebol once worked well for Korea, smaller businesses now want similar government treatments. Conflicts among interest groups and policy-making institutions abound.

The rationale seems obvious—to continue some policies and to change others. But should the ROKG be as directly involved as before? Many say no, yet everybody wants to maximize growth and high industrial values from international markets. Everyone wants prompt government intervention when in trouble.

As a result of these issues, Koreans are experimenting with policies. Take the complex issue of economic growth and development. As the economy matures, there is a shift in occupational sectors. Using comparisons for 1960–83, we see the patterns for three broad sectors. Note the changes in percentages of people for each sector: agriculture (65 to 30 percent, reduction), manufacturing industry (9 to 23 percent, increase), and service (25 to 47 percent, increase).[9] Moreover, these shifts impact both rural and urban economics. They affect economic growth, government enacted policies on managing populations, and industrial decentralization. One example is how the ROKG restricted industrial growth outside the traditional corridor between Seoul and Pusan.

The government also experiments with liberalization and tariff reductions, but more so for the manufacturing sector. Agriculture and the service sectors lag behind manufacturing and consumer-oriented products. Thus the agricultural sector is just now opening up, but not without pressure from Washington. This is a "catch 22" for the government. To yield to pressure is to incite internal unrest; not to yield is to incite more external Washington pressure.

IMPORT TARIFFS

Korea maintains a three-column import tariff schedule comprised of general rates, temporary rates, and GATT rates. There are also separate sets of concessional tariff rates relating to trade negotiations among developing countries. Very few special temporary rates, GATT rates, and TNDC rates are now in effect. One special tariff schedule, the Emergency Tariff System, is designed for three purposes: (1) to protect economically critical domestic industries, (2) to discourage specific undesirable imports, and (3) to correct tariff inequities resulting from industry structure. Since 1984 nine items have been listed here: isononal alcohols; diiosodecyl phthalate; alginic acid and its salts and esters; lubricating oils; chorofluor methanes; sorbitol; other pneumatic ties for passengers cars; table and kitchen glassware; and copper scrap.

Tariff announcements are now made public. In an attempt to strengthen Korea's industrial competitiveness in international markets, the Korean government has reformed the nation's tariff system. Two examples are (1) overall reduction of tariff rates to lessen the current excessive protection tariff rates for a total of 977 items, or 42.6 percent, and (2) reduction of tariff rate differentials.

Customs surcharges remain. By law the government may impose import surcharges. They go up to a uniform rate of 30 percent of the dutiable value of imports; that is, whenever balance-of-payments considerations dictate that import levels should be controlled. Likewise, defense taxes remain. Taxable items range from commodity imports to luxury consumer goods and services, property, and corporate incomes. The defense taxes are assessed at the rate of 2.5 percent of the CIF (cost, insurance, freight) value of all imports, excluding those imported duty free. CIF is a pricing term indicating that these costs are included in the quoted price. Since these activities are based on the Foreign Capital Inducement Act, readers might want to read the act.[10]

Since 1976 the Korean government has carried out an overall tax reform on a grand scale. The ROKG introduced a value-added tax (VAT) and special excise tax system. It enacted or amended eighteen tax laws under the reform. Before then, the traditional indirect tax system included a cascade-type of business law. It was replaced by the consumption-type value added tax and the supplementary special excise tax system. Such procedures simplified the tax system and administrative requirements. At present, a flat rate of 10 percent is applicable on all imports of items subject to the value added tax (VAT = 10 percent of CIF value + customs levies). Finally there is a consumption tax on luxury items (e.g., jewelry, fur, and gold), durable consumer goods (e.g., air conditioners and refrigerators, automobiles, pianos), and other items the government wishes to control. The range is 10–100 percent levied whenever such commodities are sold or imported.

IMPLICATIONS AND CONCLUSION

Corporatism exists in Korea. That is, the private and public sectors work closely together in a collective fashion. Certain umbrella groups represent the private sector to the government. These are the Federation of Korea Industries, the Korean Chamber of Commerce and Industry, the Korean Federation of Small Businesses, and the Korean Foreign Trade Association. Groups such as these represent business needs—approval on loans, tax breaks, or bailouts in tough times. In return, the ROKG has worked out its foreign policies to gain access to raw materials and capital good that can benefit everyone—public officials and private citizens.

At first this corporatism established a bridging strategy of power and exchange with the Korean private sector. Ironically, through its export trade policies, the ROKG began to exert less power over both its trading partners and its own Korean companies. Conversely, Korean business gained power over its government through coordinated access of resources. Nevertheless, the ROKG still maintained enough power over the regulatory and restrictive nature of trade policies to execute policy. Such political power is not generative, but functional. After all, the ROKG's power depends upon needs and resources, such as consumers' markets and competitors' products.

The ROKG continues to regulate negotiations and exchanges within business trade arrangements. It engages directly in all transactions. It also places constraints on negotiation through tariffs, exemptions, financing procedures, taxation, and promotions by acting as intermediaries to the business. This corporatism is much like a big orchestra—the ROKG directs the Export Import Bank, systems of general trading companies, exporters associations, and the Korea Trade Promotion Corporation.

Through these agencies, ministries, and policies, Korea has built its defense industry. Initially the investments came from two primary sources: externally, from U.S. grants and Asian bank loans; and internally, from exporting textiles and clothing. Early on the ROKG used import substitution and Korean industrial firms to obtain the necessary technology and raw materials. The government obtained foreign investment capital for heavy industry and chemical products. Later the ROKG revised its five-year economic goals to allow for social developments. Initially these import strategies freed Koreans from the heavy demands of research and development.

The role of the ROKG has changed nationally and internationally. In the sixties, the ROKG directed business, now it guides it. Then Korea was a U.S. patron, now a partner. Those are the results of competitive industrialization. Trade policies spurred by increasing state-centeredness brought it about. Perhaps Korea is a latecomer to industrialization and government intervention. Their survival instincts and years of waiting gave them the skills they need. Internal strategies were designed to meet external needs. Some labor sectors suffered. Because the state existed autonomously, the unions and labor suffered immobility. Self-sufficiency was replaced by international mobility and interdependence. Yet the world system accommodated these latecomers. Korean policies took the shape of substantive goods, as the ROKG prepared a rationally planned intervention strategy. Increased production and government planning went hand in hand.

Corporatism for South Korea is not the same as unification. To understand Korean policies and how they affected trade is to realize that the division of the two Koreas is unique. Looking at other recent breakups, such as Vietnam and even Germany (Willy Brandt's *Ostpolitik*), suggests that Korea is indeed unique. These two nation states are themselves aligned with international politics and world systems. Their division into two sovereign nations demonstrates just how much internal structures of Korea are determined by external forces.

Korean corporatism has miraculously "multiplied the fishes." The miracle on the Han River is there for everyone to see. Paradoxically, it's somewhat rooted in an American tradition. It should be noted that President Wilson's policy of self-determination has continued. In principle Americans usually do not enter into the internal working of politics. The principle of "sovereign equality of states" still guides American foreign policy. Yet the external factors of foreign aid and military weapons affected Korea's government. If estimates are correct, Korea obtained some $12.6 billion in aid from 1946 through 1975. Professor Burmeister ties the development of Korea into U.S. policy and vice versa. Through foreign aid, Korean presidents had resources they would otherwise have lacked. Simultaneously, they achieved rapid economic development that occurred concomitantly with international market development.

It is ironic, too, that once Korean trade policies were set in motion, they contributed to their own unexpected demise. As Korea achieved international prominence and maturity in economic development, it also entered into an economic order based on closer scrutiny. The results are obvious. Future trade developments are now more tightly associated with international decisions.

It is expected that Korean trade policy will change more in response to these external demands. It's true that Korea has followed "policy issues development—foreign capital penetration, industrial organization, capital/labor relations . . . determined increasingly in more plural-istic national and international decision-making arenas."[11] Yet these constraints affect everyone, all countries. If political decisions about Korean trade policies have served their country's needs so effectively for twenty-five years, then these tested policies speak highly of the framers who confirmed them.

NOTES

1. Emily Morison Beck, ed. *John Bartlett Familiar Quotations* (Boston: Little, Brown, 1980), 890.

2. Arthur M. Whitehill, "America's Trade Deficit: The Human Problems," *Business Horizons* (January-February 1988):23.

3. Chung-In Moon, "Complex Interdependence and Transnational Lobbying: South Korea in the United States," *International Studies Quarterly* 32 (1988):74.

4. T. W. Kang, *Is Korea the Next Japan?* (New York: Free Press, 1989), 34.

5. Moon, 76.

6. Danny M. Leipziger, ed., *Korea: Transition to Maturity* (New York: Pergamon, 1988), 1.

7. Peter A. Petri, "Korea's Export Niche: Origins and Prospects," in *Korea: Transition to Maturity*, ed. Danny M. Leipziger (New York: Pergamon, 1988), 54.

8. Sak Onkvisit and John J. Shaw, "Marketing Barriers in International Trade," *Business Horizons* (May-June 1988):64.

9. Kyung-Hwan Kim and Edwin S. Mills, "Korean Development and Urbanization Prospects and Problems," in *Korea: Transition to Maturity*, ed. Danny M. Leipziger (New York: Pergamon, 1988), 167.

10. Kyung-Cho Chung, Phyllis G. Haffner, and Fredric M. Kaplan, *The Korean Guidebook, 1989* (Boston: Houghton Mifflin, 1989), 553–66.

11. Larry L. Burmeister, *Research, Realpolitik, and Development in Korea* (Boulder, Colo: Westview Press, 1988), 172–73.

11

The Importance of Culture

There is probably no subject in this book that can be so deceptively simple as this one is on Korean culture. It is risky business, indeed, for anyone to try to distill the essence of the Korean way of life. But let's take the risk, because some basic information about culture is better than no information at all.

Korean culture prescribes the way things get done, or don't get done in Korea. Whether in the corporate office asking for favors or at the GaMu (specialty shops) in the Myongdon district of Seoul drinking coffee, Koreans conduct business and negotiate deals in a certain Korean fashion. When in Korea, it is advisable for American exporters to do as the Koreans do.

In Taegu one U.S. company of health supplies and equipment hired the first Korean agents they contacted. These Koreans were instructed to sell their product line to Korean hospitals. These agents, who weren't from Taegu, lacked the appropriate contacts to enter that market. They were Taegu outsiders in a country where people value regional identities. Contacts with old class mates and family friends, though seemingly insignificant to those living in the United States, can often make the difference in closing Korean business deals.

MISUNDERSTANDING KOREAN CULTURE

It was at the 1919 Paris Peace Conference that President Woodrow Wilson advocated the principle of "self-determination of weak nations" for countries such as Korea. Shik-Man Rhee, a student of Wilson, went to Versailles to get Wilson's support. The principals of that meeting, however, took no note of Korea. Consequently, nothing happened to Japan when it failed to recognize the principle of self-determination and annexed Korea.

When Korean students heard this, they published a document demanding freedom from the Japanese. This document, spearheaded by thirty-three patriots, became the rallying cry at the Pagoda Pak in Seoul, where crowds gathered to hear the Korean "Declaration of Independence." The purpose of that meeting—to become free of Japanese intervention—never materialized for the Japanese reacted forcefully and brutally. These figures reflect just how brutally: 6,000 Koreans were killed, 15,000 wounded, and 50,000 arrested.

In 1919 President Wilson failed to realize the importance of a fundamental relationship in the Confucian society of Korea: the respect Korean students have for their teachers. Yet in 1991, U.S. business executives could easily make similar mistakes. Their mistakes would obviously not be on the magnitude of international diplomacy, but they could be as costly to them personally and to their firms professionally.

In negotiating business deals, exporters should realize the importance of cultural differences. Adjusting to Korean culture becomes critical not only to the success of long-term business relations, but also to the size and scope of profits. Without that understanding, there may be no closing of initial deals for U.S. exports. These assumptions, along with a declining U.S. dollar, have drastically changed the international equation and the plight of American business today. Consequently, U.S. exporters of all businesses need to understand how Korean culture influences trade practices.

HIDDEN DIFFERENCES

How Koreans act in given situations is influenced by their unique Korean culture. It creates differences in societies and business practices. We'll look at just six characteristics of these hidden differences. First, justice is defined by a standard of what's good for the whole Korean society. Korean law tends to combine Confucianism with certain nationalistic tendencies. From their perspective, fair trade relations are determined by how much they affect Korea.

Therefore, the way for business executives to deal with the trade problem is with sensitivity. "Remember," the Koreans say, "Korea is small compared to Japan." It does have limited resources, making it more difficult for it to compete. Furthermore, Korea has only recently achieved any measure of surplus in exporting.

Second, Korean culture is based more on emotions or sentiments than reason. Koreans tend to give less emphasis to rational analysis. In contrast to Americans, they do not ask why something happens or does not happen. They would never ask their parents why they behaved a certain way. Nor would they ask their boss why he imported one product over another. Therefore, they deemphasize national analysis in community and business relations. This emphasis on emotions does not negate their emphasis on the rationality of technology or science.

Third, Korean culture reflects a hierarchical family system, not a horizontal one. In this vertical society there is less room for individualism. Just as children submit to their parents, so also workers submit to their bosses. This is a tightly controlled society where individual efforts are limited. Individuals who go over or around bosses are considered serious violators of the Korean way to get things done.

Therefore, behind every company is a strong Korean figure who makes company decisions. In Korea this individual is known as the "strong man behind the black curtain." Those working outside the black curtain defer to the strong man.

Fourth, Korean culture incorporates an element of suffering and humility. Koreans don't want to continue suffering with lingering feelings of foreign dependency. That lingering feeling of humility means that Koreans don't always publicly express their own views. Therefore the true feelings about foreign companies are mixed. Many Koreans accommodate these businesses out of feelings of foreign dependency.

Fifth, Korean culture is rapidly changing from its traditional ways to modern ones. Changes are most evident among students, city dwellers, politicians, bankers, and farm migrants. Some students resent foreigners, because they have controlled Korea too long. These students want the reunification of the two Koreas at any cost. They seem willing to make concessions to North Korea, but those in authority do not. In 1980 the city of Kwanju was under martial law due to student riots. By the conflict's end, hundreds were killed, leaving mixed feelings about these issues.

City dwellers worry about Seoul's traffic problems, high prices, and pollution. Politicians are getting their first taste of true democracy. Instinctively, they push for more power, while bankers worry about financial restructuring.

Besides these concerned groups, farmers want to be as rich as city folk. Migrants from rural towns get impatient for the good life and eventually go to the city. Because they don't have skills and don't fit in, they get into trouble. Koreans describe their situation this way: "these young people become too competitive." As a result of having neither money nor the ability to compete, they get lost in crime, drugs, or pornography. The Korean public is greatly concerned about these negative conditions.

Sixth and finally, the Korean culture is uniquely linked with Confucianism in two ways. First, Confucius (550–478 B.C.) taught ethical social relationships: (1) Children practice filial piety toward their parents and ancestors. (2) People are loyal to rulers or kings. (3) Wives respect their husbands. (4) Students esteem teachers. (5) Finally, people support their friends. Second, he emphasized these three qualities: love of humanity, sensitivity for feelings, and justice for society.

How do these hidden differences of culture impact Americans? Anti-American sentiments are here because of increasing nationalism and rapid economic development. Nationalism brings exclusivity and success independence. Anti-American feelings have also resulted because former presidents, who were harsh dictators, aligned themselves militarily and economically with the United States. One symbol of frustration and resentment now comes from the 750-acre American military base in the heart of Seoul. If all goes according to plans, however, by 1991 the United States should return this land, along with the eighteen-hole golf course, to the Koreans.

Most of the older generation responds favorably to the United States. They still remember the Korean War and American sacrifices during and after that war. But still, relations are strained, almost in direct proportion to Korea's economic successes and to the rising spirit of nationalism. Above all, Koreans don't like arbitrary force or the highhandedness that they see on bilateral trade issues.

"Most Americans have no idea how heavy they and the U.S. come across," says Dr. Horace Underwood, grandson of the founder of Yonsei University. "Our way of thinking, and arguing especially, is not part of the East Asian culture, where there is more deference and fencing," he says.[1] Even with these disagreements, though, both countries continue to work together in areas of economics.

BENEFITS OF UNDERSTANDING

What President Wilson learned as a statesman, Pearl Buck learned through personal experience. Young Pearl Buck once held negative attitudes toward the Koreans. Writing a 1939 Asian article, she described Koreans as passively living in "a nation already subject to sloth and

Figure 11.1
Benefits of Cultural Understanding

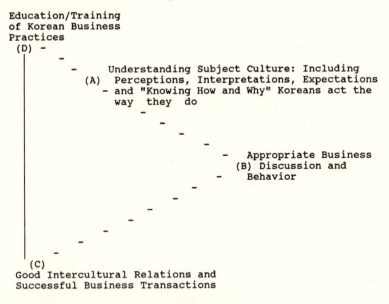

```
Education/Training
of Korean Business
Practices
  (D) -
         -
            -       Understanding Subject Culture: Including
                (A)  Perceptions, Interpretations, Expectations
                  - and "Knowing How and Why" Koreans act the
                    way   they   do
                       -
                          -
                             -
                                      -    Appropriate Business
                                      (B)  Discussion and
                                        -  Behavior
                                -
                          -
                       -
                 -
            -
  (C)
Good Intercultural Relations and
Successful Business Transactions
```

effeteness before the coming of Japan."[2] Her attitude, however, changed as she began to understand this Asian country. In 1942 she reassessed her views and began recording them (1960) in a historical novel based on extensive travels in Korea. During these trips, she assembled maps, visited villages, observed social customs, and traced change at the turn of the century.

Her efforts resulted in the 1963 best-selling novel *The Living Reed*. It is a story about four generations of the Kim family (1881–1952). More important to our discussion is how personal exposure and cultural awareness caused her to change her prejudice toward Koreans. In a nine-page preface, she begins her historical note: "Korea is a gem of a country inhabited by a noble people."[3] Obviously, her stereotypes of Korea had changed. The older, more mature Pearl Buck became both a champion of mutual cultural understanding and an advocate of active support for Koreans.

Barriers to exporting business vary with an understanding of the target country. As U.S. exporters learn to appreciate this rich 5,000-year-old heritage, they reap some unique benefits in commerce and trade. Cultural training and education predictably contribute to that process (see Figure 11.1). Knowing etiquette and trade practices (A) increases a firm's understanding of Korean business. That understanding (B) assists Americans in knowing "how and why" Koreans act as they do. Then perceptions and interpretations will more nearly match the Koreans.

This process affects business deals, making discussions and behavior more culturally appropriate (C). Finally, that predictable process increases the quality of good relationships in social and business settings (D).

Figure 11.1 is cultural general, which means it could be used for any setting, whether Korea or Germany. In each geographical location business leaders must adapt to business protocols. As such, this figure does not account for politics or for conflicts, either between North Korea and the United States or between South Korea and Russia. However, the issues of establishing good intercultural relations and successful business transactions would work between South Korea and the United States. This model works best in fairly neutral exchanges, business transactions, say, between South Korean importers and U.S. suppliers.

LEARNING THE ASIAN CULTURES

In Asian cultures intercultural relations—the importance of harmony and structure—are usually preferred over innovation and experimentation. Consequently, negotiations characterized by argumentative and adversarial exchanges are less effective methods for conducting business. Koreans may appear to acquiesce over differences of opinion. This appearance of harmony does not, however, mean agreement. Rather this perplexing behavior indicates the value of social relations as ends, not means to ends. So personal trust extends beyond the business to reinforcement in a more social atmosphere. But even here, let the Korean hosts take the lead and set the pace—a strategy that requires flexible schedules and agendas.

Generally speaking, there are about six approaches to crosscultural training.[4] Each is classified by the type of exposure. On the low end of cultural involvement is the method of fact gathering. This exposure (information or fact-oriented training) has to do with geographic and historic facts about the country of destination. The next level (attribution training) is the application of these facts. That is, an identification of the problems encountered by people living in that region. The third level (cultural awareness) engages the trainees more than the other two. Here trainees compare differences in the new culture from the old one. Those moving abroad should begin to internalize cultural differences.

The last three approaches give trainees greater exposure than the first three. At the fourth level (cognitive-behavior modification) trainees begin to examine the types of behavior that are encouraged and not encouraged. The next training opportunity engages people directly (experiential learning). They learn from field trips, simulations, or videos. And finally, the most exposure comes from interacting with another person over cultural differences. New arrivals are assigned to those experienced in the culture. The two interact about happenings (inter-action approach). Since people learn best by imitating the behavior of others, the sojourner approach works well. Newcomers are able to engage and accurately interpret events simultaneously. They understand differences much quicker through the help of another. Significant others coach them in what to do next and how to respond.

Donald Macdonald, a foreign service core member with over ten years service to Korea, predicts the eventual emergence of an Asian alliance based on similarity of cultures, especially in "facing the North American and European blocs."[5] As Asian countries—Korea, Japan, Hong Kong, Singapore—face these regions with common cultures and economies, they might unite. At present individual countries show more flexibility than do regions. "One of the reasons for Korea's development has been the extraordinary flexibility of Korea's economic planners."[6] But Macdonald warns that if these advantages of flexibility are offset by European and U.S. economic blocs, then the Koreans might look for other alliances in Asia.

CONCLUSIONS

It is too easy to overlook distinctions about the Korean society and culture. Those who do may suffer severe consequences. Successful U.S. exporters can take full advantage of Korean opportunities by adjusting to Korea's business community. In a political sense, Americans face difficult trade decisions about Korea—decisions that will affect the interactional and diplomatic status for years to come.

Americans have three choices in prioritizing Korea's culture. Two choices have negative consequences. Having not given priority to Korean culture and not wanting to now doesn't make sense socially or economically. The third choice—validating Korean culture—should lead to harmonious relations and healthier markets.

Giving priority to Korean culture, it is argued, should better prepare negotiators for closing business deals. Exporters learn that knowledge about cultural differences becomes critical, not only to the success of long-term business relations, but also to the size and scope of business profits.

What is important for the business executives to know? It is argued that the bottom line is cultural and social. It matters not whether U.S. exporters learn about how Korean business and political leaders pick their successors. It matters neither whether they learn about how "feudalistic thinking" affects the chances of democracy, nor whether they ever view the Korean elite as a type of upper class in a feudal society. These "whethers" are insignificant to most business executives. What matters is that exporters know how to interact with business leaders, how to interpret the high status that Koreans give managers, and how to get the job done while there. That's the bottom line.

The pull of cultures in the Pacific Rim may be much greater than recognized. Those who travel and experience the culture first hand probably understand the weight of this assumption.

Those who travel internationally also know something else. Such travelers can see similarities in the Korean socialization process and the one that produced their strong economy. The taken-for-granted values found in the United States are certainly different. Nevertheless, beyond these basic values, there is the process of how things get done at home, at school, and at work. The process affects Americans—their behavior and mannerisms—just as it does the Koreans.

Through the experiences associated with travel, people come to value, even more than they did earlier, their own culture. After all, culture is at the heart of learning. And the values—those things people think important—of a culture, like the history of every country, begin in the heart of each man and woman, boy and girl. For the most part, the heart of Korea is dominated either by outside forces or inside ministries.

NOTES

1. Richard Gourtay, "Koreans Point an Accusing Finger at Uncle Sam," *Financial Times*, June 15, 1989, 5.

2. Pearl S. Buck, "He Who Lives Wins," *Asian Magazine*, November 1939, vol. 39, p. 635.

3. Pearl S. Buck, *The Living Reed* (New York: John Day Company, 1963), 9.

4. Dan Landis and Richard W. Brisin, *Handbook on Intercultural Training* (New York: Pergamon Press, 1983), 9.

5. Donald Macdonald, "Korea Through Western Eyes," *Business Korea*, April 1989, 38.

6. Macdonald, 39.

The Dominance of Government

Many positive developments now underscore the joint efforts of the Korean and U.S. governments to increase U.S. exports to Korea. While the government involvement tends to be viewed negatively by nearly all American businesses and some Korean ones, that is not always the case for those exporting.

Historically the Korean government exercised direct influence not merely on trade policies but also on particular business decisions. Both patterns fit the Korean pattern of vertical integration. Koreans tend to think of others as superior-subordinate where employees are loyal to their bosses. In exchange for that loyalty, the superior ones protect those under them. As a result, technology transfers have been carefully planned and implemented in Korea. The agency closely overseeing the operations is the Ministry of Trade and Industry (MTI), an agency that surveys and monitors technological developments. As new technologies emerge, this government agency coordinates with the private sector to encourage or discourage technology transfer and development.

IMPLICATIONS FOR U.S. EXPORTERS

According to Boye De Mente, these patterns have at least three direct implications for American business executives doing business in Korea.[1] First, in dealing with Korean government officials, Americans don't get far using only the practical, rational, and logical approaches to policies. As a general rule, each export problem tends to be solved on an individual, case-by-case basis. Not only that, officials in one agency may give one interpretation, while those in another give yet a different one.

Second, in seeking refuge from Korean laws and ethics, Americans soon discover an entirely different system. Their system places less emphasis on an objective outside standard and more on one that is part of the business agreements themselves. The result is that Americans have complained bitterly and long about violations of copyrights, patents, and contracts. As just a side note, most lawyers don't practice law in the same manner as in the United States. Traditionally the Confucius society assumes that differences over business transactions, if there are any, should be handled through personal established channels of business. Such practices worked best in the feudal system, in a homogeneous society. But they are less effective for today's international trade if they preclude the use of attorneys. This pattern is slowly changing as a dominant pattern in Asian business relations.

Third, in finally reaching an agreeable solution about an export matter, many U.S. exporters suddenly watch the whole deal come unravelled. The reason is less obvious to Americans than Koreans. But the explanations go like this: business deals begin and end in personal relations. Therefore, contracts are more important than people's ability to discuss matters currently affecting business deals. As social conditions change, so do the needs to renegotiate business deals.

Frustrated by countless examples, U.S. exporters sought government support and leverage to balance the equation. Comparatively speaking, Japanese and Korean exporters have fewer problems bringing their goods into the United States than American exporters do into Asia. Americans go through countless ministries, agencies, and procedures to get exports into Korea. If you ever have these problems in Korea, remember that one U.S. exporter of drugs to Japan completed 312 documents, struggled with 62 administrative procedures, and finally gained approval. It came only after three years of determined effort. Frustrated by such practices, Americans sought for and obtained U.S. Government assistance.

TWO DIFFERENT VIEWS

In the United States scholars have found at least two usually divergent views about the proper relationship of government and business. Woodrow Wilson held one view; Calvin Coolidge held another.

Wilson looked askance at the monopolistic control of the business enterprise. The political force of combined capitalists and manufacturers, he thought, usurped individual freedoms. Addressing the Senate in 1917, Wilson advocated a community of power. By contrast Coolidge idealized the business community. He said that the advancement of civilization depends upon business success. That comes best when government leaves business alone. In 1925 he addressed the American Society of Newspaper Editors saying, "the chief business of the American people is business."

Although these two presidents differed in their attitudes, they each realized the importance of business enterprises. Both recognized the potential of business activities for either good or bad. The potential is there, it just depends upon how it is channeled. Consumers can be exploited, so can producers; employers can take advantage of the work setting, but so can employees; Exxon can ship needed oil from Alaska, or its tankers can spill oil in the process. Even with pressing environmental problems, however, most citizens prefer a system of voluntarism in which businesses assume some social responsibilities over one where the government consistently exercises some type of coercion.

Could we safely say that both presidents, before their death, recognized how history shaped the U.S. policies on government-business relations? It is a known fact that with the process of industrialization also came capitalists who preferred a laissez-faire type of government. It was during Wilson's administration that the U.S. government reacted to monopolistic exploitation of big business. It was then that Congress passed the antitrust laws, established regulatory agencies, and applied criminal sanctions against those whose activities violated the law.

And finally, though both had different political views, they agreed that business practices reflect our way of life because social life influences business practices. Would not Coolidge have agreed with Wilson that a strong business economy strengthens our national and spiritual lives?

Publicly debated political views are not found in Korean tradition. Traditionally, the government dominates the people. If rulers were cruel, the people revolted. Otherwise, they obeyed. The type of participatory democracy whereby individuals express their individual views is foreign to Korean tradition.

Since World War II Korea's political confidence, along with military and economic developments, has been growing. In those early years a single political leader, often a former military general, took charge. After Lieutenant General John Hodge assumed control of Korea's government, he and his staff adopted the Japanese system of rules, a policy which offended the Koreans. Three years later, on August 15, 1948, General Douglas MacArthur recognized the Republic of South Korea. Not surprisingly, American military rule combined with an Asian tradition of military exploitation contributed to the development of Korea's government.

From 1946 to 1975 Korea received more than $12.6 billion in U.S. aid, of which half was for military assistance. Without that money, the repressiveness of many Korean presidents would have been more difficult. But with the declaration of national self-determination by Wilson, U.S. policymakers find it difficult to control the international policies either of Korea or of other governments.

KOREAN POLITICS

In principle, Korea has a free market economy based on private owners who control both the means of production and distribution. But in fact, the government controls the process throughout. The government owns several companies: Agriculture Development Corporation, Korean General Chemical Industry Corporation, Korean Electric Power Corporation, the Korean Broadcasting System, and Korean Telecommunication Authority. More important, however, is the traditional role the government plays through its overall economic development plans, specific industry expansion plans, price controls, and other special economic measures taken to achieve stabilization and growth.

After the Korean War, President Syngman Rhee became increasingly dictatorial. He dominated the government through his dominant parliamentary group called the Liberal Party. He proclaimed martial law and arrested those who opposed him. He became increasingly intolerant of criticism and later rigged the elections. He was eventually forced out after serving as president of the Republic of Korea until April 1960.

Demonstrators forced his resignation. Then the New National Assembly named prime minister Myon Chang as the president. Though his office was characterized by democratic tendencies, Chang was ineffective. He was overthrown by an army coup led by Major General Chung-Hee Park. General Park became president, moving the country forward toward economic development until he was assassinated.

Prime Minister Choi took control, at least until General Chun forced him to resign. After several years of serving as president, Doo-Hwan Chun also resigned. Both his family and associates were involved in a corruption scandal. His brother stood trial for bribery and misuse of government funds.

President Chun picked Tae-Woo Roh as his successor. But Roh elected to hold elections. In December 1987, Roh barely managed to win. Since that election, President Roh has distanced himself from the tainted image of former President Chun. Ironically, the picked successor to Chun asked for new elections. Roh won, then disassociated himself from his predecessor, the one who picked him in the first place.

Government offices, agencies, and ministries tend to be paternalistic toward business leaders, who may not comply with regulations unless they want to, for there are no laws compelling business leaders to follow all government initiatives. But business leaders do respond to most government directives because of social, not legal, pressure. Such pressure works.

Government agencies exert pressure to conform by refusing business proposals, using so-called quotas, and limiting imports. Through these means they gain compliance by the local business leaders. Since the ROKG maintains representation in the Korea Trade Promotion Corporation and the Korea Exchange Bank, they also control markets and foreign exchanges. The ROKG implements policies in other ways: national budgets, the regulation of particular markets, the establishment of its own enterprises, and the supply of credit through price stability policies.

The ROKG enforces price stability policies. Both the consumer price index and the wholesale price index have been kept to the one-digit range since 1982. The consumer index has fluctuated from 6.1 percent (1987) to 7.2 (1988) to 5.0 (1989); wholesale index, 2.7 percent (1987), 2.3 (1988), and 3.0 (1989). So far this policy has worked. The Korean government boosts productivity and import liberalization, while keeping industrial prices and service areas down even as the won has appreciated. However, were agricultural prices and wages to continue rising, it would ultimately affect price stabilization.

Since costs of agricultural products, inflationary tendencies, and wage increases affect price stability, the ROKG wants to balance this economic equation. Consequently, it supports policies—corporate productivity, import liberalization, currency exchanges—that should both stabilize the price of industrial goods and keep the inflation rate within 3–5 percent for wholesale and retail goods.

Interest rates and money supplies are also controlled by the government through certain policies. As of January 1989, commercial banks lend money at 12 percent per annum. Financial institutions now establish their own policies. Because the government wants to simplify import procedures, it is also easing special restrictions on imports. Previously, testing and inspection procedures were specified by twelve laws and statutes. Now all import procedures are applied uniformly to the same products. From importers' perspectives, such simplifications are good news. In 1988 the ROKG also abolished the import surveillance system. Devised in 1979 to alleviate international competition, importers viewed this approach as an unfair barrier. With a surplus in trade, it became unnecessary. Still some thirty-four items, agricultural and fishing products, remain intact, ready for implementation if U.S. imports cause undue hardships. The government plans to abolish the import deposit system, to shift tariff evaluation from CIF to FOB, and to expand items eligible for installment payments.

The government explored six other ideas that could lead to more profitable imports: (1) to strengthen import information (through organizations and computerized systems); (2) to improve functions of private companies (give shares to private companies, promote general trading companies); (3) to activate the Korean Federation of Small Business (KFSB) for joint purchasing of raw materials (raise procurement funds); (4) to increase reserves of a raw materials procurement fund; (5) to encourage the import of raw materials; and (6) to promote overseas consignments to overseas Korean distributors.[2]

As the economy grows, Deputy Prime Ministry Woong-Bae Rha believes government control will wane: "A few bureaucrats cannot control it." In a move toward greater democratization, many policies originating from both the trade minister and finance minister are being questioned by the National Assembly. Such checks and balances should eventually lead to greater distribution of wealth. Already one controversial policy is to pressure chaebols to dissolve their cross-holdings, limit their borrowing power, dissolve laws that protect them, and distribute new opportunities to smaller firms. The trends seem clear: chaebols served their purpose. But with new, emerging internal domestic demands, the ROKG wants to limit their growth while encouraging the growth of small businesses through the KFSB.

THE AMERICAN CHALLENGE

It has been argued, after years of successful economic progress, that a mismatch now exists between how American economics works and how international business works. Historically, Americans believe that economic policies should be off limits to government jurisdiction. The less corporations have to do with government, the better off they are. Business takes care of economics, and government handles politics. Each realm of activity has its own values: free access versus control, free markets versus restriction, prosperity versus equality, and exporting opportunities versus government nonintervention.

These values go back to our early history, where they served as checks and balances whenever either side dominated. At the turn of the century, mass production techniques generated monopolies that resulted in government controls and restrictions. The rivalry of both groups continues today. However, a united front is emerging, and it must if American products are to survive. We need to develop a new international economy so characterized: On the one hand, it is organized by a highly competent labor force and an innovative organizational structure. On the other hand, it is characterized by a responsive government structure and political negotiations where leverage is needed.

The problems we face are largely outside our national boundaries. Since World War II, Germany, England, Japan, Korea, and Taiwan have recovered economically. They now compete internationally with American products. As a result of increased international competition, our international environment has drastically changed. Our world is a more interdependent one, where most national governments openly direct the private sector. They make no distinction between public or private sectors. Consequently, increased government involvement puts American goods at a disadvantage.

To compete internationally, Americans must cooperate in the workplace and coordinate from a common place. Workers need more than a pay check; companies need more than techniques for negotiating with the Koreans. The private sector needs the public sector, especially if we as a country ever hope to adjust to international politics, as they presently exist. What worked for Americans in the past seems to work less well now because in countries like Korea the government dominates trade. The only way that U.S. exporters can overcome these political barriers is by using politics themselves—by seeking the political leverage of the U.S. federal government.

This is a pragmatic decision. But remember that pragmatism is the foundation upon which American business operates. Its motto goes like this: "What sells in the market place determines what is sold." It is right that U.S. exporters to Korea use the federal government's help because of the benefits. In only this way can Americans ever hope to enter all the Korean markets and compete with Japanese exporters. The benefits far outweigh the disadvantages. And it's happening, whether we admit it or not.

The importance of foreign trade developed after 1965. That fact has progressively changed, as our products were increasingly shipped abroad: 6 percent in 1970, 19 percent in 1980. U.S. two-way trade totalled $763.4 billion in 1988: exports $321.8 billion and imports $441.6 billion. Our trade deficit shrank from the 1987 peak by 212 percent to $119.8 billion. The U.S. exported 5.4 percent of its GNP (1988), while Japan exports about 10.5 percent, the United Kingdom 19.3 percent, West Germany 25.9 percent, and Canada 25.1 percent. U.S. exports comprise 79 percent manufactured goods, 12 percent agricultural commodities, and 9 percent primarily mineral fuels and crude materials. Capital goods and aircraft lead U.S. exports, followed by industrial supplies and materials, then foods, feeds, and beverages, automotive products, and other consumer products.

What worked in the past evidently is not continuing to work. From 1891 until 1970, the United States recorded an unbroken string of trade surpluses. After 1970, however, deficits were recorded for every year but two (1973 and 1975). We must act while we are still the world's largest economy, the largest market, and the leading importer. Together with West Germany and Japan, the United States leads the world in exports. According to U.S. Chamber of Commerce reports, U.S. exports contributed to 41.2 percent of real U.S. GNP growth. The present growth in U.S. economy comes in large part because of exports to other countries. It is feasible that a closer working relationship between the public and private sectors might work. It could once again result in fair play in the international market arena. Until then, U.S. exporters are at a decided disadvantage, even with Asian countries like Korea. The steps that should make for improved bilateral relations have already begun, as shown by the number of U.S. government agencies that actively support international trade.

SUMMARY

In summary, international trade is affected by two different types of governments—the Korean and American. The ROKG directly intervenes in business affairs, while the U.S. government does not. Each of these governments approaches business relations in such a way that it can be explained historically based on unique traditions and politics.

The Korean government dominates business for several reasons. First, there is a tradition of vertical integration. Second, this system works. As new technologies emerge, this government coordinates with the private sector to encourage or discourage technology transfer and development. Third, Koreans borrowed their military bureaucratic model from the American military. After all, the Koreans had three years to analyze how that military rule worked. Fourth, there is an Asian tradition of military exploitation, which also contributed to the development of the ROKG. The Koreans were influenced by the prominent Japanese institution, *zaibatsu*, which began with the industrial and financial companies of merchant soldiers.

Both governments present barriers and opportunities for trade. The ROKG is frantically working to lessen restrictions, making its markets open and accessible for American exports to Korea. Nevertheless, U.S. exporters can expect at least four problems. First, in negotiations Americans don't get far using only the practical, rational, and logical approaches to policies. Unwritten rules of government ministries are applied differently. Second, in seeking refuge from Korean laws and ethics, Americans soon discover an entirely different system. Koreans place less emphasis on an objective standard. Third, in reaching an agreeable solution about an export matter, many U.S. exporters suddenly watch the whole deal come unravelled.

Fourth, in seeking fair play, U.S. exporters could seek government support and leverage to balance the equation in cases of unfair trade practices. It is a fact that Japanese and Korean exporters have fewer problems bringing their goods into the United States. Both governments lend support where needed, but state-run enterprises definitely have an advantage. Until these issues are resolved, the ROKG remains the final formulator of economic policy, even though Korean businessmen freely pursue profits wherever they want. Their system combines free enterprise and government control simultaneously.

Effectively putting these suggestions or others into practice begins by asking the right questions. "How does their system work?" is one question. But there are others. "What about making business deals?" is another. "How are U.S. exporters affected by the market place, attitudes of the Koreans, and inside deals in a one-on-one exchange?" is a third. These are some of the questions handled in the next chapters.

NOTES

1. Boye De Mente, *Korean Etiquette & Ethics in Business* (Lincolnwood, Ill.: NTC Business Books, 1988), 43–44.

2. Sun-Ki Lee, *A Guide to the Korean Import Market* (Seoul: Korea Trade Promotion Corporation, 1979), 23–34.

_____ *IV*

*Observe Those
Practices*

13

Korean Import Market Characteristics

In 1988 two Korean firms, SKC America and Lucky-Goldstar International, began operations in New Jersey. The former company built an assembly and distribution plant in Mount Olive; the latter established an international headquarters in Englewood Cliffs, New Jersey, from which they conduct worldwide operations.

U.S. companies in New Jersey are strategically located between New York City and Philadelphia. From here they implement two strategies. One strategy attracts more international investments, such as SKC and Lucky-Goldstar of Korea. The other strategy increases their exports, definitely to Korea but also to other countries as well.

Either way, importing or exporting, the strategies are paying off for U.S. residents and Koreans. New Jersey now ranks twelfth in total export volume, tenth in export-related jobs. Last year alone some seventy-five foreign-owned firms invested in this state. The Japanese and Koreans are flocking to New Jersey, while the residents are exporting $4.1 billion worth of manufacturing goods abroad (January to October 1988) and $302 million worth of service or nonmanufactured items abroad.[1]

That strategy should work elsewhere for other exporters, especially to Korea. But only under certain conditions. Exporters should know at least four aspects of doing business in Korea. First, international managers should know about specific characteristics of Korean markets. This information shows them where the markets are and whether they will want to get on board the export ship. Second, they should know how to conduct business in this Asian country for one very important reason. Whether U.S. exporters realize it or not, they are compared with the Japanese, who have exploited this region for over a century. The Japanese set the pace on properly dealing with the Koreans and conducting business deals.

The third and fourth aspects of doing business concern how U.S. exporters access the Korean markets and how they conduct business. Exporters will want not simply to gain access to Korean markets but also to get inside business deals. All four aspects of doing business comprise the four chapter headings found in Part IV titled "Observe Those Practices."

Earlier chapters should have given you some guidance by providing basic information on this market. A summary of those early chapters (1–12) is found below:

1. No two companies have the same export potential for Korea.
2. Each develops Korean markets using individual strategies.
3. Start by matching your products with import demands.
4. Realize that Korean policies and culture influence trade.

This next information can be as valuable to Americans looking for Korean markets as to Koreans looking at the gilt-bronzed seated Buddha in Seoul (National Museum at Kyongbokkung Palace). It should assist exporters who want more specific information about the market itself and how to trade there. This chapter begins by developing several entry mode strategies that companies might select for exporting goods to Korea.

KOREAN IMPORT VOLUME

Korean consumers, regardless of socioeconomic status, show strong preference for foreign-made brands because of their increased standard of living and the Westernization of life style. Most consumers—75 percent surveyed by Korea Chamber of Commerce and Industry—expressed satisfaction with foreign brand goods as measured by quality, status, and prices.

Consumers listed the foreign items they purchased: electric home appliances (28.1 percent were foreign made), cosmetic and beauty (15.5 percent), food stuffs (15.3 percent), kitchen equipment (12.7 percent), sporting goods (7.5 percent), personal accessories (7.2 percent), pharmaceuticals (6.9 percent). Armed with this knowledge, you as exporters (sales team, Korean agents) are able to check not only your competitors, but also the total volume of what is selling. Since this survey measured attitudes of Koreans toward foreign items, international managers know more about designing international marketing plans. This would obviously include the marketing mix profile for Korea and markets for candidate products. You can use this information in considering not only the product but perhaps even promotional considerations.

Obviously consumer/users have different preferences and needs. The consumer survey mentioned above identified some of those Korean preferences. Since Korea is a small market country, it is advisable to use market aggregate, not market segment. A market segment identifies specific groups of consumers/users rather than grouping them all together.

Korea has a small market compared to the ones found either in the United States or in Europe. Nevertheless, its potential is expanding rapidly. As the Koreans raise their standard of living, they will buy more sophisticated consumer products. For now, however, put consumers in aggregate form, at least until you have some familiarity with the Korean market.

Information about end users (consumer attitudes) should help you in designing marketing plans. But other types of information are also needed. Some of that comes from commodity groups. In the next paragraph you can see the imports from the United States by commodity group (machines, chemicals, farm) (1987); you can use this in your market plans. Foreign target markets depend upon a firm's ability to identify the total market, say for Korea. From that information, firms develop their own market strategies.

The machinery category (electric and electronic goods) represents about a fourth of imports (22.7 percent). Chemicals ($3.82 billion) totaled 32.6 percent of total imports, an increase from 1986. Machinery imports ($1.78 billion) rose 36.6 percent from 1986. Of the total amount of machinery imported from all countries ($6.99 billion), almost a fifth of that ($1.34 billion) comes from the United States. On farm and fishery products, U.S. percentages show a lower amount (only 7.4 percent) than the total amount imported (18 percent). The same pattern in reverse is true for steel and metals. Koreans import more from other countries (43.4 percent) than from the U.S. (5.2 percent).

Table 13.1
Importers for Largest Volume of Chemical Products

HS	Description	List of Korean Importers
2601	iron ores	Pohand Iron & Steel LTD C.P.O. Box 36
2701	mineral fuels, oils	Ssangyong Corporation C.P.O. Box 409
2709	petroleum oils	Honam Oil Refinery Co. Youido P.O. Box 525
2710	petro oils bitumius	Sungkyong Magnetic Limited C.P.O. Box 4861
2711	petro gases	Karahm Carbon LTD. C.P.O. Box 5946
2933	heterocyclic compound	Dong Oh Corporation C.P.O. Box 9132

Table 13.2
Importers for Largest Volume of Raw Products

HS	Description	List of Korean Importers
7204	scrap iron	Korea Sangsa Co. LTD C.P.O. Box 8632
7208	iron flat rolled	Pusan Steel Pipe Corporation C.P.O. Box 2293
7219	stainless steel	Korea Iron & Steel Works, LTD. 475 Mangmi-dong, Nam-gu Pusan
7601	aluminium, unwrought	Choil Aluminum Mfg. 550, Sawoi-dong, Susong-gu Taegu

THE LARGEST VOLUMES

Either countries can choose to reduce imports through a variety of 850 methods (until recently, Koreans could "be fined if they are found in possession of foreign cigarettes"[2]) or countries can open their doors to trade. "South Korea has performed well by promoting industries that exhibit superior performance as a result of their export activity."[3] Some of those Korean importers seek large volumes of chemical products, raw products, and machines. Table 13.1 provides readers with both a description of the product and a list of Korean importers. For example those who want to export iron ores could contact the Pohand Iron & Steel of Seoul, Korea.

Table 13.2 also provides lists of Korean importers for largest volumes of raw products.

These are by no means the only Korean suppliers. Nor are they necessarily the best ones to contact. These names were randomly drawn

Table 13.3
Importers for Largest Volume of Machines and Parts

HS	Description	List of Korean Importers
8445	machines for textiles	Chonbang Company, LTD. C.P.O. Box 55
8471	data process machines	Samsung Co. LTD. C.P.O. Box 1144
8473	parts # 84.69-84.72 calculating machines	Shine Korea LTD. 2nd Block of Chang Won 1Nd. Complex, Changwon-shi Kyongnam
8479	machines not elsewhere	Goldstar Electric Company LTD. 20 Youido-dong, Yongdungpo-gu Seoul
8522	parts #85.19-85.21 heads for recording	Tanashin Korea Company LTD. 366 Tangjong-ri, Kunpo-up
8529	parts #85.25-85.28 tuner for color	Nam Sung Electronics Corporation C.P.O. Box 2907
8356	switching apparatus	Maxon Electronic Company LTD. P.O. Box 126 Kurodanji
8540	cold cathode	Anam Electric Industry Company 316-29 Hyosong-dong Puk-gu Inchon
8541	diodes transistors	Jinnha Electronics Company LTD. 65-9 Samsong-dong Kangnam-gu Seoul
8542	integrated circuits	Yung San Industrial Company LTD. C.P.O. Box 6686 Tel. (02) 275-1291
8708	parts motor gear boxes	Tong Il LTD. Mapo P.O. Box 300
8802	aircraft vehicles helicopters	Korean Air Lines LTD. C.P.O. Box 864

from lists provided by the Korean trade associations. The purpose is to show you how the procedure works. You could, if you wanted to, even contact these Korean importers. After all, they are listed as legitimate firms.

Table 13.3 contains a long list of product descriptions and Korean importers. You may want to get more exact information on HS description, so they conform to your expectations.

CONSUMER PRODUCTS

Consumer production is increasing in Korea. In the late sixties, the sacred consumer items for Koreans were for basic household needs: electric rice cookers, washing machines, and electric fans. After wide distribution of these household items, more elaborate gadgets developed for the late seventies, including private automobiles, color televisions, and room air conditioners. Now, in the nineties, Koreans want property in the United States, overseas air travel, and spaciously built, private homes and resorts.

Where do these consumer goods come from? They come from the two-tier level of companies already discussed. Hyundai group and its 32 affiliates account for almost 5 percent of the GNP; Sansung has 35 affiliates. Large company (chaebol) productions include electronics, steel, petrochemicals, automobiles, textiles, and ships. Together they buy and sell thousands of different products, everything from noodles to weapon systems.

Smaller companies also produce consumer products. Service industries are rapidly expanding in Korea, especially restaurant chains, wholesale and retail operations, and fashion merchandising. The smaller companies are also developing high technology assembly plants. These include fast foods, special toys, sportswear sporting goods, housing materials, and educational books.

Whether small or large, U.S. suppliers should try to match their products with those compatible with Korean ones. Some Korean companies want Western technology, others want to gain profits from investments. Don't overlook the smaller companies, they do have several advantages. These include tax benefits, special government treatment, and greater cooperation. Sometimes the business accounting for these small companies isn't as efficient as that of the larger ones. To select a company with similar products could be a mistake because of different business practices.

Finally, Korea's consumer products find their way into international markets. What the people who buy them don't realize is that to produce these consumer goods, the Koreans combine Asian principles with the religious fervor of Confucians. Consumers may not realize where all the Korean products go. They now produce commercial activities in North America and Europe, as well as goods for Third World countries. They ship light manufacturing industries and products to Latin America and the Middle East. The Koreans, as much as the Japanese, have sensed the dynamic international division of labor. They work well in close relations with others.

Throughout the world, people are becoming more impressed with Korean products. They find a much better quality product than just a few years ago. Their technology and knowledge-intensive specialties have improved considerably. Take electronics, computers, integrated circuits, fashionable automobiles, and boats. Their assembly techniques are also impressive: communication networks, air condition controls, prefabricated housing, and spacious warehousing. But for them, new directions seem inevitable: software development, video systems consulting and adaptation, and information systems for office and company development.

Though crowded in many ways, Korea can boast of better health, longer life, a solid consumer economy, low unemployment, better wages, and a society built on hard work. Similarly, as the web of interdependence extends throughout the world, Korea can meet the needs of other, less developed countries. Of interest to our discussion is how Korea and America have achieved international prominence. Such successes occurred as both countries became integrated into the world's economic web.

Any country can plan long-range accomplishments, but exactly how to carry them out is another matter. The process of strategic planning involves several steps. The first concern must be directed toward human resources. Both in the United States and Korea, education is highly valued.

The second step of increasing international sales is through mass produced high technology. Koreans do that. They study engineering and other high technology fields. They work with the ROKG policies that favor international trade. Without that guidance, many qualified engineers would be restricted. Korean policies seem more favorable toward business than those in the United States. With a highly centralized and coordinated joint effort, the ROKG works closely with business leaders and research scientists.

Obtaining these two previous steps does not necessarily produce results. That is, unless the products are slanted toward local markets. The Latins must have a chance to buy Korean products. Those Korean-made South American shirts are tailored for Caracas, with its unique blend of Caribbean tropical traditions.

Sometimes it is risky not knowing what products to develop. Some technologies take long-term planning and developmental work. But even so, Korea views increasing productivity as more than increasing volumes, as more than increasing quality. It takes a concerted effort. Korean business executives, under the guidance of the ROKG, examine every aspect of strategic planning and implementation. They work together to experiment with various aspects of human resource development, mass production, and mass marketing in several international markets. They deliberately plan, as they start out on a given course. Everyone in society is involved, whether consciously aware of it or not.

Aside from preserving customs and habits of the people, this philosophy is also consistent with the philosophy of Confucian teaching. Confucian thinking emphasizes social order and harmony, but it also allows for division of labor and authoritative rule. If the decision was in the best interest of Korea and the Koreans, then it was permitted in a Confucian society.

CONCLUDING BENEATH THE MARKETS

Country comparisons emphasize cross-cultural differences. People do live quite different life styles. What appears strange in one society is commonplace in another. For example, most Americans are familiar with the story of Tom Sawyer and Huckleberry Finn and their boat ride down the Mississippi River. For Tom and Huck fishing was simple enough: live bait, fish hooks, and pieces of string. Yet those who live on Cheju Island know another way to fish. Women divers (known as *haenyo*) plunge into the cold sea to retrieve edible seaweed, shellfish, and octopus. Located 60 miles south of the southern coast, it is acclaimed as one of the world's ten most "unspoiled tourist paradises."

City residents in any country get impulses to flee. They want to return to earlier times, live off the land, and catch fish, whether in America or Korea. Mark Twain wrote about *The Adventures of Huckleberry Finn* in 1884. This tradition of deep-sea diving for sea weed dates back for centuries. People in both places fish, but the cultural differences vary considerably.

The theme throughout this book is that both social habits and cultural customs shape the national character of people. Over time social habits change more readily than cultural customs do. If social habits change enough, then finally traditional customs also begin to change slightly. Equally important is the idea that our characters are formed not only by our social and cultural settings, but also by interaction with other societies. Because of international trade and development, the cutting edge of change comes from multinational or transnational organizations.

To summarize, exporters can begin to understand biographic data of Koreans by recognizing their status, which is often based on their hometown and college attended. By spending time in Korea, exporters can also begin to recognize different customs and traditions. By comparing their way of thinking with those of the Koreans, they begin to see through the Korean cultural lenses. They understand why the Koreans are hard workers and intensely committed to action. To understand the people, not just products and markets, makes good business sense. Knowing that lower level can make sailing on the surface easier. Nevertheless, let's close with some practical notes about the characteristics of Korean markets.

1. Observe those practices surrounding and defining market characteristics. This serves a marketing purpose: how to gain access to the Korean markets.

2. The Korean market is not saturated for many industrial groups. Think about developing your international marketing strategy by matching your products to those the Koreans are importing.

3. Preliminary screening should include some profile of the consumer/user. In order to do that, you should estimate the market size and preferences of Koreans by regions.

4. In later screening estimate your industry market potential. The annual real growth rates tell you something about what's happening in the countryside.

5. Once you've established base-line data, match market size with annual growth. That's the start toward estimating the general market potential and your particular company potential.

6. Many other factors affect your sales potential. These are competitive products, market shares of competitors, comparisons, facilities, government tariffs, channels, prices, supply information, and importers.

7. Look at these products: rolling mills, metalworking and printing machinery, office machines, valves, bearings, textile processing machinery. Consider these other items which are also showing export increases—electric machinery, generators, motors, transformers, rectifier relays, radiotelephonic equipment, passive electrical components, and switches.

NOTES

1. David Gill, "Expanding Markets," *Business Journal of New Jersey* (April 20, 1989): 58.

2. Sak Onkvisit and John J. Shaw, "Marketing Barriers in International Trade," *Business Horizons* (May/June 1988):65.

3. Onkvisit and Shaw, 72.

14

U.S. Suppliers Compared to Japanese

At Tiananmen Square in the summer of 1989 Deng Xiao Ping, senior leader of the People's Republic of China, forcefully contained student unrest. After that military reaction and subsequent political purges, both Japan and Korea are more significantly positioned for greater international affairs. U.S. foreign policy experts now confirm this belief by high level policy analysts.

"In the 1970s and the early 1980s, the United States tended to think that stability in Asia led not through Tokyo but through Beijing," said a high-level Bush administrator.[1] Now, however, U.S. foreign policy has shifted its emphasis from the People's Republic of China to Japan. According to foreign policy officials, that means that "we have to avoid doing stupid things, like driving the Japanese away."[2] Ties with Japan and Korea are more politically important to that region's stability.

Political shifts also contribute to economic shifts toward East Asia. But these occur for more than political reasons. Unless the private sector acts to capitalize on opportunities or unless the government encourages economic development not much development occurs. The best way to isolate market influences is through various comparisons. That way researchers can better determine what makes the difference in success or failure. Country comparisons are made by other countries all the time. Japanese compare themselves with Americans quite often. Likewise, Koreans compare Americans with the Japanese, especially in light of their import diversification program. Judgments made on the basis of such comparison, in turn, affect an exporter's entry and pricing strategies to those respective countries. In all cases potential exporters compare their products at various levels.

To evaluate exports is to compare one society's approach with another's. It is to ask significant questions about competitors and company markets. Learning about competitors begins with questions such as these: Who are our competitors? What about their products? What is their quality image? How are our competitors similar and different? How much market share do they hold? What market segments belong to major competitors? How do their sales promotions and advertisements work? How do Koreans' selling, pricing, and discounting policies work? And finally, how do all these competitive issues affect major developments and market potentials of Korea?

Marketing professionals also ask these questions about company markets: How important is "after service" to increased sales? Does service affect the Korean's perceived quality of exported goods? Do the "little extras" in service ultimately pay? What do Koreans expect from U.S. exporters?

Fortunately for exporters, market researchers have already asked some of these questions. One firm changed its approach. After extensive evaluation of competitors and market issues, executives at Texas Instruments (TI) reached this conclusion. They saw the value of viewing service and quality, not as separate entities, but as one and the same aspect of a market. Through an integrated market proposal, these executives began to view competitors and markets as flip sides of the same coin with service and quality. So they changed their policies.

As a major company policy, TI strives for both quality products and service. Both make the difference to competitors, increased markets, and potential buyers. Those margins mean more differences in perception; they also can mean greater profits. President Jerry R. Junkins explains the corporate philosophy and how all of these comparison fit together. "The scope of quality has been expanded beyond manufacturing to include all aspects of the relationship between a supplier and his customers."[3] Everyone assumes a responsibility for implementation.

As a corporate policy, product quality extends into personal relationships. It is left neither to chance nor the TI employee's imagination. Quality, according to Mr. Junkins, is an all-encompassing term. He believes it highlights the suppliers' obligation to their customers in the following manner:

(1) understanding the customer's needs, (2) designing products and services that meet those needs, (3) building products so that they will perform as the customer expects, (4) packaging them carefully, labeling them correctly, (5) selling them at prices which reflect their true value, (6) delivering them as scheduled, and (7) doing whatever is necessary to assure trouble-free performance in the customer's application.[4]

Why does Mr. Junkins worry about quality? Poor quality is costly. According to a recent industrial survey, most *Fortune* 500 executives estimate that poor quality accounts for 10 percent of losses in gross sales. Experts push that figure upward, more toward 20 percent or even 30 percent. The reasons are obvious. First the consumer's perception of quality ultimately determines the product's financial performance. And second, consumers tend to evaluate quality of product with quality of services, whether the firm recognizes it or not.

What is true in the United States is equally true in Korea, especially as Koreans continue with their policy of diversification. Korean importers want after service along with the products themselves. They have come to expect it from the Japanese. And if American exporters are to be successful, they must follow suit. What follows are exhibits that give percentage of respondents by classification of decision makers, their preferences and motivations. This chapter reveals other insights about how information is accessed from sources other than those in Japan, including other supply sources. Finally, this chapter provides useful data for exporters interested in evaluating cost and noncost factors that influence importer preferences.

KOREA QUALITY SURVEY

The latest survey of Korean executives engaged in international trade yielded some surprising results. In 1987 in conjunction with Yonsei University, the Korean Foreign Trade Association conducted a survey to learn why Korean importers (over 2,000) preferred imports from Japan.[5]

The survey sample represented the major Korean importers. The following exhibits and motivations as well as the competitive factors of costs and noncosts as they affect market success.

But these findings should be understood in a broader context. Traditional animosity exists between these two peoples. Given that fact, what were the incentives for importing from Japan? Are there secrets that others should put into practice? The answer came from the Korean

Table 14.1
Preference for Japanese Imports

Classification	Percentage of respondents
Quality	44.6
Prices	39.1
Delivery	11.1
After-care services	3.1
Willingness of suppliers to accept small orders	1.3
Other requirements	0.8
Total	100.0

Foreign Trade Association. They surveyed Korean executives about Japanese and American importers.

By understanding the problem, the Korean Foreign Trade Association hoped to solve two problems. They bought too many Japanese products, while they sold the Americans too many Korean ones. The survey revealed the primary reasons why Koreans imported Japanese products by classification: quality, prices, delivery, after-care services, and so on (see Table 14.1). Overall the findings revealed how U.S. exporters could improve after service and sales. The Japanese did such a good job that both U.S. and the European Community (EC) exporters failed to live up to those expectations. Korean importers went so far as to state that sluggish growth in U.S. exports was directly related to poor performance in after service. Consequently, now the ROKG hopes to change Korean business opinions by strengthening after service.

The ROKG is concerned about trade imbalance. Therefore, it gave money to promote U.S. products over Japanese ones.

THE COST OF COMPETITION

Japanese firms, unlike those in the United States, export short distances to Korea. If American exporters think their costs of competition are high, then let them compare their motives with those of East Asian traders. Both Japan and Korea compete internationally in order to survive. Asian traders engage in international trade simply because they have to. Neither country has an abundance of land or natural resources. Consequently, they depend upon large imports of agriculture and minerals just to meet minimum population needs. Considering the ratio of these two countries' population to cultivable land, experts place Japan and Korea among the top of most densely populated countries. That means they must trade. They are even more dependent on basic imports than are India and Egypt (countries with high density populations). All

Table 14.2
Cost Comparison

						percentage of items*
Reasons	Machinery	Electric & Electronics	Chemicals	Textiles	Steels & other Metals	Total
Higher FOB Price	78.4	76.5	60.0	50.0	64.3	72.9
Higher trans. & insur. charges	21.6	23.5	40.0	50.0	35.7	27.1
Total	100.0	100.0	100.0	100.0	100.0	100.0

*January 1987.

of these Asian countries depend upon foreign oil reserves to meet their needs. That is why petroleum products rank so high among imports for both countries. They don't have any oil reserves. Thus Japanese firms, unlike U.S. firms, import most of their oil.

Asian countries, while short distances apart, are on the other side of the globe from America. Although close together, each country has its own unique culture and language, strongly influenced by China. Confucian and Buddhist thought permeate these respective cultures and ways of doing business. From an American perspective, exporters should note similarities, not differences. From U.S. exporters' perspectives, it's the factor of geography that figures high on cost comparison (see Table 14.2).

That's also why cost must be rigorously controlled. In 1985, TI recorded steep loses. To correct that problem immediately, CEO Jerry Junkins encouraged his international managers to see the big picture, not the one they normally saw. They worried mostly about their own limited turfs. Their solution linked the organization symbolically together. Computer networks link 40,000 terminals in 50 countries. Yet behind all this technology stands the relationships. Just as the networks are all encompassing, so too are the strategies for quality. They highlight the suppliers' obligation to their customers. They combine the two ideas—quality and service.

Managers should know enough about customer needs "to invest in the manufacturing technologies that will satisfy the greatest numbers of buyers, no matter where they come from."[6]

Such strategies are nonprice competitive ones, but when fully implemented they should bring profits. At least for TI they did. TI recorded seven consequent profit quarters.

Do those ideas about quality and service work in Korea? (See Table

Table 14.3
Comparison of Non-Price Competitiveness

			percentage of respondents		
	Preference Japan		Preference U.S.	Similar	Total
Quality	36.0		16.4	47.6	100.0
Delivery	89.4		1.3	9.2	100.0
After-care	82.4		3.3	14.3	100.0
Sales & marketing capability	84.3		2.2	13.5	100.0
Acceptance of small orders	82.9		1.1	16.0	100.0
Total	80.4		6.3	13.3	100.0

Table 14.4
Motivation for Importing from Japan

Classification	Percentage of respondents
Marketing survey results	40.7
Technical and joint-venture ties	21.8
Foreign customers' preference	12.7
Lack of information	4.5
Preference of company engineers	3.9
Others	16.4
Total	100.0

14.3.) Koreans preferred Japanese products over U.S. ones on a nonprice comparison. Once Koreans ranked Japanese products higher in many areas. Why did Koreans make these distinctions?

We learn why in Table 14.4. It specifies the motives for preferring Japanese imports. What can U.S. suppliers learn? While giving responses to the structured questions, Koreans also expressed other concerns that U.S. suppliers should keep in mind. Americans should engage in (1) offering more competitive prices; (2) improving production quality; (3) accepting small orders more readily; (4) developing products specifically adapted to the Korean market; (5) providing catalogues exclusively for Korean buyers; and (6) lowering import expenses for inland transportation costs.

After service is a two-way street. To be successful U.S. exporters need some help. In a recent publication, the Korean government promised "to support the strengthening of an after service system for machinery and equipment imported from the U.S. and the European Community."

Exporters from these regions, by contrast with the Japanese, ship their products around the world. But Korean businessmen also point to the lack of after service as the main reason for the sluggish growth of imports from these regions. Americans argue too that customs clearance procedures on after service must continue to be simplified. Storage areas must be built. The Korean won has going up continuously since 1986. At that time, 860 wons equaled one U.S. dollar. The 1990 rate (680 wons) reflects both a 14 percent revaluation and upward trend. Koreans are also encouraged to accelerate U.S. imports.

COMPARING DIFFERENCES IN ASIA

Japan and Korea resemble each other in several significant ways: Both trade to survive. Both lack enough land or natural resources. Both are strongly influenced by Chinese traditions and religions. Both received U.S. assistance. Yet these facts alone do not account for their successes. For U.S. suppliers to understand the Japanese and Korean country markets, they should recognize the differences each country used both to achieve its full measure of success and to restrict its markets from U.S. imports.

Exporters to this region often complain about their inability to penetrate the market. Ann Hardee of San Antonio complains about government red tape. To sell medical supplies in the U.S. domestic market takes about three pages. To sell those same medical products in Japan would take 700 pages.[7] Goodyear International Corporation recently paid a $250,000 fine for violating the 1977 Foreign Corrupt Practices Act (this prohibits U.S. corporations from bribing foreign officials). Yet many competitors of Goodyear do cash "commissions to maintain good relations in France, South Korea, and Japan."[8] Gary Kohake, director of Farmland's export markets of fresh pork, tells about the need to meet particular consumer needs.

"For instance," he says, "the Japanese can't handle as much salt content as what Americans are used to."[9] Consequently products must be altered to meet consumer needs. The Japanese gained control of the marketplace differently from the Koreans. Table 14.5 shows those two differences when compared with the United States.

This table also highlights the major country differences for the United States, Japan, and Korea in several key categories. Starting with the first row, you note that the political system is different. Exporters to this region soon realize that the capitalism they confront here is politically differently structured.[10] That structure contributes to the problems.

Until recently, U.S. firms wanted limited government intervention in their international affairs. In fact, the private and public sectors were competitive rivals and ineffective partners, not allies in trade. It worked

Table 14.5
Comparing Country Differences

Category	United States	Japan	Korea
Politics	Competitive Rivals	Cooperative Partners	Political Capitalism
Relations	Independent Acts	Intermarkets	Large Conglomerates
Philosophy	Individualism	Clan Ideologies	State Confucianism
Process	Authority	Consensus	Impersonal Manager
Motivation	Achievement	Acceptance	Compliance
Markets	New, Established	New Products	Capital Venture

in the opposite direction. Government policies, according to Ferguson, were too rigid and short-sighted. The U.S. government relied on "tax and economic policies biased toward consumption; a fragmented political and economic structure that impeded long-term technologies and strategic coordination."[11] Further, too many policies allowed for "asymmetric access" to trade, research, education, and technologies.

This condition contributed to the United States's international decline. But a few other factors, including external competitive pressure, finalized its impact. This happened as Japan used a formula of "cooperative partners," while Korea used political capitalism to accelerate the internationalization of Japanese and Korean industries. This is where the terms "Japan Incorporated" and "Korea Incorporated" come from.

Few debate the fact that there is greater cooperation between government and business in both Japan and Korea than in the United States. However that does not imply that industry is protected from failure. It is not. What it does imply is that strong state relations do contribute to rapid industrialization. For example, in Korea important business operations are controlled by government bureaucracies. That is not quite the case in Japan, where business firms and networks are free of direct government control. Nevertheless, the Japanese firms cooperate with the state's guidance.

As we've seen earlier, their political systems are public-private cooperatives. Both the Korean and Japanese prototypes go back to Japanese industrial policy at the turn of the century. The ROKG actively intervenes in both the public and private sectors by centralized planning and implementation. Historically, the Japanese have maintained separate powers, yet they maintain cooperation because each ruling group sees itself responsible to the people and subordinates itself to them. In each country American exporters confront a united Asian effort, even in the private sector.

By contrast with the importance of relations, U.S. firms work closely neither with other U.S. firms nor with the U.S. federal government. International trade, like other business, is fiercely independent. Japan uses "intermarket strategies" to gain competitive advantage, while Korea uses "large conglomerates." All strategies, whether in the United States, Japan, or Korea, come from cultural values and philosophies: U.S. individualism, Japanese clan ideologies, or Korean state Confucianism.

Over time religious values become the basis for group process and individual motivation. Here are other differences: Americans follow an organizational authority model; Japanese work from a consensus model; Koreans respond to an impersonal manager. Koreans give more emphasis to the scholar-official role than the Japanese. This peculiar development came from American involvement after the Korean war. Moreover, many of the leading Korean government officials were educated in the United States. Thus for Asians, the vortex of political power is upward toward the government. It is a modified type of structure, combining the ancient Confucian ideology with modern American management styles.

The two Asian cultures emphasize the importance of the family, obedience to authority, the centrality of education, and the desire to achieve success for the family name. Workers' motivations differ as well. Americans work from an achievement motivation framework; Japanese want group acceptance; Koreans comply with the government (up to a point).

As a result of these differences—politics, relations, philosophy, process, motivation—the market strategies for each country vary as well. After World War II, America developed a system of business that openly shared technology. American policy promoted free international trade and overlooked the aggressiveness of Japan. Politicians emphasized military alliance over economic issues. Industry tended to emphasize domestic consumer markets by mass production. Besides, international trade was small, so American technology was freely shared.

According to Ferguson, "U.S. firms would develop new technologies, only to find themselves defeated in market competition by the superior manufacturing and financial power of Japanese imitators or licensees."[12] Overall the American industrial system met the needs of a slow changing market. With the advent of information-intense technology, the separation of research and design from the manufacturing plants and market strategies proved less effective. In other words, international environments were less suited to American mass production techniques than to Asian consumerism.

The Japanese combined consumerism with their government policy. Barriers excluded American products, yet imported American technology, and then exported it back to American markets. Their manufacturing systems were geared to quick change, small markets, and new products. The Japanese excluded foreign competitors, borrowed technology, and used low-cost mass markets to gain a competitive edge on U.S. exporters to this region. As a result, Ferguson thinks we now face a challenge more serious than any since the Cold War. He suggests that Americans must (1) improve their economy through productivity and product performance; (2) reform their approaches to military procurement and defense industries (no longer freely sharing advanced technology with either Korea or Japan); and (3) manage Japanese relations better. "The U.S. must learn that these issues of high technology and Japanese industrial policy, not just Soviet warheads, will determine the future national security of the United States."[13]

"The large Japanese corporations specialize in a product area and, through research, development, and marketing strategies, attempt to create new commodities and consumers for those commodities."[14] By deliberately controlling the direction of product development, the Japanese government holds a competitive advantage through their technology and network systems. Thus they operate on the cutting edge of product development. It works.

Twenty years ago, Japan began with low-cost consumer electronics. In the last ten years, they achieved 49 percent of the world's semiconductor market. Now they control about 90 percent of the world's market in the newest generation of semiconductor memories—the 1-megabit DRAMS. Their efficiency rates exceeded both American and European standards. They excel in the use of robots per manufacturing units. Their manufacturing plants seem to handle a more varied and complex production mix than plants in either the United States or Europe.[15] Industrial success is measured in other ways. Their banking industry ranks among the top seven banks in the world, includes four of the largest securities firms, and encompasses the largest insurance and trading companies in the world.

By contrast, Korea is now trying to overtake some of Japan's lead. Nevertheless, Japan still holds the edge on electronic products. They do so because they hold the patents and components needed for production. At the same time, Koreans want to become independent of Japan and its domination in electronic components. Consequently, the Koreans are beginning to design their own products and parts. Most of the Korean development depends upon extensive capital investment (steel, construction, automobiles). The driving force comes from coordinated efforts in which capital provides the energy resource. Until now the major industries for exports did not require much research or development. They were the lowest cost strategies a developing country could take. Internationalization changes how the Japanese and Koreans perform.

For, among other reasons, their citizens begin to demand better medical services.

CONCLUSIONS

Medical costs in Japan and Korea are soaring. Both industry and government are looking for ways to cut costs. Until now Japan and Korea have bought reusable stainless steel medical products. That practice is changing. A fledgling San Antonio-based medical export supplier is responding to the similarities of these two country markets. The practice of product reuse leads to high infection rates for both Korea and Japan · because of poor sterilization procedures. To eliminate the spread of disease and infection, industrial leaders and physicians prefer cheap disposable medical supplies.

"The sky's the limit," said Ann Hardee, cofounder of Rann-Med. "There's not much competition out there."[16] However, relations must be cultivated.

In her travels to increase market sales, Ann Hardee discovered why the Koreans prefer Japanese products. It all comes from people. She believes that personal relations are paramount to export success in Asia.

"In Japan," she said, "who you know is very important. They have to get to know you on a personal basis before they'll deal with you."

After traveling to Japan three times in 1988, she began to make some export headway. Only after these trips, which she used to establish relationships, did she begin to close business deals and complete customer orders. She concluded that letters of introduction about her trustworthiness were crucial to her establishing good reliable customer relations.[17]

In terms of geopolitical and trade dimensions, both Korea and Japan gained status after the 1989 purges by Deng Xiao Ping in the PRC. Learning about Asian competitors and these two countries is basic to any market success. The Koreans expect quality products and after service—both depend upon good close relationships. To compete successfully in Asia requires a high level of commitment similar to the Japanese model. It's expected, not only because of the Asian culture, but also because of economically developed societies. Customer needs rank high because of a sophisticated interplay of factors. But equally important are the realities of diplomacy.

NOTES

1. Jim Mann, "U.S. Asia Policy Places Top Priority on Ties With Japan," *Los Angeles Times*, May 21, 1989, 3.

2. Mann.

3. Eugenia S. Hunter, "Quality—A Consumer Perspective," *Business America*, May 9, 1989, 10.

4. Hunter, 10.

5. The study (1987) was conducted by Yonsei University for KOTRA.These findings are still relevant for U.S. exporters. However, since that survey, the value of the Japanese yen against the dollar has increased considerably.

6. Andrew Kupfer, "How to Be a Global Manager," *Fortune*, March 14, 1988, 48.

7. Paul H. Carr, "Medical Supply Company Signs Its First Export Contracts," *San Antonio Business Journal*, May 5, 1989, 12.

8. Ruth Marcus, "Goodyear Unit Admits Bribes, Fined $250,000," *The Washington Post*, June 2, 1989, 1.

9. Kelly Alston, "Heartland Products, Service Ring Up International Sales," *Kansas City Business Journal*, May 5, 1989, 21.

10. Christopher Winship and Sherwin Rosen, "Organizations and Institutions: Sociological and Economic Approaches to the Analysis of Social Structure," *American Journal of Sociology* 94 (1988):S52-S94. While their original study focused on structural comparisons among Taiwan, Japan, and Korea, I have limited my discussion to the latter two countries.

11. Charles H. Ferguson, "America's High-Tech Decline," *Foreign Policy* (Spring 1989):124.

12. Ferguson, 127.

13. Ferguson, 140.

14. Winship and Rosen, S55-S56.

15. Ferguson, 128.

16. Paul Carr, "Medical Supply Company Signs Its First Export Contracts," *San Antonio Business Journal*, May 5, 1989, 5.

17. Carr, 12.

Gaining Access to Korean Markets

Were the statement "Know Thy Market" one of the ten marketing commandments, then "Know Thy Consumers" would be its corollary.[1] The truth of the matter is that both—markets and consumers—go together like walls around the traditional Korean cities.

If U.S. exporters do not know Korean consumers, they must depend upon their Korean agents. That was the case for Jim Maxton, Manager of International Marketing and Sales (Kustom Electronics Inc. of Lenexa, Kansas). Therefore, he took painstaking care in selecting his Korean agents. In fact, his firm spends six to eight months preparing for trips overseas to meet prospective agents. Consistent with a long-term export development program, his company has carefully selected seventy-five agents in sixty countries. This select body of representatives accounts for 20 percent of all the firm's production.

Their search begins with lists from the U.S. Department of Commerce's Agent/Distributor Service and other sources. They want to find just the right person at any cost. Just before Jim takes a trip abroad, he

corresponds with prospective representatives. But even after a prolonged search, he goes a step further by asking prospective agents to
arrange appointments for him with end users. This puts the agent to
the test. "It helps the agent and the end-user to see the equipment and
put their hands on it and to be able to ask questions about it,"Maxton
said.[2] These agents should know what and where to sell.

Prospective exporters to Korea with little knowledge of business practices, trade laws, or procedures for import success are advised to contact
trade organizations or other outlets for assistance. Only representatives
would understand the new community movement (*Saemaul Undong*) and
how much this effort contributed to eliminating rural poverty.Only an
agent would know about either the Korean tiger or the fact that Koreans
call their homeland *Kumsu Kangsan* (beautiful landscape) and their national flower *Mukung-hwa* (the everlasting flower). More important than
this, though, local partners and agents know how to do business, how
to gain access to Korean markets.

Griffin believes that "the choice of a Korean business participant is
the single largest determinant of success in doing business in Korea."[3]
It does not matter how one is selected. It could come from the American
Chamber of Commerce or the British or the Germans. Agents can be
contacted through consulting firms, accounting firms, even banks. Get
advice and assistance in locating the best qualified, most able Koreans
as partners and agents. Don't forget the U.S. Embassy, Commercial
Office (82 Sejong-ro, Seoul, Korea), the American Chamber of Commerce
(Chosen Hotel, 3rd Floor, Seoul, Korea), or U.S. Department of Commerce (14th Street and Constitution, Washington, DC).

If local representatives determine successful penetration, then get the
job done in whatever manner necessary. There are several strategic
options for getting access to Korean markets. The major concern is with
importers, agents distributors, and selling techniques.

THE MECHANICS OF GETTING INTO KOREA

Whether international traders want to export into Korea or later export
their products from Korea, they must be invited to do so. Korean regulations specify that business proposals precede any business deals.
After preparing the proposal, those wanting to access Korean markets
must submit their proposal either to a business institution or business
firm. Assistance comes from either side: U.S. Department of Commerce
or the Korean Foreign Trade Association, the American Chamber of
Commerce or the Korean Chamber of Commerce and Industry.

The process takes several steps. First, the invitation, then the association. The most effective Korean organizations are the Korea Foreign

Trade Association (licensed traders) and the Korea Trade Promotion Corporation (licensed traders). Others are the Korea Chamber of Commerce and Industry and the U.S. branch banks in Seoul. By law only registered traders can import goods in their names. The only exclusion is for goods brought in under foreign economic assistance programs, goods imported in connection with foreign private investment, raw material and components imported for processing and then reexporting, and government procurement.

Twenty-two U.S. trading firms in Korea handle a diversified line of products and represent primarily U.S. suppliers. Some see these as an advantage; others do not. It depends upon their volume and attentiveness to clients. To get lists of prospective firms, contact one of the nine U.S. offices for Korea Trade Promotion Corporation (KOTRA) (see the appendix).

U.S. suppliers seeking representatives can do what Jim Maxton did. Get lists. The Agent Distributor Service (U.S. Department of Commerce) offers advice on representatives for a nominal fee. The U.S. Trade Center at the U.S. Embassy offers special visitation services, includingtemporary duty-free entry for demonstration equipment and samples, identification and contacting of prospects, and hiring of a qualified interpreter/secretary for the account of the U.S. firm. The effect is a temporary office and staff in Korea.

Moreover, exporters should ask for the 1989 publication,108 *A Guide to the Korean Import Market*. Or ask for *A Directory of Trade*. What the exporter wants to do is make contacts with the appropriate Koreans who can assist in entering or penetrating the market.

After establishing these procedures, the exporter drafts a proposal about what he wants. The proposal should give some introduction about the exporter's firm, what he wants to sell, how he proposes to ship it, and what technical assistances are needed.

In 1988 only about 534 items, using the Harmonized System (HS) 10-digit standard, required some type of import regulation. For primary goods this restricted list included "meat, dairy products, fish and vegetables." For manufactured goods, it listed "precious metals, raw silk, silk yarn and silk fabrics."[4]

Griffin suggests that proposals should be translated into Korean. This third step is optional, however. Griffin says it is a "polite gesture which can save time and demonstrate goodwill."[5] It is absolutely not essential to do this, for most Koreans speak English, or they know someone in their organization who does. The fourth requirement is to get Korean visas. Remember to get a notarized letter from the Korean contact. That letter, along with some financial arrangements and an estimate of time necessary for the trip, is all that is needed.

THE MECHANICS OF PENETRATING KOREAN MARKETS

Certain conditions exist for gaining access to Korean markets: (1) if exporters, or their selected representatives, can sense the culture of beliefs, they will then be better able to find hidden motives about why Koreans prefer their courses of action; (2) if exporters can observe culture as patterns of behavior, they will be less likely to neglect market segments; (3) if exporters can serve the culture of taste, they should be able to define subtle messages for advertisement.

Multiple conditions interact with business activities. If U.S. exporters seek new markets and eventually penetrate them, they probably will increase sales and profits by decreasing costs. The reverse is also true. As U.S. exporters develop Korean markets and rationalize them, they increase costs. Conversely, they'll increase sales volume, which should eventually offset these costs. And finally, as U.S. exporters invest in manufacturing and marketing products, initially they will incur added costs. Yet through marketing strategies, they'll be better able to maintain their share of Korean markets. It is obviously risky to develop or to promote new products. However, as Korean consumers increase in sophistication and as Korea's industries import higher levels of technology, risks are reduced.

Foreign firms seeking business presence and entrances into Korean markets may establish a liaison office, a branch office, or a joint venture. Liaison offices are low-profile establishments that, while limited in scope, do not pay Korean corporate taxes. Expenses are paid from U.S. operations, simply because no money is generated by the sponsoring firm. Additionally, liaisons are limited. They purchase goods, store them, promote them through advertising, and perform auxiliary functions.

Because of these limitations, most U.S. firms use the branch office, which reports to the Bank of Korea and registers with the court. Branches are authorized for specific business endeavors. Sending earned money back to the United States presents some special problems. The same is true in manufacturing and conducting foreign financial exchanges. Those business activities require other authorization, which originates in the Ministry of Finance. Both methods are used with varying degrees of visibility. The big difference is that liaison offices, unlike branch offices, are not allowed to do any profit-loss business activities.

As an alternative business structure, U.S. firms can invest in Korean companies as subsidiaries or joint ventures (JVs). There are both advantages and disadvantages to this. On the plus side, JVs require less capital while allowing U.S. exporters to gain partner's expertise. That saves time (a quicker entrance), gives a local presence, and provides some trade benefits, as in the case of investment incentives. On the negative side, profits and control are shared, which can lead to conflicts and, in some cases, the creation of another competitor. Another drawback in Korea is that the ROKG must approve all expansions. It limits autonomy. Also, in the case of branch offices, any remittance of business profits must come from the Bank of Korea. Establishing foreign investment firms requires authorization by the Ministry of Finance under the Foreign Capital Inducement Act. For further information, see appendix.

Usually the home office personnel appoint one of the U.S. trading firms in Korea as their representative, select registered trading firms to act as their agents, or have registered offer agents act in their stead in Korea.

THE MECHANICS OF STAYING IN KOREA

One should find Korean agents who are paid commissions by foreign sellers. However, to do that each time would be cumbersome. Consequently, there are four ways of establishing local commission agents in Korea:

1. Offer agents—these people issue offer sheets on behalf of foreign suppliers (a commission basis). There are over 2,354 offers agents with 81 branch offices (22 American, 18 Japanese, and other countries).

2. Sales agents—their business concerns sales promotion activities and after service.

3. Offer-sales agents—their work includes issuing offer sheets and sales promotion activities.

4. End-user agents—those who issue offer sheets for importing only those raw materials, machinery, and equipment necessary for promotion purposes.

What this means is that the authority of agents varies, depending upon the type of arrangement.

Let's suppose that American firms want to export one of these fastest selling types of machinery. They would first determine if their products are in demand. If so, they would then contact one of the Korean importers who has a trader's license and who can serve as an offer agent.

Sellers and agents work together. The sellers initially establish the arrangement with their agents. They could, if they wanted, give agents power over the terms of the offers, the authority to negotiate, and the power to promote the products.

Agents handle most imports into Korea (78 percent). There is a growing number of offer agents. Effective agents receive a $30,000/year commission. Knowing this, prospective U.S. exporters should select the best, most effective agents (those with the highest commissions). Registered

Table 15.1
Top Ten Korean Advertising Agencies

Korea First Advertising LTD. Central P.O. Box 1580 Seoul	Oricom Inc. Central P.O. Box 289 Seoul
Union Advertising Kwanghwamun P.O. Box 1408 Seoul	Korea International 35-36 Yoido-dong Youngdungpo-gu Seoul
Daehong Advertising Kwanghwamun P.O. Box 373 Seoul	LG Advertising Central P.O. Box 1088 Seoul
Diamond Advertising Kwanghwamun P.O. Box 1087 Seoul	Nara Advertising Central P.O. Box 1894 Seoul
Samhee Advertising 111-5 Sogong-dong Chung-gu Seoul	Dongbang Advertising 114 Nonhyyun-dong Kangnam-gu Seoul

traders, or agents, usually receive a 3 to 15 percent commission. In some cases they earn more, say from 5 to 30 percent. The price the end user pays for imported machinery is usually about 20 percent higher than the supplier's initial price quotation.

ADVERTISING

Effective advertising is a prerequisite to successful marketing in Korea. Most consumers (68 percent) say that advertising influences their purchasing decisions. The advertising industry in Korea is dominated by a few agencies: Korea Broadcast Advertising Corporations for television and radio; the Korea Newspaper Association for newspapers. Magazines, however, pay commissions to all agencies. Korea has three TV networks, four commercial radio networks, six national dailies, two economic dailies, two sports dailies, two English-language dailies, and more than 2,000 magazines. Contacting these advertising agencies can be crucial to business success. Two encouraging aspects of advertising are the current open-door policy of the Korean government and the new opportunities for exports to Korea. Domestic advertising is relatively recent in Korean history.

In 1987 the amount paid for commercial advertising in Korea totalled about 1.4 percent of the total GNP. The top ten Korean advertising agencies are listed in Table 15.1. These, along with others, advertise products and services through the media. The 1988 breakdowns by classification and percentage are: food and beverages (19.2 percent); pharmaceuticals (14.7 percent); kitchen equipment (12.7 percent); sports, leisure, and services (9.9 percent); personal accessories (7.2 percent); cosmetics and beauty supply (7.1 percent); electric appliances (6.5 percent); clothing and textiles (4.9 percent); chemicals and industrial machines and tools (4.2 percent); education and medical services (4.2 percent); the publication industry (3.5 percent); and others (5.9 percent).

In 1988 Korean firms paid $1.869 billion in advertisements, representing an increase of one-third from the previous year. A breakdown of expenditures shows the media share by and percentages per dollar: newspaper (36.2 percent, $677 million), television (34.8 percent, $650 million); magazines (5.1 percent, $95.3 million); radio (4.0 percent, $74.8 million); overseas ads (2.1 percent, $39.2 million); and others (17.8 percent, $332 million). After the 1988 Summer Olympic Games, foreign advertising agents used these markets much more than before.

The basic media for advertising in Korea are the newspaper, radio, television, magazines, and movies. Since 90 percent of Koreans are literate, written materials are commonly used for advertising. Radio is second because there are over 25 million radios, 54 radio stations. Prime time is from 7 A.M. to 9 A.M. and noon to 1 P.M. during the day. TV is now more important, especially after the 1988 Summer Olympic Games. About 7 million sets are owned by Koreans. Magazine circulations total 240,000 pieces. Motion picture theaters also run short commercials.

STRATEGIES FOR DISTRIBUTION CHANNELS

Even before selecting distribution channels, exporters must begin concentrating on sales. To be competitive, U.S. firms should be aware of recent survey findings about problems Koreans are having in transferring import sources. Effective sales operations compensate for these problems, regardless of the product line. They consider what Koreans expect of U.S. suppliers, even as they did from the Japanese.

Table 15.2 reveals where the problems are in transferring import sources. By percentage of respondents, the Koreans believe U.S. goods are not competitive in quality and price (a third of the sample). Delivery problems also exists (25.5 percent). U.S. goods have a reputation among Korean buyers. But until now the Korean consumers bought Japanese or other products. That is all changing with the policy of trade diversification. Korean business is now shifting import resources from Japan to the United States. U.S. exports grew by 43 percent from January to May of 1988 due to changes in policies.

Seven other problems were cited:

1. U.S. suppliers furnish no samples.
2. U.S. suppliers demand expenses for estimates.

Table 15.2
Problems in Transferring Import Sources to United States

Reason	Percentage Respondents
-Noncompetitive quality and price	27.7
-Problems in delivery	25.5
-Lack of information on suppliers	13.1
-Unsatisfactory after-service	11.3
-Difficulty in placing small orders	8.6
-Technical and capital reliance on Japan	8.3
-Others	5.5
Total	100.0

3. Difficulties in measurement and interpreting exist.

4. U.S. suppliers demand cash or advance payments.

5. U.S. suppliers exhibit an unenthusiastic attitude toward exporting to Korea.

6. Korea has an exclusive arrangement with the Japanese for all imports.

7. There is indirect importing by Japanese suppliers through dumping.

Table 15.3 gives some examples of the problems of certain products. Distribution channels depend upon having competitive prices, fast delivery, and good after-sales service.

Personal contacts are important not only because of the value placed on personal discussions in the Orient, but also because such discussion serves to bring the end user in touch with new processes and equipment. Manufacturers may not be aware of new product developments for equipment. Korean firms looking for expansion and modernization may not be aware of what products are available. American exporters should keep these business relations in mind, because the Koreans certainly do. Table 15.4 offers some solutions to U.S. suppliers.

The ability to deliver goods in a prompt and timely manner is a positive factor for the Koreans. Shipping transit time from Yokohama to Pusan is twenty-four hours and from Kobe to Pusan eighteen hours, while goods shipped to Korea from the United States take considerably longer. Although little can be done to reduce transit time, the possibility of maintaining stocks of rapid-turnover goods requires more serious consideration, as will other methods designed to combat competitive advantages of proximity. At present, only a few agents for U.S. firms stock equipment in Korea. Additionally, U.S. exporters should provide more and better information to Korean importers, improve after-service, adopt marketing procedures more in conformity with Korean practice, accept small orders more readily, and dispatch sales missions to Korea to promote priority.

Koreans offer other suggestions for potential U.S. suppliers:

Table 15.3
Examples of Problems by Product

Products	Problems
Machine Tools	Noncompetitive prices, slow delivery & poor after-sales service.
Automobiles and Parts	Lack of information about U.S. suppliers, noncompetitive prices, slow delivery, poor after-sales service, Korean manufacturers' technical tie-ups with Japanese products, insufficient marketing activities by U.S. suppliers.
General Machinery	Noncompetitive prices, slow delivery, technical tie-ups with Japanese makers, insufficient marketing activities by suppliers.
Textiles	Noncompetitive prices, slow delivery, insufficient marketing activities by U.S. suppliers, negative reactions by U.S. companies to small orders.
Consumer Goods	Noncompetitive prices, lack of sufficient information about U.S. suppliers.

Note: Korean marketing analysts obtained the above information from major import companies and end users.

Table 15.4
Problems Requiring Solution by U.S. Suppliers

-Expedite deliveries	29.4
-Provide more and better information	24.1
-Improve after-service	17.5
-Adopt marketing procedures more in conformity with Korean practice	14.6
-Accept small orders more readily (e.g. through stock sales)	8.3
-Dispatch sales missions to Korea to promote priority import-transfer items	4.7
-Others	1.4
Total	100.0

1. Offer more competitive prices.
2. Improve production quality.
3. Accept small orders readily.
4. Develop products specifically adapted to the Korean market.
5. Provide catalogues exclusively for Korean buyers.
6. Lower import expenses for inland transportation costs.

CONCLUSION

This chapter described the risks of entering the Korean markets. It is risky, because there are no guarantees about outcomes. To pass the Korean market by, however, without exploring it could be risky as well. The best one can hope for is that some laws of marketing probability bring profits. The odds of success are probably slanted toward those who work hard and gain market access through the strategic location in Asia. "Korea is the only country that shares its borders with all four superpowers: China, the Soviet Union, Japan, and the United States. [Moreover], Korea is a high priority country for sustained economic growth in order to compensate for a poor natural endowment."[6]

B. J. Bland, President of Antitox Corporation (Georgia), summarized his experiences. "You can't just sit back and place an ad or send out a flier in the mail," he said. "You have got to go there." And that's the problem, too many American executives are reluctant to go there and listen to the customers' complaints. But if the CEO goes, then the agents also begin to respond. "Very early we began overseas traveling, not just for one or two weeks, but for up to six weeks at a time," Bland said. "It is difficult to count the times when an overseas customer has greeted us with amazement that we would take the time and effort to come see him."

But that is exactly what the Koreans seem to be saying—listen. Gaining access to Korean markets takes top management commitment, not just on the front end of making initial decisions, but also on the back side of maintaining established personal contacts with the Koreans themselves.

NOTES

1. Song-Hyun Jang, "Discovering the Korea Consumer," *Korea Business World*, November 1985, 91.

2. Katherine Glover and Bill Scoutone, "50 Firms Share Export Techniques," *Business America*, September 12, 1988, 22.

3. Trenholme J. Griffin, *Korea: The Tiger Economy* (London: Euromoney Publications, 1988), 58.

4. Sun-Ki Lee, *A Guide to the Korean Import Market* (Seoul: KOTRA, 1989), 23.

5. Trenholme J. Griffin, "Doing Business in Korea: A Special Report," *Korea 1989 Guidebook* (Boston: Houghton Mifflin, 1989), 179. This text is a standard travel book, but it is more. Originally written for the Olympics, the editors have subsequently added information for business travelers.

6. Lee Chong Ouk, "Korea's Science and Technology Policy and Cooperation with the United States," *Korea's Economy*, August 1988, 3.

16

Inside Business Practices

Successful exporters to Korea already know about insider's advice. Over time they have learned more than most from interacting with competent Korean importers. They know Koreans, or other experienced Americans, who can effectively guide them to better, closer connections with Koreans. That is important anywhere, but especially here. Koreans conduct business intensely through proper connections.

Exporters should find some well-connected Koreans with "wide legs." *Bal i nul ba* is what they are called in Korea.[1] These are people who get inside business practices; they turn talk into sales because of high-level connections.

Using the right contacts makes sense internationally. Managers at Telenet Communications (Reston, Virginia) attribute their export success to an effective worldwide distribution network. They warn others to be careful in selecting agent/distributors. Before selecting consultants, know their reputation. Crystal International (New Orleans), a supplier of food products, finds the employment of nationals quite profitable.

This chapter will explore these cultural dynamics as they impact markets. Specifically let's relate the Korean language to action. After all, it describes the culture and inside business practices. Our discussion compares gestures, images, and actions for two different cultures—Korean and American. Each culture uses different symbols in organizing strategies for marketing. The Koreans have a term, *yuryuk ja*, which refers to a person's ability to get something done. Getting inside business practices explains why many business leaders come from government service. People with influence are called "big shots," or *keo mul*. Both terms suggest the importance of getting inside the business deals, where the real action is.

KOREAN BUSINESS PROTOCOLS

As for conversations, Americans ask questions. Some are difficult, others inappropriate for Asians. In Korea "yes" does not always mean "yes." "Yes" could mean "I understand your question." "Yes" could mean "I don't want to embarrass you." Or "yes" could mean "I will act." In business conversations, it is impolite to speak only with the fluent-English-speaking Koreans, unless they are the highest status.

In business deals, American executives work fast; Koreans establish relations. That is why short trips to Korea don't usually work. Long-term relations are not optional, they're essential. You don't sign contracts, you make connections.

Also, get the highest status Korean to introduce you, for your initial status is no greater than that of the person who introduces you. The word is *yeon* (personal connections whereby one person takes care of another). Yeon establishes the way this interaction proceeds to include (1) proper introductions by the right person, (2) some face-to-face discussions, both formally and informally, (3) a reasonable amount of time for eating together, (4) learning about personal history and background experiences, (5) sharing common interests and hobbies, and (6) developing trust relations.

Americans may view such practices or protocols as ancillary to business matters. Not so for Korea. Personal exchanges take precedence over business exchanges. Since Koreans tend to be formal, it is only after first getting acquainted that they express true feelings. Otherwise, the tendency of Koreans is to be polite and respectful (*kongsunhee*).

Koreans prefer to communicate formally and intuitively. Vagueness is preferred over clarity, indirectness over directness, feeling over expressions, and silence over excessive talking. Despite these seemingly limiting preferences, they maintain "well lubricated" business and social relationships. Keep that in mind as you eating *kimchi* at Kim's famous

Korea Restaurant in Seoul. Remember that Koreans don't usually talk during the meal. It's only afterward that you can ask your questions.

A bow symbolizes respect and is a form of greeting. The lower the bow (below 15 degrees), the greater the respect. Culture prescribes these patterns of behavior, and in turn, these patterns are acquired and transmitted by symbols. Koreans, like Americans, use symbols in two ways: They process symbols visually and emotionally. Consequently, to see visually is to perceive mentally with our minds' eyes. There are fixed associations with recurrent encounters that allow for public communication. In Korea there are many unwritten rules, or *naekyuu*, about what can or cannot happen.

Exporters to Korea have been frustrated about these unwritten rules applied without prior knowledge. Although frustrating, you should seek guidance from insiders. Korean executives, who serve that role, can sometimes avoid delays in customs and clearance at the dock.

Customs predispose people to certain responses. As people recognize certain symbols, they will attribute special meaning to them. Never use red ink to emphasize or correct Korean proposals. That color symbolizes death for those involved.

Within minutes before beginning the baseball world series, crowds stand for the national anthem and the American flag. Symbols make visible the invisible values of the American culture. Sacred symbols elicit strong emotional association. Christians view the cross as the symbol of the uniqueness of God-man, the mystery of life-death, and the efficacy of the crucifixion-resurrection.

In Confucianism Koreans learn to respect the past and their ancestors. Many believers regularly participate in ceremonies to honor them. Ceremonial rites and memorial services are still conducted in over 200 Confucian academies (*hyanggyo*).

With this brief explanation, you can better understand the importance of symbols for Korean practices. You'll begin to understand why most Korean firms use the morning as a time to symbolically motivate their workers. You can even associate the Korean word *chonmae* with these morning ceremonies where the national anthem is played. Whether in Seoul or St. Louis, symbols encourage appropriate business behavior. That is, assuming that you read about current events while there.

INFORMATION ON SOUTH KOREA IN ENGLISH

If you know where to look, relevant information is available to executives living in Korea. They could even become familiar with the range of published source materials before moving there. Here are the most important publications that can give the insider's view on doing business in Korea. Broadly speaking, it is important to distinguish between government publications and nongovernment publications.

Government-sponsored Publications

The *Korea Herald* claims to be the only English-language newspaper for foreign businessmen. It is a twelve-page daily newspaper published by the Korean government. It provides general coverage of political, economic, and social topics. Although the *Korea Herald* does not provide investigative reporting or unbiased treatment of current issues, it does convey the government's point of view, and it does take note of major news affecting the foreign business community.

Another government publication is the weekly *Korea News Review*, which is also useful for general political, economic, and cultural coverage. *Korea Trade and Business*, published by the Korea Trade Promotion Corporation (KOTRA), has a business emphasis.

Korea's Economy has been a quarterly newsletter prepared by the Korea Economic Institute (KEI) (Washington, D.C.). KEI is a lobbying organization funded by the Korean government's think-tank, the Korea Development Institute. It seems that the newsletter is being discontinued. But this institute provides other excellent materials, as well as contacts for networking.

Nongovernment Publications

Government news management at times produces a monotonous sameness in the Korean language media. Yet *Tonga Ilbo* has a tradition of lively resistance against censorship that dates back to the days of Japanese colonial rule.

No doubt the government would like to see more harmony and unity in economic as well as in political reporting. The complex Korean economy, however, demands accurate and timely information. This reduces, though never eliminates, government control in media and business fields. Practices of censorship have waned considerably.

The Korea Times is an English-lanugage daily newspaper. It operates less under government oversight than the *Korea Herald*, providing alternative perspectives on current events. Another publication is *Business Korea*, a monthly that reflects the Korean business scene in an attractive and informative format. *Korean Business Review* is a more restrained but useful monthly of the Federation of Korean Industries.

Objective foreign assessments are also available. The commercial section of the U.S. Embassy in Seoul makes available both general surveys of business conditions and studies of key industries. The American Chamber of Commerce (Seoul) also produces specialized reports and studies. For another assessment of the economy, see the *Quarterly Economic Review of South Korea,* published by the Economist Intelligence Unit in London. The same organization publishes an annual survey of the South Korean economy. The Mead Group (Phoenix, Arizona) publishes *Korea High-Tech Review,* a monthly bulletin based largely on interviews with American businessmen in electronics and other high-tech fields.

Those who want deeper understanding should gain access to the nongovernment Korean-language media. Korean-language publications contain information not found in the government-published English-language publications. Specialized industry publications and economic dailies provide a wealth of articles, interviews, profiles of business leaders, and discussion of pending shifts in government economic policies.

Press Translations: Korea, produced by the U.S. Embassy in Seoul, gives coverage of the Korean press six days a week. Heavily relied upon by most Western embassies in Seoul, this publication provides accurate English excerpts of current Korean press articles, editorial cartoons, and headlines and summaries of television news programming. Coverage is selective, with an emphasis on South Korean politics, economics, and current issues in U.S.-South Korean relations. This is an indispensable guide both to Korean perceptions of U.S. business activity and to the day-to-day mood of the government and media.

Another important source for current Korean news is the Foreign Broadcast Information Service, *Daily Report/East Asia* (formerly *Daily Report/Asia & Pacific*). It is published five times weekly. Back issues are available on microfiche or in the annual index of Newsbank (New Canaan, Connecticut).

Asian Business and Korean Politics

There are several Asian business publications that provide sporadic but valuable attention to business issues in Korea. These include *The Asian Wall Street Journal, Asian Business,* and *Asian Finance,* all published in Hong Kong. *Asian Finance* gives a review of the top 500 Asian corporations in its December and January issue each year. *The Far Eastern Economic Review* has good reporting on Korean economic and business issues. It also publishes an annual yearbook that contains reviews of the previous year. A publication with valuable current information and advice on doing business in Korea and other Asian countries is the *East Asian Executive Reports.* It is a monthly published in Washington, D.C., by American lawyers with Asian business expertise.

For background coverage of Korean politics and foreign relations, the *Journal of Northeast Asian Studies,* a quarterly published in Washington, D.C., and *Asian Survey,* a monthly published in Berkeley, California, are especially helpful. *Asian Survey* reviews the previous year in Korea in each January issue.[2]

THE USE OF INSIDE INFORMATION

What we've learned depends, in part, upon where we lived, where we were raised. Perhaps it's where he lives that prompted Philip Burgress to discuss the historical similarities and differences between the old and new west.[3] Affiliated with the Colorado Center for the New West, he naturally speaks about the process of business developments in the west. Before, and even after, the Civil War, many wagon trains of explorers set out for the west, hoping to find a new way of life and prosperity. These explorers sincerely believed that the opportunities were there. In order to find this life, they were willing to encounter snakes, the dessert, Indians, and outlaws.

Today there is still a "west," as a symbol of opportunity. In one sense, though, it's different now, for the world symbolizes opportunity, not just the western United States. But in another real sense, the process hasn't changed all that much. Before venturing out into the unknown, people must collect information about their options. What is available and where is it? How do we get there and when do we leave? What does it take to get started and who will help? What adjustments should be made along the way and how do we make them? Just as explorers once moved west to find land, now entrepreneurs move east looking for international markets.

"You're looking at a $3 trillion market in the Pacific Rim," Burgress said. "It's increasing at a rate of $3 billion a week."[4]

Measured by growth rates, these statistics exceed the European Community (EC) projections of $4.2 trillion. With projected increases in East Asia, it will outpace the EC, especially after 1992. Those who take advantage of the opportunities should combine government and business resources. Taken together, firms have much better chances of success these days. Today firms must respond to emerging, rapid changes in technology and international competition. Some examples are those who come up with innovations about how to capitalize on everything from software production to economic "mining" with new technology.

While Burgress speaks in general terms about opportunities, those at Heartland Products (Kansas City, Missouri) deal with specifics. Exporting for these professionals is more than world travel and exotic cultures. Everyday their business center coordinates the shipping of their produce to world ports, including Asia.[5]

In just two years, the Japanese reduced tariffs on fresh pork (from 25 percent to 10 percent). As a result of these changes in global markets, "the potential is tremendous, particularly in the Third World countries

Table 16.1
The General Electric Screen

Business Strength Factors	Market Attractiveness Factors
relative market share	market size
company image	market growth rate
production capacity	demand segmentability
cost of manufacture	competitive climate
financial resources	ease of entry
extent of integration	industry capacity
R & D	industry capacity use
patent protection	industry profitability
product quality	investment intensity
distribution system	regulatory climate
sales/customer service	environmental climate
advertising	market quality
sales promotion, pricing	accessibility

and the Pacific Rim,"[6] says Jajko, a marketing specialist in agriculture. "When the markets are ready, we'll be set to capitalize."[7] The Koreans are following the pattern of the Japanese in reducing tariffs.

How do companies develop marketing strategies that allow them to get inside Korea with minimum costs?

STEPS TO GET INSIDE KOREAN MARKETS

To implement marketing proposals requires several steps. Begin looking for leads into the Korean market using all available avenues. Since the government controls the economy, determine what it is planning. With renewed emphasis on small to medium size businesses, target these.

Another step is to look at the strength-weaknesses of your firm versus the opportunity-problems. The strengths are those capacities that allow you to reach marketing objectives. Weaknesses are organizational deficiencies that usually get less attention, have fewer resources, than other clearly visible activities.

One technique for analysis is the General Electric Screen. This allowed executives at GE to determine their strategies. The process lists business strength factors with market attractiveness factors (Table 16.1).

Develop good product and market segment mixes. Marketing professionals make sales forecasts using (1) Korean government data, (2) U.S. Commerce information about the Korean market, (3) state data accumulated from an economic development government unit, (4) extrapolations from historical data of similar firms, (5) surveys conducted by the Korean or U.S. governments, and finally, (6) insights from Korean experts, sales personnel, or the Korean customers themselves.

Recognize gaps between the projected analysis for market objectives and expected results. Compare what should happen versus what does happen. Consider advertisements. One way to decrease the gaps of marketing expectation is by increasing sales through the Korean media and advertisements.

Look for product life cycles based on performances of your competitors. Know where your best opportunities are. If the expanding opportunities are in manufacturing, find out who is already there and what they do in volume. Continue to scan, looking for places where competitors leave out segments of untapped markets.

In summary, look at the characteristics of either successful joint ventures or foreign affiliated companies in Korea. Usually those who succeed explore Korean markets despite real constraints, difficult obstacles, and red tape. Does your firm have characteristics that make for success? This is essential to your chances of success.

Those who show strong do so because they are confident. They enter the Korean market with something special to offer. Their products are resource-driven (coal), or technological breakthroughs (stucco), or new ideas (integrated circuits), or differentiated marketing strategies (Korean festivals).

These are only generalizations, and this is risky. But one fact has stood the test of time:

Foreign companies which carefully investigate the Korean market and enter with well-defined objectives are nearly always the most successful. Companies which come to Korea looking for profit from both domestic markets [sales in Korea] and trading [sourcing products from Korea] will also have a considerably greater chance of being successful. By adopting this dual purpose strategy, risks are diminished and government support [because of the exports] is virtually assured.[8]

Those who survive take definite action. They do not send only new employees or old ones passed over. They demonstrate long-term commitment by sending their best people. These suppliers, not frightened by obstacles, continue to look objectively at difficulties with one exception. They tend to see problems as creative challenges and look for solutions. These firms display competitiveness through well-researched marketing plans. Even as they enter or expand their Korean markets, they combine strategies with sound rationale.

In conclusion, to get started right is to begin constructing your own Korean analyses. That information saves time because you'll already have a flexible marketing plan from which to approach Korea as an evolving industrial complex.

CONCLUSIONS ABOUT THE COMPLEXITIES OF KOREA

Holograms show small pictures that are exact replicas of larger pictures. In this discussion, we contended that Korean insiders operate through complex networks. Obviously, exporters have many more questions than they can answer. "So just find a company that has an active export operation and ask them questions," said an executive from Southwest Hide of Boise. Learn about their export methods and about Korean business practices, even as they learned from their exporting experiences.

Also learn from Koreans. After all, the Koreans know more about their markets than others do. Go to trade fairs. Take the advice from Sandco, a Tulsa manufacturer of printing supplies and equipment. Its export managers attended several international trade shows where they met country dealers interested in their products. By attending such events, these exporters found Koreans with "wide legs." Those contacts allowed them to step inside business practices where the real action was.

These suggestions become all the more important in our global economy where events interconnect. In 1988 Samsung celebrated its fiftieth anniversary. Were Samsung an American company, it would rank fifteenth in the *Fortune* 500. It employs 150,000 people who contributed to its $24 billion in revenues (1988). Companies like Samsung make winners of their employers.

The Korean GNP per person should reach $5,000 by 1990. Both white collar professionals' and blue collar wages are slowly increasing. Manufacturing wages show a steady increase: 50 percent since 1980, 20 percent (1987), and 15 percent (1988). Naturally, wages affect Korean domestic markets. But for those 42 million people living in a country the size of Indiana, there are major social problems—labor unrest, military threats, government corruption, student demands. Despite these changes, the Korean economy is strong.

Prosperity for the Koreans is something new, especially for those born at the turn of the century. The founder of Samsung, B. C. Lee, was born in 1910, the year that Japan annexed Korea. The son of a wealthy farmer, he studied in Tokyo at Waseda University. After returning to Korea, he started his trading company in 1938, but he always depended upon the Japanese for business advice. Pil-Gon Rhee, now president, tells exactly how that worked. "When he returned from Japan, he would gather directors of the relevant companies and tell them about his ideas."[9] What he learned about inside trading, he implemented, and it paid off. Samsung's models for exporting and managing, not surprisingly, were patterned after the Japanese.

Since there are few natural resources here, Korea must depend upon her workers. They must work in the right climate of cooperation to achieve their successes. Both technological innovations and the free spirit of international development have contributed to the emerging of a new epoch of international trade. Others, like Korea, have accepted the challenges of this new era of automation and computer technology. They either contribute to good will or bad. International marketing and managing represent the greatest challenge. To manage a machine requires some skills, but to manage people internationally requires even greater skills. Too often, we do not balance the dimensions of our similarities against the differences in our cultures and language. "I have a dream," Lee once said, "to build Samsung into a world-class company, a genuine multinational company."[10]

The international traders may be the key figures in this delicate operation. Too much emphasis on the individual leads to self love or social isolation, while too much emphasis on respect and duty in organization may repress creativity and innovation. It is not one or the other, but both. This is the challenge. Both human survival and the maintenance of human dignity compel us to combine business practices found in East and West. We desperately need an international harmonious world filled with managers sensitive both to real-world issues and consumer demands.

The jumping off place could be Korea. Koreans have a history of demonstrating courage and loyalty within the confines of Asian traditions. Yet their cultural distinctions also prepared them for recent high tech industries and scientific accomplishments. Since the Korean War, they have achieved phenomenal successes. Who knows what they can do with continued American business interests?

Neither their early strategies of borrowing Western technology nor the later ones of isolating themselves from U.S. imports works. Another new, yet less known, challenge awaits these two different countries. The real issues are to be found in guiding each other inside business practices and in not encouraging a type of Japanese *keiretsu*, which would limit international trade opportunities. No one wants protectionism. Nor does anyone desire a world where reciprocal trade agreements are not encouraged. Export managers will play a crucial role here, especially as they spend time in Korea.

"Visit your overseas agents and customers. Something is missing if you only try to communicate entirely by mail."[11] That advice comes from V. P. Maxon Corporation, a successful exporter from Muncie, Indiana, and it's not a bad idea for U.S. exporters to Korea.

NOTES

1. Boye De Mente, *Korean Etiquette & Ethics in Business* (Lincolnwood, Ill.: NTC Business Books, 1988), 122–53.

2. This section came from Bill Shaw (Ph.D., Harvard University). I first met Dr. Shaw while he was on a Fulbright Scholarship lecturing in Korean at Seoul National University, Law College.

3. Imre Nemeth, "New West Capitalizes on Shared Opportunity," *Alaska Journal of Commerce*, March 13, 1989.

4. Nemeth, 1.

5. Kelly Alston, "Heartland Products, Services Ring Up International Sales," *Kansas City Business Journal*, May 1, 1989, 21.

6. Alston, 21.

7. Alston, 21.

8. Trenholme J. Griffin, *Korea: The Tiger Economy* (London: Euromoney Publications, 1988), 132.

9. Andrew Tanzer, "Samsung: South Korea Marches to Its Own Drummer," *Forbes*, May 16, 1988, 87.

10. Tanzer, 85.

11. Katherine Glover and Bill Scoutone, "50 Firms Share Export Techniques," *Business America*, September 12, 1988, 22.

_____ V

Follow That Protocol

17

Customs and Traditions

Edna M. Hennessee learned the importance of Korean customs and traditions six years ago. As founder and chairman of the board (Cosmetic Specialty Labs of Lawton, Oklahoma), she has adjusted to them. After she got serious about Korea and other foreign markets, she began exporting her aloe vera products overseas. Today 20 percent of her business comes from overseas markets—her goal, to reach 50 percent.

Since cultural boundaries can affect territories, she adjusts to the environment. She learned, as Avon Industries did, that door-to-door selling does not work in Europe, where women consider such behavior an invasion of their privacy. Culture affects not only distribution channels, but also channels for products and their promotion. Those at Cosmetic Specialty learned how promotion and culture work best in Japan, Malaysia, Singapore, Taiwan, France, Honduras, Brazil, Guatemala, and Korea.

High volumes, high profits? Yes, but not without careful promotion. Cultural errors disrupt advertising and profits the most. But these Oklahomans know that. So they distribute through established outlets and with appropriate advertisements. These two are determined by customs.

Color in magazine ads affects sales. Sensitive advertisers know that they should not use much white in Asia. It signifies death. "Cultural sensitivity takes a lot of patience," Mrs. Hennessee said. "It is the number one requirement for exporting success."[1] Americans are not noted for their patience or for their cultural sensitivity.

"Americans tend to get in a hurry, unlike people in other countries who take their time," she said. "It takes a long time and much paperwork to get into foreign markets. You have to keep at it."[2] Her son Odus shows patience, not merely as an international manager who has to learn about customs and traditions, but also as the president of the firm who evaluates promotion methods for Korea. It seems that success comes quicker for those, like her son, who are punctilious in their dealings with foreign nationals and the Koreans.

"We end up liking most of our foreign customers very much. Most come to visit us in Oklahoma."[3] Evidently these Oklahomans sincerely care about their customers and sales representatives. Relations such as these don't just happen, they must be cultivated. Neither iconoclastic attitudes, nor duplicity in business, works in international settings.

"You have to learn about the customs of each country," Hennessee explained, "you get to know the personalities of the people." It pays off.

While profits are high, their true export volume is much higher than what they cite. This firm counts only direct sales—not resales under a different product label. Edna attributes her firm's success to its emphasis of knowing country customs and traditions. Cultural sensitivity begins with the process of preparing business trips. But it also continues throughout negotiation.

Exporters who finally travel to Korea will be interested in developing a marketing plan, one which follows a protocol. The etymology of the word "protocol" means the first leaf glued to a manuscript. That first page describes the content. For us and our purposes, it's the social context where Korean business takes place. By learning about protocol, international managers follow the customary procedures of negotiating with the Koreans. As stated earlier, since the consumer is ultimately the Korean, U.S. exporters should learn as much as possible about Korea and its people.

No company operates in a cultural vacuum. Executives must take time to analyze their corporate cultures—their internal and external capabilities. To invade new markets is to compete. Outdistancing your competitors may mean expanding product lines to meet changing consumer needs. To expand overseas markets depends upon how Koreans value your product or service. You should know not just about your corporate culture, but also about the Korean culture. Fortunately the Koreans generally have a favorable attitude toward Americans.

PREPARE FOR BUSINESS TRIPS

Korea now boasts some of the best hotels, not only in Seoul, but also in Pusan, Dyongju, and Cheju Island. There are 55 tourist hotels in Seoul alone, not counting the 184 hotels across the country with more than 25,321 rooms. And you have a choice of selecting Western or Asian accommodations.

One hotel you might want to consider is the Korean-style inn called *Yogwan*. Here is found authentic Korean living: the Korean bedding-mattress, *Yo*, the quilt known as *Ibul*, and a hard pillow. Here is where you, as traveling executives, discover how Koreans traditionally heat their homes using the *Ondol*. Such hotels do not have their own restaurants, but finding one is no problem. If you stay in this type of inn and can't sleep with the hard pillow, ask for a regular one. Other accommodations include indoor bathrooms, hot water, and color TV. Such experiences highlight the customs and traditions of Korea, even more than for those who don't venture out to the Yogwan.

Planned trips to Korea accomplish several things. Through means of travel, you can locate and cultivate new customers, improve old relationships, and communicate with current foreign representatives. As for Korea, nothing works like face-to-face meetings with customers and agents. But getting there fit and alert is another matter.

Jet lag is not caused by the enclosed compartments of aircraft. It comes from disruption of time, place, and well-being. Flying from the U.S. to Korea disrupts the body's sense of time. To be in Korea is to flip flop your days and nights (some thirteen hours forward). That change affects certain biochemical responses and interaction patterns. What people take for granted—daylight versus night, eating patterns, and conversations—changes. If possible, schedule flights to avoid sleep deprivation. Try to arrive in Korea during their active period. If you go east, fly as early as possible; west, fly late.

A well-planned itinerary ensures the best use of time abroad. As a rule, business decisions move slower in Korea. One U.S. executive put it this way: "We didn't plan ahead or expect things to take so long. The Koreans knew when we were to leave; they kept stalling about the contract until the day before we were to leave," he said. "What are you going to do then?"[4]

Korean geography and climate probably differ from your own locale. Contrast very cold winters with the monsoon rains, pleasant springs with hot muggy summers. Business negotiations also affect your sense of well-being. Negotiating for electronics exports one businessman said,

"It was the coldest winter I ever remember. The snow was bad enough, but the wind made it worse. Our negotiations took place in an old tin building near Pusan where the ship building yards were. I finally got to a place where I would do anything to get out of that cold. They seemed to sense my frustrations as well."[5] By the way, he didn't make that same mistake twice.

Accomplish as much as you can by getting names, arranging appointments, scheduling transportation, and booking hotels. Keep a flexible schedule for unexpected problems or opportunities. Consider holidays. Travel agents help plan the itinerary, check on hotel rates, and make suggestions about country travel. However, don't forget about translator services or anything else that would maximize the value of your time in Korea.

RECOGNIZE THE DRIVING FORCE

Stored up feelings—*hahn*—when released, create energy. Hahn refers to the emotional energy of the Korean people, energy that was suppressed for centuries. According to the Korean definition, only recently have they been able to release their deepest yearnings of artistic creativity and economic innovativeness. Until now adverse situations were collectively accumulated in the form of sentiments. Because of their geographical position Koreans know about invasion, domination, and submission. Throughout their history, the Koreans have suffered from foreign occupation and poverty. Korea has often been regarded as little more than a cultural conduit between China and Japan.

Yet the peninsula possesses a unique and rich culture, one that is socially shared, along with their grief. The country abounds in royal tombs, palaces, and majestic gardens. Korean arts and technical achievements are varied to include the early development of the unique blue-green *celadon* pottery, the invention of movable type printing, and the creation of the phonetic Hangul alphabet. Korea is also the source of inspiration for several schools of Confucian philosophy. But that is not the only religion in Korea.

Koreans have a long tradition of religious syncretism. Over the years many sophisticated religions have developed such as Taoism, Confucianism, Christianity, and Islam. The largest number of people adhere to Buddhism, followed by Protestantism, Confucianism, Catholicism, and some native religions such as Chondogyo, Taejonggyo, and Wonbulgyo. The late Yale anthropologist, Cornelius Osgood, observed that the Koreans, among all Asians, were indeed the most religious. Perhaps this explains why the national anthem of Korea contains these words: "Until the East Sea is drained, and Paektu is no more, May God preserve this Land as one, May it last ever more. Land of rose-of-sharon, The

fairest land! May God preserve this fold as one, The people of Taehan."[6]
This cohesive factor counterbalanced their exploitation and preserved
the hahn feeling of survival. Once released, hahn finds expression in
education and the family traditions. Both institutions bond the society
tightly together.

Education is highly valued for two reasons. First, Koreans value it
from an intrinsic desire to gain knowledge and wisdom. Second, education is also seen as an avenue to social mobility, wealth, and power.
The illiteracy rate in Korea is almost zero. The school systems are organized into six years of elementary school, three years of middle school,
three years of high school, and four years of college. Rigorous discipline
in education, however, begins in the home.

The family perpetuates Korean culture and civilization through extended groups of multiple generations. The force of both family bonding
(duty and obligation of members) and filial piety (willingness to fulfill
duties toward parents and family) is one of the greatest Korean virtues.
It is true that younger, urban families resemble Western ones. Both have
abandoned the extended family for households consisting of parents
and unmarried children.

But underneath religion, education, and the family flows a quality
much deeper and more vast. It flows from the tensions of exploitation.
Either those tensions (hahn) find collective release in Korean customs
and traditions, or the core of grievance and rancor accumulates. It is a
powerful force of creativity for overcoming poverty, oppression, and
dependence. Education and modernization did their work, but some
argue that hahn propels the Koreans to achieve. Does this emotional
energy explain much of Korea's economic miracle?

ADJUSTING TO KOREA

Korea has four distinct seasons that are similar to the northeastern
and central areas of the United States and the central southern part of
Europe. The conservative clothes that Koreans wear are suitable; they
correspond to the distinct seasons. The average temperature in January
is –4.9°C (23°F). April brings with it an average temperature of 13°C
(55°F). July is the hottest, most humid month, with the temperature
averaging 25°C (79°F). The October temperatures hover around 17°C
(62°F). Monsoon rains are the heaviest from June to September, when
almost 70 percent of the annual precipitation occurs. The weather can
be quite harsh—either extremely cold and/or wet.

Just as U.S. exporters must adapt to the climatic conditions of this
country, so they must also adapt to jet lag and cultural shock. The former
conditions demand less than the latter. Both are important. Those who
know Korea's culture of dos and don'ts gain the competitive edge in

business deals. Since customs and traditions influence business deals, they're equally important as you prepare your business trips and exports.

Before 1945 the traditional attire was the *hanbok*, a comfortable, loose fitting gown. However, that dress is more of a ceremonial costume worn on special holidays, such as Lunar New Year and Full Moon Day. White-clad people symbolized purity and innocence, and that's still the case.

About Korean cuisine: it's deliciously different. If you don't think you'll like it, you can find any type of food you like. Dishes come from all over the world. Nevertheless, Korean cuisine remains unique: vegetables steamed and seasoned; braised meat or fish; and *kimchi*, a fermented vegetable dish that is highly seasoned with red peppers and garlic. It is a must for everyone. We suggest you try the milder variety until you learn to like it.

Some other dishes include *Pulgogi*, a popular beef dish (literal meaning "fire beef"—the practical meaning is "Korean Barbecue") comprised of tender beef slices, soy sauce, sesame seeds, garlic oil, and seasonings; *Kalbi* (short ribs); *Bujolpan*, which is much like a French hors d'oeuvre tray with Korean pancakes in the center with cooked meat and vegetables; *Shinsollo*, a mix of meat, fish, vegetables, and bean curd over which beef broth is poured; *Kalbitang*, a rich beef-based soup served as a main course along with rice, side dishes, and a special kimchi known as *kkakttugi* (turnips diced into bite size pieces, seasoned with red pepper and garlic); *Manduguk*, a meat dumpling soup much like Chinese wonton soup (the dumplings are bigger); *Pibimbap*, cooked rice mixed with meat and seasoned vegetables; *Naengmyon*, cold noodles served on hot summer days; *Hanjongshik*, a full course Korean meal that includes much of the above.

Domestic air travel is under the exclusive domain of Korea Air. Service is to Seoul, Pusan, Cheju, Kwangju, Taegu, Yosu, Sokcho, Chinju, Ulsan, and Kangnung. The Korean National Railroads operates a super-express train—the Saemaul—along these routes: Seoul-Pusan, Seoul-Mokpo, Seoul-Yosu, and Seoul-Kyonguy (Taejon, Taegu). Trips from Seoul to Pusan are about four hours. Express busses number 1,768. No reservations are needed. The new subway system runs four lines. These are: Line 1, which runs through the main portion of Seoul; Line 2, which is a circular route connecting downtown with points south of the Han River; Line 3, which runs northwest to southeast on both sides of the Han River; and Line 4, which runs diagonally opposite (northeast to southwest). It is the seventh longest, most modern system in the world. It is also possible to drive rental cars or to rent a chauffeur-driven car.

THE FAMILY ESTABLISHES TRADITIONS

The Korean family life is the school for society. The mother and father prepare their children for social life. This takes a special type of responsible socializing. If the young generation goes astray, the society blames the family, not the school. Because Koreans think of life as being hazardous, they train their children to seek some special help from others to survive. Both the family and society are family oriented. Thus Koreans tend not to think about personal needs, which means that every topic is open to the whole family. Similarly at business, Koreans tend to discuss salaries, wages, and the practice of giving bonuses openly. No subjects are hidden matters. Both systems of group life are tightly controlled, both obligate members to loyalty. The communal life of this society tends to suppress expressions of individualism. This explains why Koreans, more than Americans, are less concerned about keeping secrets, whether at home or work.

The family system mixes sternness with joy, though. While members respectfully honor their parents and elders, they also joyfully share special occasions with them. Koreans enjoy celebrations; they're quite hospitable. They frequently hold banquets for several reasons, as welcoming receptions for newcomers, as beginnings of the new year, as celebrations of contract signing, or as farewells for people leaving. The biggest holiday is in late January or early February. Called *sol*, this is a time when all family members, dressed in their best clothes, celebrate together. The purpose is both to enjoy a feast and to respect the elders. Another holiday is *taeborum*. During this time, the fishermen and farmers celebrate their successful catches and crops, while the children play special games.

Koreans learn from their families that the world is hierarchical and insecure. They learn that close friends, influential patrons, and special contacts are necessary for them to succeed. Because Koreans maintain close family and friendships, they frequently apologize for their offenses. Some even write letters expressing their mistakes. Of the two methods, they prefer face-to-face interaction over the written. But regardless of the method, they usually present positive friendly faces, being careful not to hurt anyone's feelings or offend. Through their lives, Koreans devote much time and energy to their network of friends. As a way of maintaining close ties, they spent the holidays with them, often singing together.

Koreans have several family holidays. One hundred days after the birth of a child Koreans celebrate *paegil*. One year later, they celebrate *tol*, the first birthday. *Hwan-gap* is the time to celebrate the sixtieth birthday, and *kohi* represents the seventieth birthday. Other holidays are the New Year, Independence Movement (March 1), Arbor Day (April 5), Children's Day (May 5), Memorial Day (June 6), Constitution Day (July 17), Liberation Day (August 15), Armed Forces Day (October 1), National Foundation Day (October 3), Han-gul Day (October 9), and Christmas (December 25).

Identification, as previously mentioned, tends to be vertical. Koreans identify upward with parents and elders, because, according to them, ranking of people and institutions, even countries, forms a hierarchy of relationships. As a result of these differences in perception, Koreans start from a very different approach in communicating with others. Those over them, they respect; those under them are subservient.

Koreans attentively observe bodily reactions as measures of true intentions. They gauge these reactions of others (*nunchi*) as important signals of intent. Because of these abilities, Koreans sometime give communication priority to the insights of visceral feelings over appearances. Based on their perceptions of others' reactions, they react. Perhaps that is why Koreans prefer personal dialogue over written forms or attorneys' documents.

KOREAN NAMES AND CULTURAL IDENTITIES

Some mistakes by foreigners are overlooked. Mistaking names is not one of them. The Korean names are arranged backward from names in the West. They consist of three Chinese characters, each given a special distinction. In Korea the first name given is always the family name: Kim Soo-Nam, not Soo-Nam Kim as I have used for Western readers (an exception is China's Deng Xiao Ping). To Koreans the personal name is also important, because they believe it carries with it good fortune. The name *Soo-nam* means a "man of long life," or *Soo-bok* (long life and prosperity), or other such designations—wealth, nobility, happiness, goodness, greatness.

Since there are only 300 family names in Korea, there can be some confusion. It is proper to refer to Koreans only by their last names. In fact, only close friends know first names. Even in the family itself, younger members call older ones by their family name, not the given name. Remember too that married women in Korea do not take the name of their husband. They retain their family name.

Families exert significant influence on society, its customs, and traditions. It's the school for society, the place of discipline and celebration. It's the launching pad to a hierarchical and insecure world. It connects members to influential patrons. But more than that, Korean family patterns extend into networks, regions, and companies. Professionals identify with organizations, not so much occupations. That fact has two business implications: (1) Crossovers from one business to another are difficult, and (2) ethical restraints depend mostly upon group loyalty. Identity is linear and restrictive, but not of equal value.

Since society is an extension of the family, its purpose is to encourage mutual cooperation between the family, business, school, and village. Teachers are also highly regarded and respected by training and as contacts. After all, teachers open doors for successful upward mobility.

In Confucian society teachers are respected, even as elders are. Yet nationalism has always bound all distinctions together.

That pride for Korea produced a common cultural history of arts and crafts for 4,000 years. Artistically minded, the Koreans, though borrowing from the Chinese, nevertheless developed an artistic culture of their own. Ancient Korean paintings were usually drawn on pieces of paper and silk cloth using India ink and water colors. Calligraphy, the art of writing in brush and India ink, ranked high among learned men and women not only as a favorite hobby but also as a symbol of social accomplishment. The Korean Folk Village, just south of Seoul, is a reconstructed village, designed and devised to preserve many of these Korean traditions.

Koreans have always expressed themselves through music and dance. Osgood thinks they are more musically inclined than either the Chinese or the Japanese. Traditional Korean music, using the five-tone scale, sounds simpler than Western music, which uses seven tones. Korean folk dances are well known for the delicate movements of limbs and shoulders. Korean drama consists of mask plays, puppet shows, classical opera, melodramas, and modern drama. Because Koreans haven't been able to express themselves freely, self expressions became bottled up frustrations. Korean sufferings allowed them to identify with one another even in boycotts. They wave flags, express nationalism, and yearn for freedom from outside constraints. These yearnings are called hahn, people's psychic energy.

CONCLUDING OBSERVATIONS

As employees Koreans are sincere and honest. Their personal work relations are essential to them and their family members. Just as Koreans have sacrificed over the centuries, so they continue to at work. Workers learn to make sacrifices for the company. Koreans have several sayings that imply they view themselves as an industrious people. During a peak work period, Koreans describe the urgency of work this way: "We must be busy, for the grasshoppers will eat their food." Another expression about working hard is this: "After the lamp goes out, little work will be done." Or sometimes they say that someone is as "busy as a bee." Koreans also talk about how skilled and nonskilled workers make sacrifices, or they relate how Korean managers rotate to different regions of the country. Older managers, like regular workers, geographically move for training purposes. Korean business partners tell you how all workers—managers and laborers—constantly improve themselves and their business.

Since they have faced social injustices, they know first hand about failures. Perhaps that is why they cling to one another and those they know best—their friends and family members. They now know about success too. But after centuries of exploitation they, even more than others, realize just how frail their successes have been and can be. They realize the extraordinary measures—hard work, overtime, steady production—that are essential for their success to continue. Such bipolar emotional profiles—dread of success and reality of failure—make for interesting and unusual trade relations. Yet to be discussed is just how much these insights apply to business operations.

NOTES

1. Katherine Glover and Bill Scoutone, "Exporting Pays Off," *Business America*, May 9, 1988, 24.

2. Glover and Scoutone, 24.

3. Glover and Scoutone, 24.

4. This was a private conversation. I spoke with an experienced exporter to South Korea about problems they confronted in dealing with the Koreans.

5. Glover and Scoutone, 24.

6. Korean Overseas Information Service, *Facts about Korea* (Seoul: Samhwa, 1988), 210.

18

Korean Business Etiquette

In 1989 the Tandy Corporation of Korea witnessed continued labor unrest. After releasing 1,400 workers, Tandy property protestors (Masan, South Korea) expressed their sentiments symbolically. An American flag on a large sign read "Step on the Yankee monopoly."

Such sentiments by Korean workers are becoming more common. IBM, Citibank, and Motorola all recently experienced labor problems. Violence has been avoided, but only because of concessions to unions. Even with 40 percent salary increases, tensions remain. Some executives worry, even though most incidents involving foreigners are under control. Who is to blame? Some Koreans say the Americans.

"In the sixties, my country was poor," said Byoung-Hoon Lee, a union leader who expressed his views. "We needed foreign capital, and so foreign companies came here and had many benefits."[1] Lee thinks Americans owe Koreans. If companies pay, then Lee will become a faithful worker. "I am a Korean and an IBM worker, so I want my company to contribute to my society," says Lee. "Then I will be proud."[2]

Some blame unions; others point to social inequity. This chapter evaluates export impacts by recognizing that etiquette varies with cultural changes. Social undercurrents precipitate turbulence, yet establish Korea's business life. Permissible standards are being scrutinized as Korea assumes greater international roles. If Washington and Seoul can agree on bilateral negotiations, then both benefit. If not, there will be economic trouble ahead.

This chapter and the next take two directions: first toward Korea's social context; then toward how leaders make decisions. The social context frames cultural understanding; Korean's decision-making styles frame practical matters. The former material—Korean etiquette and how to use it to conduct business—should prepare you for acceptable business conduct while in the Republic of Korea. The latter—Korean investments, business, and government relations—provides an explanation on how Korean business works. That explanation describes who makes decisions, how import procedures flow, what bureaucracies help or hinder business, and which alternatives of funding work best in given circumstances.

KOREAN ETIQUETTE

Labor management problems are not new to South Korea, but they certainly do not fit our images of Asian etiquette. When we think of socially correct behavior in business settings, we usually conjure images of how U.S. traders should greet Koreans. Men bow slightly, then shake hands. Women avoid handshaking. Because of crosscultural differences, and corporate culture policies, inexperienced travelers to Korea might be misunderstood. Certain normal behavior in Texas is unacceptable in Korea. Take the Texan with the loud mouth and the ten-gallon cowboy hat. His animated behavior of slapping Korean executives on the back, loudly telling jokes, and laughing out loud is incorrect behavior. His behavior should be contrasted with the soft-spoken, gray-haired, distinguished-looking senior Korean executive who promptly greets the Texan with a business card. The Texan has forgotten his. So he calls his Korean counterpart by his first name and gives him a big bear hug.

This account is exaggerated, but the point is this: carry a name card at all times. Koreans adhere to a predictable pattern of greetings, dress, and schedule. In initial greetings both the bow (thirty to forty degrees from vertical) and the exchange of name cards are the first items of business. The business card locates individuals in this neo-Confucian society. Identity determines one's place in society.

The next item is to address the Korean as Kim Sa-Jang (President Kim). The title is affixed to the name. The VIP titles bring privileges at the office and in social settings. The president sits at the head of the table and rides in the back seat of the chauffeured car. As for dress, be conservative. The Koreans wear white shirts with blue, brown, or grey suits. They take pride in how they dress and in their work schedule. Therefore, be on time for meetings. For large companies the day begins at 9 A.M. and may last until 7 P.M. or later.

At the first meeting be prepared to tell about yourself. You will have a chance to tell about your family, your favorite sports, and your age. Koreans want to know this because age, position, and rank determine seniority. On that first meeting let the Korean counterpart set the pace. Shortly after the meeting, coffee or sodas are served, followed by more informal discussions. Should your host invite you to a restaurant, remove your shoes before entering. You may sit on a cushion, so cross your legs. During the conversation, it is best to avoid certain topics: communism, politics, and socialism. To show respect lower your eyes. Eat with a spoon and chopsticks. When you are finished, place your chopsticks across your dish. As for gifts, be modest. Offer music tapes, art objects, U.S. stamps, Western belt buckles, or framed photos of historic sites.

As a foreigner who does business in Korea, your products and service depend upon business etiquette. Yet a fine line exists between condescending and cooperative attitudes toward Koreans. Their etiquette is based on a 4,000-year-old tradition of greetings and exchanges. Yet they are the ones forced to do business in English. Speak slowly, repeat words, and use notes for later references on specific business deals. "Sensitivity to your Korean counterpart's etiquette patterns is one way to achieve [business] success."[3]

USING KOREAN ETIQUETTE

Louis Brandeis, Boston lawyer and former Supreme Court Chief Justice, recognized the source of serious controversies. They come from misunderstanding the viewpoints of other people. If that is true in our culture, it is much more true in different cultures. Successful business interaction depends upon whether executives understand the conventional way of doing business in Korea. Exporters expect good profits. Yet these fantasies, unless countered with cultural understanding, may not be realized. Most Koreans are pro-American; they'll import American goods. If U.S. exporters use business etiquette to resolve partner conflicts or plan company training, the import volumes could increase.

First, U.S. business executives can use Asian etiquette to resolve partner conflicts. John C. Condon describes how ignorance of culture leads to differences—differences in perceptions of goals, differences in interpretations, differences in expectations.[4] When recognized by merchants they experience discomfort. Stress creates not only negative responses, but also poor business relations. Differences emerge both in friendly conversations and international deals. And while Koreans accept internationalization of their economy, they want to be independent of outside constraints. They want a stake in policy development and business decisions. Americans want short-term profits; Koreans want a long-term market share.

Then there are problems over promotion, salaries, customers, and selling practices. Etiquette, socially acceptable behavior, can prevent or help resolve these problems. Communication of true feelings prevents the problem, especially if both parties know each other's family and friends. Developing common interest outside work means a lot to Koreans. At the foundation of any relation is mutual respect and trust. Once a conflict develops it pays to control emotions, yet get them out in the open. The Western logic does not always work in Korea. Since this is a vertical society, the head's opinions might resolve the issue. To establish rules of fair play in advance gives alternatives to resolving conflicts once they begin.[5]

Second, business executives should use Asian etiquette in promoting Korean employees and their business. While the training etiquette varies from firm to firm, the Koreans interpret orientation training much differently. First, Koreans place more emphasis on attitude than action. They want loyalty and dedication, not just performance. Loyalty and commitment to the corporate philosophy takes precedence over abilities. Jang suggests that company training emphasize team spirit to include identity with the business and its destiny. Professionals, sometimes retired professors, can speak on life goals and hard work. Mix up the training sessions, using a variety of speakers inside and outside the organization. Foreign language training, whether in English or Korean, is always useful. Nothing instills team spirit like good public relations. When an individual is promoted, cite the accomplishments of local employees. When the company has a picnic, get out a story on that. Write about new products, head office sales, scientific seminars, and export volumes.[6]

DISCOVERING INADEQUACIES

Through recent interviews and a survey, it is evident that Americans fall short of Asian etiquette. In interviews Condon discovered the most glittering, ignorant irritations of that etiquette. Here are how East Asians describe some culturally insensitive Americans: "they talk too much, they interrupt other people, they don't listen, and they seem to think that if they don't tell you something you won't know it." Furthermore, "they are too direct in asking questions, giving opinions, and poking fun, they fail to express thanks and appreciation sufficiently, they are

Table 18.1
Information Routes on Supply Sources Not Japanese

Classification	Percentage of respondents
Commission agents	47.1
Branch offices of foreign companies	23.0
Fairs or exhibitions	10.8
Foreign buyers who import Korean goods	5.1
Public agencies of foreign countries	2.2
Other means	11.8
Total	100.0

reluctant to admit faults or limitations, they seldom apologize or seem polite, they give more attention to individuals than to groups, they do not appreciate the importance of certain formalities, and they are too time conscious."[7]

THE CONDUCT OF KOREANS IN BUSINESS

In a recent survey conducted by Yonsei University, the researchers learned how Korean suppliers gather information. The Korean importers, those shifting their supply sources from Japan to the United States, needed to know how to find U.S. exporters, not Japanese, who can supply them with products. The ROKG, through its diversification program, required that Koreans export from U.S. suppliers where possible. Table 18.1 shows the sources of U.S. suppliers.

This two-year study gives us some insight on how Koreans conduct business. Usually they prefer mediated, personal contacts as they begin formal ones. Introductions are important as much to them as they are for them. They prefer direct contacts over telephone calls. Calls may be necessary to make appointments for face-to-face discussions. Koreans respect U.S. exporters outside their sphere of influence, but expect familiarity and closeness to evolve. Until that happens, their business etiquette and business practices are rather paternalistic.

Since age is crucial in this society, it is proper to show respect for the elderly. That is why U.S. companies are usually advised not to send their youngest employees as country managers. To the Koreans, such people are lower status; individuals should accept their proper place in society and at work. Despite what others say, the general culture and norm of Korea still shape both organizational behavior and expected responses.

KOREANS' VIEW OF FOREIGN BUSINESS

As an increasingly pluralistic society, Korea has many groups who express their views about foreign business. It is not possible to get a consensus. But it is possible to see what angle particular classes of Koreans take.

According to Jang, both foreign products and foreign workers permeate every facet of the Korean economy. Still there remain many differences between American and Korean cultures. The Korean system of etiquette is designed to protect the honor of individuals, their families and their companies. People do not speak out to disturb that honor.[8]

The fact is Koreans want more than money from their jobs. Their achievements and successes depend upon group effort, not individual ones. The prestige of American firms is not enough to guarantee satisfaction now. Koreans continue to be concerned about the image of their company in the broader community. That was why Mr. Lee wanted the IBM workers to contribute to the Korean society. Geographic locations of offices carry status and speak volumes about respectability and honor. Worker loyalty is reciprocal. It is given to those U.S. firms who make firm commitments to their workers.

So far we've discussed general patterns of behavior and typical responses. However, foreign companies hire almost a million Korean workers. Through these experiences, Koreans are much more sophisticated than formerly was the case. The official elites—government leaders and intellectuals—realize that international activities are changing their society. They accept foreign businesses because they are more liberally minded. They know about the spirit of reciprocity, government sanctions, and trade pressures. But still, according to Jang, there must be some face-saving measures for these elites to survive the pressures from their own society—the students, interest groups, and other business leaders.

Korean businessmen are conservative. They, much like the farmers, want protection. They take a pragmatic view about their businesses. What does not affect them immediately is less their concern; however, when import items affect their profits, these same business leaders work with their government to control disruptors.

Once it was prestigious to work for foreign subsidiaries. This is no longer the case for a couple of reasons. First, many Koreans who joined these firms did not feel they were given equal opportunities. Second, when frictions over work occurred, Koreans thought they were later overlooked.

GESTURES

Proper gestures conform to social etiquette. Through body movements, people express themselves. These gestures may be formal, such as bowing, or informal, such as the Koreans' habit of putting a hand over their mouth when speaking.

Koreans maintain the etiquette of *myongham*, using name cards; *yu-haeng*, being well-dressed; and *sonmul*, giving gifts. Name cards are more important because many Koreans have the same family names and positions determine protocol. They wear the latest styles of business suits, especially at the first business meetings. Here they give gifts as expressions of gratitude for small favors. The gifts of value, *myungmul* (those with name brands), are prized. Since Koreans give gifts when they travel, U.S. executives could exchange small gifts as symbols of their products or regional affiliation. If in doubt, check with locals about the appropriateness of gifts.

People communicate by content and style. They reveal content by what they say, and style by how they express themselves through gestures. What people say, or intend to say, varies with the culture. Initially Korean business executives and government leaders formally interact (*hyongshikchogin*) with Americans. While it is polite for Koreans to give compliments (*chansa*), men should not compliment women. That is considered a taboo, reflecting strict gender protocols.

Americans emphasize status equality; therefore, they freely express appreciation for others. This practice, however, may appear rude, at least to Koreans, who feel compelled to respect high status dignitaries. In contrast to Americans' emphasis on equality, their society is vertically structured. Koreans give respect (*chongyong*) where due. Americans could adjust their thinking away from informal business dealings.

Style, as well as content, differs. Gestures differ: Koreans neither pat workers nor touch another of higher rank. Putting an arm on the shoulder is considered disrespectful, except in informal gatherings with close friends. Personal contact violates the Korean norm of respect. Even conversations are ordered by status, not by freely exchanging information back and forth from one person to another. Americans, not Koreans, are often rewarded for speaking out.

In stating true intentions, Americans strive for clarity in writing and speaking. Brevity and clarity are valued in science and business. Since disguised gestures are less valued, most Americans speak out honestly, regardless of the impact. Were Koreans to do so, without regard for true feelings or face, they would be called *mailmanta*, or talkers. The term suggests cold reason over personal feelings, offensive encounters over subtle gestures.

CONTRACTS AND CONFLICTS

In speaking with others, even foreigners, Koreans may use gestures that don't communicate their true feelings. Koreans have the ability to understand without words. It refers to heartfelt, emotional feelings that come without anyone speaking a word. Boye De Mente coined the expression "cultural telepathy." How is this type of communication possible? Because of their rather homogeneous and long-surviving history, this type of communication is practiced and refined. Perhaps this preference for intuition over logic comes from either religious communities or from Koreans' emphasis on meditation. It may even arise from those who live in close geographic proximity to others, thereby increasing the likelihood of intuitive communication. Whatever the explanation, it is easy for Americans to overlook communication of true feelings without speaking.

Because of their strong emphasis on relationships, it has been stated that Koreans negotiate relationships, not contracts. Contracts signed in Korea are usually honored by all parties. Yet at the same time, Koreans, like other Asians, distrust contracts. To them signing an agreement means in effect "I intend to do this," not "I agree to do this." To them the names or reputations of the parties involved carry more weight than the signatures.

In Korea small losses or disagreements are handled privately. It is an internal matter, not one for the courts. The accepted practice is to handle most contracting work and disagreements internally. At the heart of any contract is good will. That is where the vitality and closeness of the relationship comes from. In negotiating an agreement, the parties first establish credibility about getting the work done. Remember that Koreans tend to be overly optimistic about establishing new relationships; therefore, U.S. exporters should take care to learn what's expected and what's involved.

According to Griffin, this requires three steps. (1) American businessmen should know the meaning of the agreement before signing it. Although the words carry import, understanding of the conditions and what they mean to each party should be carefully discussed. (2) They should themselves accept and ensure that the Koreans agree to comply with the entire agreement, not just the summary statements. This may take some time, even after reading the report and after meeting to discuss its meaning. Be prepared to hold several meetings over compliance. Finally, (3) neither party should consent to change the agreement or its terms without both letting the other party know and making some compensation for costs incurred. Realize too that to sign such a contract, even after discussing it at length, does not necessarily mean this prevents disputes.[9]

BUSINESS IN HISTORY

The department stores and arcades in Myong-dong stand as monuments to a rich heritage dating back almost twenty-four centuries before the birth of Christ. Midopoa, Shinsegye, Cheil, Saerona, and Lotte department stores border Myong-dong just as early kingdoms did. A single kingdom known as Chosun (Land of the Morning Calm) came together fifty-seven years before the birth of Christ. Eventually, three kingdoms (Silla, Kokuryo, Paikche) struggled for power. These tribes, like the new residential areas of Youido, Yuongdong and Chamshil, struggled for prominence. Beginning in 935 A.D., the power of Silla was turned over to Wang Kun. This began the Kingdom of Koryo, from which Korea, the Western name for the land, was evidently derived. (Koreans call their nation HanKuk.)

Even today in Seoul one can find evidence of the Chosun Dynasty (1392). Although founded by General Sung-Ke Yi in Kaesong, the capital was later moved to Seoul. At the heart of the capital city, the Kyoingbok Palace has few modern equals. The Palace, the royal family's court, continues to exude a regal charm. Even the Tongdaemun Market a short distance from East Gate does not lack vitality and simplicity. On the palace grounds are the National Museum and the Folk Museum. Both house an impressive collection of 5,000 years of Korean art and cultural artifacts, including the first movable metal type (half a century before Gutenberg's famous printing press).

Who would even guess now, however, that Korea was known as the "hermit nation"? And who would think, after walking a short distance from the Namdaemun (South Gate) with its popular open market, that things were not always this way? At one time (1592–1876), Korea advocated a policy of complete isolation. Only after 1876 did Japan force a trade treaty with Korea, a treaty that precipitated one with the United States in 1882. Or if you are at Insa-dong, the antique district, you wouldn't guess that the signs came from a period dating back to 1446. It was then that King Sae Jong invented a purely phonetic alphabet system for the Korean language. On October 9 of each year, foreigners learn about Korean Language Day. They learn that Korea is probably the only country in the world that observes a special day commemorating the origin of its written language. To watch the Japanese tourists in the busy department stores or duty free shops, one would never guess that Japan invaded Korea in 1592. That Japanese invasion of Hideyoshi Toyotomi brought not only 150,000 troops to Korea, but a response from Admiral Sun-Shin Yi who used the first "turtle ship" (ironclad warship) to gain a stunning victory in sea waters against the Japanese, who outnumbered the Korean sailors and ships.

KOREAN ETIQUETTE SUMMARIZED

The ultimate standard in business etiquette concerns the society. Justice is measured against the good of society. Furthermore, law combines both Confucian and nationalistic tendencies. For these reasons, we could safely say that morality is determined by social factors that override all social concerns. It is less of a philosophical principle of right or wrong. Such ideas have historical roots only in American culture.

Still, Korean business etiquette establishes the standards in Korea's official business life. That etiquette is a mixture of deep-seated traditions about rules despite change. Although the Korean upheaval is great and foreign influence prevalent, there are still rules of governance, rules whereby Koreans evaluate what's proper and what's right.

Nevertheless, ignorance of cultural etiquette leads to different perceptions of goals, differences in interpretations, differences in expectations. The final outcome—conflict. To ignore an etiquette that emerged from the cultural context of friendly conversations, raising children, socializing, and doing business is to neglect the fundamental aspect of being human. Koreans conduct business through mediated, personal contacts, which form a whole unit. Collective participation prevails, not individualism. And while young Korean men and women, especially those in the cities, act more independent and assertive, don't let their stylistic fashions and appearance mislead you. The roots of Confucianism go deep.

U.S. exporters should know about Korean business practices such as name cards and family names, people's titles and positions, ceremonies and bows, greetings and tipping. Koreans do not tip. Service charges are automatically added to hotel bills and restaurant charges. Koreans do, however, show respect for others by being punctual.

The protocol is simple enough—be on time, be prepared, and attend all business functions. In the case of negotiations, where many business leaders are involved, the senior person enters first, then the Koreans introduce their party members. This is followed by American introductions from the senior executive. Recognition is given to those with any expertise. Formality, respect, dignity, and order—these qualities matter. In a vertical society, these things are more important protocols than in a horizontal society, where everyone is considered equal.

Griffin recommends that American executives know the meaning of agreements, assure compliance, and pay any compensation for later changes.[10] Fair play—even attempts at fair play—brings light; high-handedness brings fog to business relations.

NOTES

1. Peter Maass, "Foreign Firms a Target in South Korea," *The Washington Post*, 7.

2. Maass, 7.

3. Song-Hyon Jang, "Business Etiquette in Korea," *Korean Business World*, January 1987, 81.

4. John C. Condon, *With Respect to the Japanese: A Guide for Americans* (Yarmouth, Maine: Intercultural Press, 1984).

5. Song-Hyon Jang, "Resolving Partner Conflicts," *Business Korea*, June 1985, 6.

6. Song-Hyon Jang, "Company Training in Korea," *Korean Business World*, September 1986, 91.

7. Condon, 64–65.

8. Song-Hyon Jang, "How Koreans View Foreign Businesses," *Korean Business World*, April 1987, 60–61.

9. Trenholme Griffin, "Negotiating Agreements with Korean Businesses," *Korea's Economy*, May 1986, 10.

10. Griffin, 10.

19

Korean Business Relations

Korea and U.S. relations continue to promote business deals. Over 100 years of U.S. diplomacy and trade should reap dividends into the twenty-first century. U.S. exporters, especially those with strong Korean business ties, are benefitting from industrialization of this region. It happened that same way elsewhere. The process of industrialization began in Europe (the Atlantic era) 300 years ago, before it spread to North America (Pacific era). In the upcoming Pan-Pacific era, three nations—China, Korea, Japan—will be decisive. In the summer of 1988, Korea was "front and center" on international television. As viewers watched the opening and closing ceremonies at the Seoul Olympic Stadium, they also saw the announced coming of the Pan-Pacific era and the importance of Korea. Problems for exporters remain.

One major concern for U.S. exporters concerns tariffs and taxation of their goods. These charges go "on the value of imported goods pyramided on top of the tariff."[1] This raises the costs considerably. "The final Korean sale price of a commodity will include a defense tax in the amount of 2.5 percent of the dutiable value; and a value-added tax (VAT) in the amount of 10 percent of the dutiable value plus the actual duty in addition to the duty. Depending on the items involved, special consumption taxes and education taxes also may be imposed."[2] Thus an exported U.S. automobile would cost the Korean customer 312 percent over the base price and 42 percent more than a comparable Korean auto. Korean business relations can lead to profits.

FOREIGN INVESTMENTS

The Goodyear Tire and Rubber Company now owns a $100 million investment in Korea. Evidently they're not the only ones who have their sights on Korea. U.S. direct investments are now over $1 billion. The accelerated flurry of joint business ventures no longer favors the Korean side. Philip A. Spanninger, formerly Director of Technology and Venture Management, applied to the Ministry of Finance for approval of a Korean business plan. Although the investment process is governed by the Foreign Capital Inducement Law, other government ministers give their opinion through the referral process. The law serves as guides for the MTI and other ministers who represent Korean industries.[3]

Spanninger believes the climate is right for Korean investments. "The volume of foreign investment controlled by foreign investors (i.e., more than 50 percent equity ownership) has increased over the past two years," he says. Even as the Eastern sea of Korea accommodates large ships, so too Koreans have learned that the high tides of joint ventures provide sources of capital for an expanding economy.

Foreign licensing agreements are also on the upswing. From January through October 1988, Korean companies signed 513 technical licensing agreements. Of these, U.S. firms represented about a third (138 total or 26 percent). Geographically known as the "Land of the Morning Calm," the Korean economy is anything but that. Their economy is more like the ever changing, hydroelectric producing power of the Yalu River. Just as those in the western half of Korea harnessed this great river, so too those in the Western Hemisphere want to release it through their investments. Some U.S. exporters realize that Korea is now a place that is almost completely open to foreign investments.

After three years of negotiating with the Koreans, Spanninger is an expert on what to do in business relations. Here are his recommendations:

First, define your firm's objectives from the Korean viewpoint. For people who trace their origins back 5,000 years, things look much different from those "who brought forth their nation," just over 200. As a bridge between China and Japan, Korea has learned not to look for comfort. However, as they have looked for business deals, profits and comforts have come—not as their primary object, but as byproducts. The Koreans have learned that those who only look for comfort may find neither profits nor deals—only hot tubs, long trips, and not much else.

Second, broad business relations are established in their country. Their preferences are different—everything from business location to bonuses. That means both parties must know what to do and how things get done. Early in the negotiation process, Goodyear realized that clarity counts the most in Korean business relations. Be very clear about Korean managers' responsibilities because Koreans, more than others, go for control and power. "Remember that a shareholding beyond a third of a percent will give the Korean partner a blocking minority," Spanninger emphasizes. If a U.S. firm wants to maintain absolute control, it should own two-thirds of the business. Regardless of investment percentages, Koreans still want in on the action.

Third, think positively, even when you don't feel like it. Spanninger is a "possibility thinker." Beginning with an assumption, such as "what if," he then estimated where that thinking, if put into business practice, would lead. That pattern of thinking worked well for him and Goodyear. "What if we could," he thought. "What would we really like to do?" he asked. And it works. Koreans respond to big thinkers and big planners. Yet we know that such thinking falls short and can even be dangerous. And that's when the real test, the test of "tenacity in defending your position," actually begins. The other part of it is only a warm up for the real bout. Once in the so-called "Korean ring" it's a slug out, a give and take exchange. Here is his conclusion about possibility thinking. "Get to know the people you are dealing with," Spanninger says. "That's basic."

Fourth, as an experienced innovator, Spanninger still sought advice about decisions and insights into Korean actions. The best advice is often free. Using the assistance of embassy personnel is the same as expanding your own staff, at no cost. Then there is the other side—the Koreans. The Korean networks, like thick spider webs, allow for many routes of influence. In Korea keep asking yourself two questions: "How much are my nets worth?" And, "Do my nets work?"

And finally, fifth, Spanninger used visuals for better communication across cultural barriers. He used slides, drawings, pictures, flip charts, and videotapes. Of course, these were dubbed with Korean expressions. He went one step further. He regularly read about Korean history and culture, because it was essential to understand their thought process.

But why should you do this? From the voice of an experienced professional, here is why he believes every exporter should know about Korea.

"You can better understand the viewpoints represented by the Korea side. This understanding will also give you some ideas on how to express the specific benefits your project offers."

PROMOTING BUSINESS RELATIONS

The following are recommendations from Korean traders who have worked on both sides of the Pacific.[4] These Korean executives recommend that Korean business relations exhibit strong personal and business relations. That U.S. exporters learn not only about Korean culture but also how to put their traditions of business into practice. Both governments and their leaders should create jobs, support businesses, provide incentives, educate the younger generation of business executives, and promote cultural exchanges.

They recommend that economic growth include provisions for human resource development. Economic growth necessitates the revitalization of both profits and people. Together government and business can provide international security and stability, especially as sensitive leaders communicate on deeper cultural levels.

Koreans want more than capital goods. Their reward comes as much from cultural esteem as from monetary rewards. Still they prefer that U.S. exporters ship raw materials and parts, along with their cargoes of capital goods and equipment. The Japanese do. Koreans also prefer foreign brands. But they don't like U.S. payment schedules. They want preferential financial arrangements if they promote or sell U.S. products. Use deferred payment terms.

U.S. trade associations could do more. They could promote exports and thus create new jobs for Americans and Koreans. According to Donna F. Tuttle, Deputy Secretary for the U.S. Department of Commerce, associations could identify "those factors which affect overseas sales, such as quotas, import restrictions, technical standards, and a multitude of other market access considerations."[5] Since 3,500 national trade associations and 40,000 local ones exist, the impact of such a service would be multiplied. In 1988 the U.S. Department of Commerce attracted 120 representatives from 70 national associations (such as American Bankers, American Hardware Manufacturers, Gas Appliances, and the American Frozen Food Institute). Curriculum included federal services for export assistance: export licensing, export and investment financing, and market information; formulating trade/investment promotion strategies; understanding intellectual property rights protection in foreign markets; and developing strategies to overcome barriers to overseas markets.

From the associations' perspective, these ideas have merit for two reasons. First they allowed the American Electronics Association to service their members. "It's important for AEA to have a universal focus to support the growth of small, high-tech entrepreneurial companies. Associations must maintain this perspective for their member companies to grow," said Richard Iverson, President of the American Electronics Association.[6] Second, this collective action makes a difference. "The old adage about strength in numbers holds true," said George DeBakey, Executive Director of the Computer Software and Services Industry Association. "It's exemplified through proper functioning trade associations."[7]

Yoo-Soo Hong believes U.S. state and local governments could do more to promote international trade relations with Korea. His ideas come from the Japanese and Koreans. Export promotion could come, as it did with Japan, Korea, and Taiwan, in three ways: "tax and tariff incentives, financial incentives, and supportive measures."[8] These countries eliminated taxes and tariffs on imported goods, which would then be exported. They also gave preferential credit to those firms exporting abroad, which in effect subsidized exporting firms' finances. And finally, beginning in 1965, the Koreans held monthly meetings for all exporting groups, known as the Monthly Export Promotion Meetings. Representatives came from the ROKG, the national assembly, banks, research institutes, trade associations, and firms specializing in international trade. Later asked to evaluate these meetings, 60 percent of those attending said these monthly meetings significantly affected their export capabilities.

FEELING GOOD ABOUT BUSINESS

Americans don't understand the Koreans' preference for intuition; Koreans don't understand the Americans' preference for rationality. Take contracts. Since Koreans expect a deep personal relationship to precede a business deal, contracts (at least in the past) have been less important. The Koreans have a term, *baik ji wiim*, to describe someone who places too much trust in white papers. Koreans know about contracts in the West, but they also speak derogatorily about what they mean. What matters are trust and commitment, which come from personal relationships. They don't want to sign business deals with those who only sign contracts.

The American culture is different from the Korean, especially in interpersonal business relationships and attitudes toward bosses. Koreans want strong personal relationships. There are five consideration factors when making friends or retaining an agent in Korea:

1. Age characterizes the differences found in generations, especially in Korea.
2. The social background of one's former post is very important in hiring.

3. Similar educational experiences remain as important.
4. The place of birth and localism sometimes affect business more in Korea than in the United States.
5. In this Confucian society, family origin and family relationship remain very important.

All of these characteristics suggest an emphasis on personal loyalty.

The Koreans put a greater emphasis on relations with the boss over relations with the company. Once again the personal bond is crucial, so naturally Koreans show this respect for bosses. The Korean style of management, known as *kwalli*, has evolved from several sources. It is more of a mix—of both West and East—than is the case with Japan. As we've already discussed, Korea had a long history of Japanese occupation at the turn of the century. After the Korean War, the country was almost totally destroyed. Because of massive military aid and diplomatic relations, the Koreans rebuilt, combining American culture with their own. So Koreans have a greater affinity toward the United States than the Japanese do. Management practices reflect this assimilated characteristic, but they also show, as American firms do, unique cultures dependent upon founders and company traditions. And that style is uniquely Korean.

Americans practice greater independence than Koreans. American workers, in some ways, compete with each other. In getting the job done, however, Americans are more rational than emotional. Managers effectively disseminate information and creatively solve problems. By comparison, Koreans conduct business in an orderly society where personal relations dominate. They are fiercely loyal to their bosses and work hard for them, perhaps harder than for their company. Managers in Korean companies process symbols intuitively, whether signing contracts or participating in ceremonies.

Feeling good about one's worth and self-esteem is crucial to any Korean business deal. To protect everyone's "face" or reputation, those business executives on the inside know about the importance of preserving good feelings, regardless of the cost. Inconsistencies do occur. What appears on the surface may not actually exist, but such appearances serve a purpose. To not appear agreeable could lead to a severe breach of courtesy that, in turn, could upset a person's feelings. The Korean word for this idea of saving face or creating good will is the same word for the concept of "face" (*kibun*). It refers to how people present themselves to others so as to ensure good will and good feelings.

CHARACTERISTICS OF BUSINESS RELATIONS

It is not possible to characterize business relations completely. However, we can identify some dominant characteristics about them. The

Koreans by and large reflect an element of hastiness. Koreans are under some pressure to make fast decisions. This could give American executives a better chance of negotiating favorable agreements. With adequate preparation, U.S. exporters have a definite advantage. Most Koreans are pro-American. They remember the liberation from Japan and defenses against the North Koreans.

Now is the time for U.S. businessmen to make Korean friends (the youth hold less positive attitudes toward Americans).

To capitalize on Korean markets, U.S. exporters should realize these market potentials. The Korean market is comparatively small; don't expect large orders on the first try. Be positive about the Korean culture before exporting. Develop special products adapted to the Korean market. Provide catalogues, samples, estimates, blueprints, and other data free of charge. Use two measurement systems simultaneously (feet and meters) in catalogues, prints, and other documents. Recognize the United States's "can-do-it-alone" days are over. Learn about the Korean initiatives. Seek Korean consultants before making final decisions about Korean export markets.

Koreans want strong decision makers.[9] Here are three tips for maintaining business relations with Koreans. (1) Determine who makes the decisions at the top of the hierarchy, because in this environment any other employee is less likely to make decisions. And even so, they must be approved later. (2) Koreans, like the Japanese, share decision events through some power personality. Their system, known as the *pummi* system, compares with the Japanese *ringi* system. Both involve forms of consensus making and creating awareness of all participants. Yet in Korea, the process is more in form than substance. Koreans lean toward the top down, one-way strategy. (3) Long-term relations, face-to-face informal gatherings, are the most important. Even with the language problems, times spent together are vital. These take the form of friendly exchanges in social activities, some of which are engaged in spontaneously. Unannounced visits imply a special relationship. If the rules and formal organizations control proper interaction, then to violate these would be as rude there as in America.

In business relations, U.S. exporters should recognize the Korean character and disposition. Koreans have a concept which captures their human dimensions. Even though it is hard to translate into English, let's try by defining the word kibun. It means "good feelings" brought about by proper morals, strong self-esteem, and recognized status. It's feeling good about what's happening around you.

Preserving Koreans' kibun promotes Korean business relations. Here are some successful and practical tips that successful executives use to do just that:

- Practice polite etiquette and greetings.
- Preserve Korean friends' self-respect.
- Enjoy Korean cultures and foods with Korean friends.
- Speak a few words of the Korean language.
- Present small gifts when appropriate.
- Visit homes with pleasure, if invited.
- Remember congratulations and condolences.
- Invite friends to the United States as business guests.

In conclusion, American business leaders are reminded that Koreans often make impromptu decisions, sometimes using only their kibun. It is an intuitive process of knowing about people and how they feel; it has been described as an irrational approach. It is not. Rather it represents a kind of gestalt, or "holistic," approach to decision making.

GOVERNMENT AND BUSINESS RELATIONS

In 1971 the Saemaul Undong new community movement began as a political venture. The purpose was to improve rural villages through three avenues: (1) spiritual enlightenment, (2) improvement of the living environment, and (3) increased income. It promoted industriousness, self-reliance, and cooperation for improvements, including everything from village clean up and sanitation to expanding rural roads and rural outlets.[10]

The program initially focused on rural industrialization. Leaders provided money for mining, manufacturing, fishing, and agriculture. They tried to balance rural development with urban.

The program impact was measured by these results: 2,740,000 rural households obtained electricity; 2,450,000 thatched roofs were replaced with tile and slate roofs; and 34,123 town halls were built for community gatherings. Later the movement spread into the cities. In 1974 development projects contributed to private enterprises and plants in urban areas. Over 3,164 kilometers of village roads were repaired or widened, and 46,631 kilometers of feeder roads were opened.

The five-year plan shifted expenditures not only from rural to urban but also from farming and fishing to education and publicity. Once the movement employed 280,000 leaders and represented 282,000 government officials.

Leaders from Africa and East and Southeast Asia visited the sites. Representatives visited the 101 community development projects. They saw landscaped communities with water-supply systems and dormitories for vocational schools. They learned that 1.4 million leaders, 288,000 social figures, and 282,000 government officials participated in community education efforts.

In one year alone some 950 high ranking government officials visited these communities and observed their development efforts. They represented over forty-nine countries of the world, especially the developing ones of Africa and Southeast Asia. Leaders of this community development effort even organized the Asian and Seoul Olympic Support Committees from these communities. The Home Ministry Office, which controls the efforts of Saemaul Undong, also used the development strategies of these programs to prepare for the international events of 1986 and 1988, namely the Asian and Olympic Games.

These efforts were enhanced by two ministers. The Minister of Commerce can delegate to special cities and provincial governors the authority to handle applications for the registration of traders. The Minister of Commerce and Industry can license any corporate entities as traders to ensure the smooth supply of essential products and raw materials, or to promote the tourist industry as a local strategy of promoting community development.

Now the Small and Medium Industry Promotion Corporation (SMIPC), as a nonprofit cooperative venture, offers new incentives for community development projects. Financial assistance is available for special programs and loans—the Modernization Program, the Folkarts Industry Development Program, the Rural Industry Development Program, and the Cooperative Program. Moreover, small communities can request technical assistance where expertise is lacking. These development efforts grant tax incentives and procurement for research and development for those communities which qualify in certain designated industrial subsectors.[11]

CONCLUSIONS

All business relations are political. They have to do with who gets what, where, and when they get it. If there is one area where politics play a significant role in Korea, it is in agricultural research initiatives and extension activities.[12] As in other areas of development, this one shows the strength and resources of the ROKG. As a type of state entrepreneur, the ROKG sets agendas not only for what happens but also the manner in which it happens.

Korean business relations are political, for the ROKG holds a special place in local and international business affairs. That is quite different from the United States. In the United States, the business of business is business; in Korea the business of government is business. The ROKG intervenes directly in all business affairs for several reasons. First, there is a tradition of vertical integration, which dominates society. People rally around leaders, not positions in bureaucracies. Second, the Korean business etiquette works. As new technologies emerge, government community development agencies, such as the Home Ministry Office, coordinate with the private sector to encourage or discourage technology transfer and development.

To increase joint ventures, markets, and imports ($38.5 billions) is to travel on two-way streets occupied by the Korean-American governments, U.S. suppliers, and Korean importers. U.S. players, however, should act strategically to promote their exports both at home and abroad. Likewise, suppliers solving problems—noncompetitive prices, limited information, and after service—increase exports. Then the United States could capitalize on Korea's focused efforts to import from America, not Japan. Exporters with little knowledge—business practices, trade laws, procedures of import—are advised to contact trade organizations in Korea or work with Korean agents.

One hundred and six years ago, Walter Townsend arrived in Chemulp'o, Korea. His private business venture, along with those of others who have travelled to Korea, has grown into broader partnerships of international security and defense, into complex diplomatic relations. What began then has continued until now—the emergence of mutually beneficial trade relations, foreign investments, and technology transfers.

NOTES

1. The American Chamber of Commerce in Korea, *United States-Korean Trade Issues* (April 1989):9.

2. The American Chamber of Commerce in Korea, 10.

3. Philip A. Spanninger, "Winning Government Approval of a 100% Foreign Investment: The Goodyear Experience," *East Asian Executive Reports* (September 1988):9, 15–17. This article is also found in *Business America*, March 13, 1989, 9. For ideas on contracting, marketing, and investing in Far Eastern countries write *International Executive Reports*, 717 D Street, N.W., Suite 300, Washington, DC 20004. They also publish *East Asian Business Intelligence*, which, among other items, lists contacts for increasing sales in East Asian countries and South Korea.

4. Korean associations surveyed traders' opinions about business relations. This information is taken from those surveys and interviews with agents who work with Americans. It is, as far as I know, unpublished in English.

5. Donna Tuttle, "Trade Associations Support Export Now," *Business America*, September 12, 1988, 7.

6. Tuttle, 9.

7. Tuttle, 9.

8. Yoo-Soo Hong, *Export Promotion Measures in Korea and Taiwan* (Stillwater, Okla.: Center for International Trade Development, 1988), 29.

9. Song-Hon Jang, "How Koreans View Foreign Businesses," *Korea Business World*, April 1987, 60–61. Mr. Jang is an international business consultant specializing in entry strategies, joint ventures, and government relations.

10. From Korean documents and public records.

11. Office of the Chief Counsel for Advocacy, *Major U.S. Trading Partners' Small Business Programs, Republic of Korea* (Washington, DC: U.S. Small Business Administration, 1989), 68–79.

12. Larry L. Burmeister, *Research, Realpolitik, and Development in Korea* (Boulder, Colo.: Westview Press, 1988), 172–73.

20

Korean
Internationalization

Every U.S. exporter wants to find a niche, one place in the grand scheme of things where the action really happens. The motive behind that wish is, perhaps, less focused on money than it is on the international adventure of success. "The desire that men feel to increase their income is quite as much a desire for success as for the extra comforts that a higher income can procure."[1]

No exporter ever lived who did not, at some time or another, fail to find, even after concerted effort, a niche for his products or services. Even some of the *Fortune* 500 corporate giants, such as Motorola, Citibank, and Northrop, have suffered embarrassing losses in Korea and the international arena of world affairs.

After a bitter struggle and a violent strike, Motorola decided that it was unwise to resist the Korean labor unions. Accused of foreign exploitation, Citibank, the largest foreign bank in Korea, finally agreed to a 45 percent pay hike for its Korean employees. While the Koreans working at Citibank wore sweaters with nationalist slogans—"I love

Korea"—workers at Tandy and Pico Electronics suffered a worse treatment.[2] Tandy and Pico also increased salaries.

Don't think, however, that problems in finding an international niche come from outside the corporation, somewhere in Korea. They do not. In 1983 Northrop hired a shrewd Korean consultant, who drove a Rolls Royce Silver Shadow. At that time he was in Honolulu; previously he'd lived in Seoul. Jimmy Shin was put on the Northrop payroll for $102,000 per year evidently to sell the F–20 jet fighter to South Korea.[3] Why him? Why this salary? Shin was once the personal body guard for the late Korean president, Mr. Chong-Kyu Park. Northrop, let's add, denied any wrong doing, saying its business deals were legitimate.

Every U.S. exporter looks for an international niche, a place like Korea where the action is. Perhaps Graeme Freeman, Director of International Business for Economic Development, described the deeper motive for such activities.

"Foreign markets will help companies in several ways," he said, "by broadening and diversifying the customer base, bringing higher profit margins, bringing potential tax advantages, and by building a corporate image that is international."[4]

THE KOREAN ANGLE ON TRADE

From the perspective of U.S. exporters, finding foreign markets benefits exporting firms. From the Korean perspective, however, it's equally important for them to promote imports from the United States.

It is true that Dr. Duck-Woo Nam, chief architect for the Korean economic success story and former Prime Minister of Korea, is concerned about getting out the trade message, information about Korean internationalization. He wants overseas firms, particularly the smaller ones, to have correct, up-to-date information about the potential of the Korean markets. If these firms (potential American or European exporters) know what is happening in Korea, Dr. Nam believes that such information would influence many nonexporting firms to respond favorably.

A Korean advertisement campaign has been developed for the burgeoning Korean market. It is not only for those new to exporting but also for those already trading in East Asia. In both cases the information should provide even greater opportunities for American firms. Knowing what Dr. Nam is doing helps us understand how he is doing it. Dr. Nam, chairman of the Korea Foreign Trade Association and the Korea World Trade Center, and other Koreans urge U.S. exporters to take advantage of Korea's progress toward greater internationalization.

Their methods include distribution of various Korean publications, Korean buying trade missions to the United States, and implementation of practical how-to seminars for prospective business leaders. Their assumption is that more U.S. firms will begin exporting to Korea if their managers know the export opportunities and how to exploit them. Regardless of the validity of that assumption, one fact is clear—Korea is on the move. Its moves have international ripple effects.

The importance of these developments for potential U.S. exporters is this: successful exporting depends upon a firm's ability to supply needed products or services at the right time and place. Reciprocally, that means that interested firms must both prepare for what is likely to come and complete what has already begun. American firms interested in Korea should explore the "what will come," even as they begin to prepare for it. And part of that preparation requires of them a backward glance. Specifically, it means that the Vice President for International Marketing, Widgets Inc., examines what has happened, so as to amend and complete the process of Korean internationalization. Exporting is a process of finding the outlet of activities, and then plugging your firm's cord into the circuit.

U.S. AND KOREAN COAL TRADE

In 1983 the Alaskan Usibelli, an exporter of steam coal, signed a long-term contract with Suneel to supply 800,000 tonnes (metric tons, 1,000 kg.) of steam coal to the Korean Honam power plant. Initially these shipments from the Usibelli remained high. They also contributed to the annual increases in coal exports to Korea (58 percent, from 1981 to 1985). After three years of operating under this agreement though, the end user and buyer of this coal—the Korean Electric Power Company (KEPCO)—renegotiated the contract. By 1986 the price for coal, as agreed upon by the original contract, was inflated because of declines both in world coal prices and in projected growth rates of domestic consumption of electricity. Thus in 1987, KEPCO reduced not only the tonnage of 680,000 tonnes (from 800,000) but also the price it paid. That renegotiated price reflected declining international markets.

At the same time that the price and amounts purchased were reduced, several other factors also affected this market. Korea is completing three nuclear plants (eighth, ninth, and tenth) designed to replace coal-fired generation, thereby reducing its capacity and demand for coal by 20 percent. Simultaneously, and since 1984, KEPCO has cut by five the twelve originally planned 500MW coal-fired units. In spite of these developments, KEPCO decided to maintain its purchases from Usibelli in Alaska. Even so, Australian producers maintain a competitive rivalry, as demonstrated in the past. It is a fact that the U.S. share of the Korean steam coal market fell from 38 percent (1981) to 1 percent (1984) because of Australian producers. Eventually these figures rebounded, but not without considerable effort (pressure) and the continued presence of international competition for all types of coal production.

The same international dynamics occur for metallurgical coal markets. International forces are both positive and negative. The logistics of interested coal exporters come from preparation based on what is happening in Korea in light of what has already happened. Part of that preparation requires a backward glance.

But because change comes from outside their country's boundaries, even the Koreans must adjust to external forces they don't totally control—world prices and domestic demands. So that while the new plant at Kwangy Bay should increase Pohang Iron and Steel Company (POSCO) annual coal requirements to 11.6 million tonnes this year, Australia and Canada stand in the background, ready to supply that need. Remember that in 1986 these two countries absorbed U.S. reductions by 900 thousand and 600 thousand tonnes, respectively. It could, and probably will, happen again.

The good news about exporting must, therefore, be balanced against the bad. Internationally speaking, both poor world steel markets and the tendency of steel mills to over purchase continue to hold down the U.S. metallurgical coal market. These trends, in turn, affect the American domestic front. Until now, most exported metallurgical coal came from the Pennsylvania Tanoma mine. As one of the strongest of the U.S. coal market areas, metallurgical coal exports to Korea increased from 15 percent in 1981 to 25 percent in 1985, a figure sustained until a recent announcement.

POSCO has decided to sell its Tanoma-owned Pennsylvania mine because the mine is a high-cost underground operation. Even so, Korea reached an agreement with American Metals and Coal Incorporated (AMCI) to buy the mine hinge and to continue importing both a lower grade U.S. metallurgical coal and low grade steam coal from other mines in Appalachia.

Surprisingly, the final outcome of the equation still looks good. Factoring all the good and bad news into the equation still leads us to a positive market outlook. According to economic experts, the U.S. exports to Korea should stay around 20–25 percent for the foreseeable future.

What is true for steam and metallurgical coal is also true for anthracite. Anthracite coal comes from fines at the old cleaning waste plant sites. Koreans use the product in home heating and small boilers. So Korea's import demand of anthracite would naturally vary not only with market demand but also with the availability of good quality pond fines. Such pond fines are becoming scarce.

The Daihan Corporation purchases anthracite from traders operating out of Hong Kong, who bring it from Vietnam, North Korea, China, and Africa. Vietnam's share of the market was around 330 thousand tonnes (7.4 percent, 1986). Because of such suppliers, the U.S. market share has dropped from its 1983 peak of 44 percent. Presently the level is around 15 percent of the market share.

Exporters to Korea should be informed before they even make decisions or sign agreements. Information takes priority over pressing opportunities. Successful exporters supply needed products or services to the right place on time. They prepare for what is likely to come and complete what has already begun. So too with potential coal exporters. They should know that coal supplies 35 percent of Korea's total energy consumption, that all bituminous coal, steam and metallurgical, must be imported.

Internationalization is one thing, how to tap into the Korean market is another. Successful exporters go below the surface of normal information. Those who would be successful know that the Korean export coal market is controlled through licensing of Korean trading companies. In exchange for this controlled market, these Korean companies comply with and carry out certain government policies. Whoever would export to Korea must deal with three principal purchasers of imported coal: POSCO, KEPCO, and the Daihan Corporation. Beyond knowledge of these trading companies and an entry strategy designed to make contracts with them, there are other, not always overlapping, barriers.

Yet for exporters to close deals and sign export agreements, many uncontrollable factors must come together. Koreans don't determine them all, nor do Americans. U.S. exporters can establish tracking systems for collecting information about what has happened (time and place) and what might happen in world markets (trends and patterns). Exporters to Korea should do that, if they have any hope of supplying these markets.

INTERNATIONAL TRADE IMBALANCE

Presently there is a lot of hype about Korea. U.S. media stories and government promotions give exporting to Korean businesses favorable publicity. And little wonder with what we see. The Koreans will go to any length to solve the U.S. trade imbalance problem (see Table 20.1). Korea wants to reduce its deficit with Japan and its surplus with the United States. This surplus problem has developed since 1986 and was fueled by declining petroleum prices, currency realignments, and increasing Korean exports to the United States. Korea is seeking a solution to its international problems. The solution, like the one for Taiwan, has implications for American exporters. Taiwan reduced its trade surplus with the United States (from $16 billion, 1987, to $10.4 billion) by encouraging importing.

On 26 March 1989, a team of thirty-five Korean leaders, headed by

Table 20.1
Korean Trade with the United States

Trade Relations	Dollars in Billions by Year			
	1986	1987	1988	1989
Export to U.S.	13.9	18.3	21.2	23.0
Import from U.S.	6.5	8.8	12.8	16.5
Trade Surplus	7.4	9.5	8.5	6.5

Duck-Woo Nam, set out to four cities—San Francisco, Dallas, Milwaukee, and the Washington, D.C., area. They sought high tech electronic and genetic engineering industries in the Bay Area; machinery, auto parts and chemical industries in Dallas; agricultural, machinery, and paper industries in Milwaukee; and better government negotiations in Washington, D.C. Their purchases, estimated at $1.5 billion, came from a list of priorities including auto parts, petrochemicals, and textiles. One of their purposes was to cut the trade surplus from $8.6 billion (1988) to $6.5 billion (1989).

Duk-Kwan Yu, Director General for Trade Policy (Ministry of Trade and Industry), explained that for 1988 imports into Korea increased by 26 percent. As one of the delegates on this recent trade mission, Yu pointed out that "growth in our GNP and domestic spending makes Korea a substantial market."[5] The mission is not totally altruistic, though. As Yu put it, "we are trying to relieve the troubles of the U.S. government."[6]

They also held seminars on how to penetrate the Korean market. Jin-Ho Kim, a delegate of two such trade missions, went a step further in making suggestions about how Americans should approach this Korean market. "Aggressive promotion is needed from the U.S. side if these companies are to take advantage of the market opening that has been realized."[7] This type of negotiation over international trade is new to U.S.-Korean relations. We've had military intervention and diplomatic policies. But Kim advised "aggressiveness on the part of the U.S. companies in negotiations, communication and after sales services."

PROSPERITY WITH A PRICE

Could the hype over the potential of Korea's markets create a false sense of security for U.S. exporters? Possibly, for low quality products still won't sell well. But quality, price, and demand remain constant, no matter the source. Successful exporting to Korea, like the international process itself, is a rather complex, demanding, and unpredictable process that does not always lead to expected profits.

Still there are those who worry about the negative effects of Korean industrialization, a prerequisite to internationalization. Internationalization and the prosperity derived from it extract a price from both U.S. exporters and Korean importers alike.

Internationalization has also caused increasing demands for equitable and balanced prosperity. The labor movement has gained strength over the past few years. Large automobile exports have lead to calls for opening domestic markets, appreciating the Korean won, and expanding domestic consumption. Furthermore, internationalization stresses the need to balance regional growth in Korea. Farmers are worried about import liberalization. The average farm in Korea, about 2.5 acres, cannot compete internationally, especially since 20 percent of the population lives on these small farms.

Internationalization has tended to benefit the large Korean companies. The small and medium companies face stiff competition from abroad. This fact combined with increased salaries for workers and accelerating appreciation of the Korean won place an additional burden on these firms.

Finally, Korean internationalization has created a negative impression on the American public. Korea, like Japan with its $55 billion trade surplus, is often seen as an unfair international trader. With this perception has also come the call for retaliation toward Korea. Since Korea is more dependent on markets than Japan, talks of retaliation have brought changes in reevaluation of currency and elimination of many trade barriers. Surprisingly, U.S. retaliation, prescribed by the 1988 Trade Law whenever negotiations fail, included on its list Brazil and Japan, but not Korea. The Koreans continue to make concessions on tariffs and policies that, in turn, compound the issues.

Nevertheless, regional economic blocs and protectionism continue to raise their ugly heads in the face of unfair trade practices. In spite of this threat, there seems no retreat. Deputy Prime Minister and Minister of Economic Planning Soon Cho reached the same conclusion before the Foreign Correspondents Club in Seoul on 18 January 1989. "Even with these difficulties and dangers, we realize that internationalization is vital for the continued growth of the Korean economy."[8] With over 80 percent of the nation's GNP coming from trade, it seems that Korean internationalization will continue.

Yet sometimes the Koreans resist this developmental process. Perhaps this resistance results from their national identity, which was developed from centuries of subjugation and repression. Whatever the reason, nearly everyone agrees with Minister Soon Cho that "one's export growth can be sustained only when it is supported by increased imports from one's trading partners." Such exchanges are a must if Koreans continue doing international business. Yet the process is changing their national identity as the process assimilates their national customs and traditions, their business etiquette, and their business relations.

That's the irony—Korea wants what it might later find to be a destructive element to its traditional ways of doing business. Internationalization, as described in a United Nations report (Mexico City, 1987) titled "Technologies Impact on Culture," tends to dilute country cultures. Technology expands rapidly until the process literally overcomes national boundaries, pulling countries together based on new economic development classifications: the Organization for Economic Cooperation and Development (OECD), the Newly Industrialized Countries (NIC), and the Less Developed Countries (LDC). OECD represents Western Europe, North America, and Japan; NIC includes Korea and Taiwan; and LDC includes Asia, Africa, and South America. It creates a new economic order and new international cities, while at the same time, it spells the end of other cities, which serve as cultural centers. It corrodes both the ancient methods of farming and the slow paced community life found in rural areas of the country.

Simultaneously, internationalization causes upheaval and social change, the emergence of transcience, and an obsession for the novel. From this new order of relationships also comes some benefits, even though they are tagged with a high price. It is called progress because it provides jobs to so many throughout the world. It increases a country's standard of living and GNP, thereby increasing consumer consumption and international trade. From an exporter's perspective, such a condition is considered a boon, characterized by joyful exuberance and deliberate actions. On a broader scale, it invites many difficulties, while at the same time, it brings the world ever closer together in a potentially beneficial way.

SMALL BUSINESS PROGRAMS

Small U.S. exporters also want a market niche in Korea. But this is more challenging. Often these small companies have neither the resources nor the money to plan full-scale attacks.

Fortunately, there is some good news for small business both in Korea and the United States. The ROKG is reacting to charges of favoritism and inequitable distribution of wealth. So the Korean government is promoting small business ventures with small- and medium-sized firms in the United States. The Small and Medium Industry Promotion Corporation (SMIPC) has authority to act through the 1979 Small and Medium Industry Promotion Law. As a nonprofit organization, this agency implements programs that benefit small and medium enterprises.

To qualify, participants must meet the definitions established by the Basic Small and Medium Industry Act. This act defines small- and medium-sized businesses for various industrial sectors. A small firm in manufacturing, mining, transportation, and construction is one that employs up to 20 people; for commercial and service companies, it is 5 people. A medium-sized firm is defined as 21 to 300 people for manufacturing, mining, transportation; for construction the figures range from 21 to 200 employees; for commercial and service, the number varies from 6 to 20 people. For information about the program contact: Head Office, SMIPC, 27–2, Yoido-dong, Yongdeungpo-gu, Seoul, Korea. The U.S. office is SMIPC/USA, 2250 East Devon, Suite 249, Des Plaines, Illinois 60018.

The services provided by this cooperative venture range from financial assistance and business development to procurement assistance and policy input. This program provides export assistance, along with tax incentives. Finally, it offers employment assistance and research or development opportunities.

Those businesses who qualify can receive regular business loans for high growth and new technology businesses. There are special loans for a modernization program, a folk arts industry development program, a rural industry development program, and a cooperative program. Specifically these programs are geared toward assistance for parts and components in export potential firms. They also promote Korea's traditional handicrafts industry, bolster employment in rural areas, or combine resources with other firms. Business development programs provide for equipment leasing or establishing new breakthroughs in a field. The program provides for technical training and policy input at two sites: Technical Training, Small Business Training Institute, 931, Wongok-dong, Ansan, Kyonggi-do, Korea; and Policy Input, Ministry of Trade and Industry, 1, Jungang-dong, Goachunshi, Kyonggi-do, Korea.

Various laws allow small companies the opportunity for procurement assistance. Firms in the rural areas are given priority in this program. Other advantages include tax benefits for the first four years in business, reduced tax rates by 50 percent, and other tax-exemption programs. This program gives employment assistance for top management and entrepreneurship development. Finally, these effects include assistance for R&D, technology transfer, and international collaboration for select companies. The purpose is to expose small business personnel to new and advanced technologies and to help them acquire skills in developed countries such as the United States.

CONCLUSIONS

Internationalization challenges us all as Americans. At the end of World War II, the United States began to assume its role in the world. Gradually, the center of gravity for our country is shifting outward internationally. The training challenges increase in direct proportion to that movement. Professor Richard Lambert, at the University of Pennsylvania, urges a cooperative effort. If we are to expand our international trade industries, we should also support the development of global expertise.

As an integrated national strategy, Lambert identifies seven critical domains: (1) foreign language competency, (2) international expertise in business whereby we train business leaders to cope more effectively with cultural differences and global skills, (3) international specialists in other professions, (4) international information flows where the information is not piecemeal but adequate for practical use, (5) research on how to manage and utilize the expanding flow of international information, (6) overseas linkages whereby we develop programs for exchanges and training, and finally (7) international education for the next generation, by which we don't as a country correct the broader problem.[9]

About the internationalization of Korea we can learn much. Attorney Michael Palmer, specialist in foreign trade legal issues, applies these issues of internationalization to the topic at hand. "The state should help to establish contacts with foreign buyers, provide seminars on the export process, how-to-do-it training sessions, and library resources," he said.[10]

NOTES

1. Bertrand Russell, "Work," in *The Conquest of Happiness* (New York: Doubleday, 1930), 200.

2. Peter Maass, "Foreign Firms a Target in South Korea," *The Washington Post*, May 21, 1989, 3.

3. Ruth Marcus, "Goodyear Unit Admits Bribes, Fined $250,000," *The Washington Post*, May 21, 1989, 1.

4. Art Edelstein, "Weak Dollar Opens Export Markets," *Vermont Business Magazine*, April 1988, 10.

5. Ian Davis, "Korea Opens Its Doors to U.S. Firms," *Business America*, March 13, 1989, 2.

6. Davis, 3.

7. Davis, 3.

8. Soon Cho, "The Korean Economy at a Crossroads: A Blueprint for Internationalization," *Korean Economic Institute*, January 27, 1989.

9. Richard D. Lambert, "The Educational Challenge of Internationalization," *The Washington Quarterly* 10 (Summer 1987):163–81.

10. Edelstein, 10.

_____ VI

Establish Korean Outlets

21

Global Networks

Every day in our newspapers, we read about the significance of global networks. Ours is a global economy that operates through joint ventures, marketing agreements, mergers, acquisitions, licensing arrangements, supply agreements, and production arrangements. As a result of these patterns, corporate managers are extended well beyond their traditional exporting roles. These individuals negotiate transnational agreements, coordinate marketing, promote activities among subsidiaries, and transfer knowledge about high-tech ventures. Such activities encourage innovative thinking, creative research, and international cooperation. Activating global networks (international travel) stimulates creative problem solvers in such a way that they are better able to discover new solutions to old problems.[1]

What is true for Americans is evidently true for Asians as well. Back in 1968, Nobel Prize winner Gunnar Myrdal lamented the fact that Asians evidently lacked the creativity to solve their own economic problems. In his book titled *Asian Drama*, Myrdal compared Asia to Western Europe and the United States. The latter economies created high-quality, high-tech products that were later shipped to Asia.

Yet, just twenty years later, the outlook for rather prosperous global networking in Asia has drastically changed indeed. In fact, the rate of that change, when analyzed, is rather astonishing. The twenty year average rate of annual growth for each Asian country—Singapore (7.6 percent), Taiwan (7.2 percent), Korea (6.6 percent), Hong Kong (4.7 percent), Japan (4.7 percent)—exceeds the rate for either Western Europe (Austria, 3.5 percent), Britain, (1.6 percent), or the United States (1.7 percent).

We all know that their economic successes came from two elements forming one overall process of creativity. These "five dragons" exploited Western technology in an Eastern seal. What was originally planted in the West also found fertile soil in these Confucian outposts. The economic output and the creative process, however, could have been predicted all along. In 1988 the ROKG purchased its first Cray Supercomputer; Korea's car output jumped 38 percent; Korea created photosensitive resin, multifaceted industries, silicon wafer industries, the video transmitting and recording systems (VTRS), and the video. Not surprisingly, investments follow creativity. By comparison, investments made in North America ($79 million, 1986 versus $177 million, 1987) were higher than those in Southeast Asia ($7 million, 1986 versus $131 million, 1987), but lower than those made in Korea ($359 million versus $1 billion).

This is the age of ascendancy for these Pacific Rim area countries, including Korea. This nation, formerly isolated as the hermit nation, is visibly seen as the rising star. But Korea is not without its problems too—labor and student unrest, a trade imbalance with Western Europe and North America, a new form of government in which the president is elected directly, and a "levelling off" economy.

Developing creative leaders is one problem for exporting countries. Transnational companies need leaders who not only reflect their corporate culture, but adjust well to global cultures. They need leaders who can see beyond regional or national boundaries. Such leaders know the issues of finding international markets and establishing global networks. In their marketing plans they anticipate problems, develop contingencies, and access channels within reasonable established deadlines. They are corporate champions.

COUNTRY MANAGERS

As we move into the 1990s, international economics and world trade will continue radically altering the way business is conducted. Between developing and developed countries are the newly industrialized countries—the "five dragons," including Korea. These countries have achieved economic success partly because of sound government economic policies.

Because of them, U.S. exporters face greater risks now than earlier. But at the same time, the rewards can be greater. A host of international events are shaping our world—newly industrial countries (NICs), *perestroika* (restructuring), *glastnost* (openness), the unification of the European Economic Community (1992), student revolts at Tiananmen Square (China, 1989), volatile global markets, the financial and banking domination of Japan, the merger mania and paper entrepreneurship in the United States, and changes in Eastern Europe (1990).

As the nature of business changes, so must our views. Worldwide electric financial networks continue to fuse national boundaries. Through economic networks, financial managers create an ever increasing interdependence such that "decoupling no longer seems possible."[3] So the corporate world is responding by establishing its own global networks. What that form takes depends upon business strategies. But complex extensions of global networks need corporate strategies appropriate to the task. The corporation links financial institutions, government officials, trade associations, stockholders, suppliers, intermediaries, export management companies, market strategies, customers, cultures, and manufacturers. And the ones most responsible for pulling it all together are the country managers.

Country managers have no easy job. For thirty years their roles have been changing in direct proportion to the world's changes. In the sixties, they were known as "country managers." They had considerable independence and made decisions about the company products, market strategies, and selection of indigenous staff. With increasing international competition, many multinational companies shifted their strategies and focus from country to product lines. Managers coordinated products and marketing on a broader scale because corporations standardized procedures for international markets, not for particular country settings.

Now all of that is changing once again. Corporate strategies are now moving back to the concept of "country manager." But they also are moving forward toward a matrix type of arrangement. Increased international competition and the need for long-range involvement make the country focus more attractive than product line. Five recent changes prompted this refocus:[4]

1. Global Strategies (GS) stretched supply networks, thereby increasing management stress.

2. GS tended to desensitize corporate executives to local changes in markets. Indigenous managers now play a greater role.

3. GS executives restricted corporations in their abilities to respond to new foreign markets. A decentralization of function was needed.

4. GS reduced the number of alternative communication channels. This reduction occurred before the era of telecommunication and computerization. Obviously these technologies created greater flexibility for structural changes.

5. GS did not work well for other reasons. Through politics and legislation, more country leaders exercised greater control over international trade. Consequently, a change back to the concept of country managers seemed in order.

These factors contributed to the resurgence of the country managers. This does not mean the present trends are duplications of earlier ones. They are not. Rather the structural changes reflect the sophistication not only of machine technology, but of design technology as well.

According to a recent publication by the Conference Board (a business research group), country managers now take on a variety of roles. One is the staff function, which includes "responsibility within their countries as finance, human resources, and public affairs."[5] Another type of country manager is one who engages in standard operations. That means that country managers don't operate as separate divisions. They work along side global product divisions. As a result their powers are limited to sales, local manufacturing, or personnel. Other types may have more power and operate as independent international businesses. In these cases they start the process—product lines—and complete it with local modifications subcontracted out and sold through some licensing arrangement. Finally, those with the most power operate a single line or single division.

One example is General Electric (U.S.), where the country managers head single divisions. This type of country manager functions as extensions of sales. If markets expand, then several divisional managers may coordinate their divisions or single product lines under the organizational structure of a single country manager. This means, as in the case of GE, that divisional managers report to and receive guidance from the country managers. This concept works well, since the country manager can coordinate sales, products, functions, and changes in laws.[6]

The organizational structure follows the demands of international markets. The five recent changes on how corporations organize international trade also affect how exporters operate. With the advent of satellites, personal computers, and travel, these country managers extend themselves in ways their predecessors could not. All of which allows for direct contact between all the parties involved. And in a real sense the action takes place where the customers are, not back where the products are manufactured. Flex systems seem to work best in our constantly changing world.

MANAGING INTERNATIONALLY

Because of our global economy and networks, U.S. firms are now experimenting with new ways of managing exports. The old models were culture specific, that is, they were good when conducting business in one country. Also the old paradigms reflected a knowledge-oriented and analytical bias, one less appropriate for today. We need fresh thinking for the emergence of business practices in cross-cultural settings. We need models that are skill-based and process oriented to meet current needs.

Behavioral scientists can highlight the different orientations that managers bring to particular work requirements. Understanding cultures provides a framework for increasing effectiveness. Rather than blindly manage in a global situation, managers should take new perspectives.

Facing the realities of our global economy, managers must creatively communicate with workers. A model for that task varies from country to country. Neither Americans nor Koreans have the final say on effective ways of doing business. That is the reason for cross-cultural experiences. We learn surprisingly more about our own culture than the other's. Through international trade, we understand not only the inside business practices better but ourselves. If cross-cultural travel makes people more enlightened, so does exporting to Korean markets. Export managers become enlightened as they realize that the taken-for-granted, and often inflexible management practices of either the Koreans or ourselves, are culture bound. From these encounters, they hope for changes. Perhaps managers can learn to display greater flexibility as they encounter other ways of conducting business.

The truth is that the abilities of managers to lead others require both reason and feelings, abilities not entirely learned conceptually. Yet U.S. training is almost exclusively rational and logical. That process limits those trying to get inside Korean business practices. American-trained executives use only half of their potential ability. That one-sidedness limits American executives and should prompt us to learn from Koreans who have strengths that Americans lack. Gains of international trade are more than profits.

Export management is both a science and an art form. A science for rational coordination is the basis for organization. On paper that looks easy enough, but does everyone act rationally and logically? Technologically speaking, people with inferior knowledge aren't all that rational. Yet they still proudly display their product built by means of their ingenuity, tenacity, and respect. They work for the products, the profits, and the people.

Translating talents into final products or services is work. It's more difficult in Korea because Koreans think of relationships differently. Consequently, export managers need special skills and abilities if they are to build effective work teams. While export management is a science, it is also an art. It requires the same sensitivities as those for an artist. Artistic managers know that the sociohistorical traditions determine the best fit between rational organizations and community sentiments. Artistic managers use both insights (reason and sentiment) in management. This quest prompts export managers to wonder about Korean management, which begins with an understanding of their culture and them as a people. That usually comes when we contrast their culture with our own.

Without an understanding of the Korean people and their business practices, potential problems could become realities. Managers symbolize the vehicle for change and development in this new order of world cooperation. They can be instruments of unity in the midst of cultural diversity. Export managers work together with Koreans who knowbusiness practices. That can be indispensable because they know what it takes to close deals with associates they have known for years.

As a Confucian society, Koreans value politeness and respect for authority figures. They reinforce the basic social fabric of *self denial* and *face saving*. Moreover, they are proud of their culture, its contribution to world order. Because nationalism runs high, they expect foreigners to show respect for Korean history and accomplishments. By contrast, Americans view success more in terms of careers and personal fulfillment.

MANAGED STRUCTURES AND PROCESSES

Countries and companies, like melting giant glaciers, are sliding into the global oceans of networks. So even the largest companies are looking for new strategies of managing overseas assets. Almost paradoxically, those who survive respond to forces that pull toward both global integration and local differentiation. Globally, companies must be efficient; locally, responsive. Only those managed structures and processes which adapt themselves will likely dominate. Within ten years there will be two kinds of corporate leaders: those who have developed an international business strategy, and those unemployed. The choice is clear; either managers adjust to global changes or they are out of work. Managers should watch how these three requirements—efficiency, responsiveness, and transfer of knowledge—fit international strategies for their industry and their own organizations.[7]

In a five-year study of 236 managers working in companies around the world, Bartlett and Ghoshal explored the shape of organizations for the twenty-first century. The managers' tasks in transnational operations are to "legitimate diverse perspectives and capabilities (global competition), develop multiple and flexible coordination processes (multinational flexibility) and build shared visions and individual commitment (worldwide learning)."[8]

From a marketing perspective, managers should be, above all else, learners, risks takers who can estimate probabilities and conduct feasibility studies. In East Asia, the global task is selecting the best strategy, including contingency plans, for that area. Care should be taken to avoid tunnel vision, which could impede corporate goals and increase cost. On the other end, the tactics concern what, who, when, specific results, estimated costs about specific segmented markets.

Finally, the internal task is to prepare for program evaluation review and to present such plans. Just as corporations learn from observing worldwide operations, so too do marketing managers. They learn about Korea, its market limits, material needs, shipping costs, and probable outcomes, given certain advertising strategies. Managers should outline the details, use visuals, rehearse, and take charge in their actual presentation. International managers should remain flexible and able to set the stage for action.

Writing the corporate Korea marketing plan is thinking about how organizations can meet Korea's needs. In developing your outlines you'll probably include (1) an executive summary, (2) Korean marketing objectives, (3) Korean analysis, (4) Korean marketing strategies, (5) Korean marketing tactics, (6) a schedule of implementation, (7) procedures for monitoring, (8) evaluating results, (9) expected results, and (10) contingency plans.

To implement your plan, be sure to pick the most competent people, give them specific objectives, and let them go. If your plans include Korean representatives, get input from both the U.S. Department of Commerce and KOTRA on the Korean side. Find out whether the representatives relate to products, certain cities in Korea, the Korean sales staff, the Korean customers, or some government regulations. Project control comes as you tune tactics and adjust your strategies. These requirements were confirmed by Bartlett and Ghoshal in their study.[9]

This study did not address the personal side of planning. But it did show that international managers form a team of interdependent players. They relate to top managers, others in their marketing department, and sales managers, as well as those in advertising, market research, and management information systems. In large corporations other relationships include those in corporate planning, operations, R&D, law, accounting, finance, and personnel.

Those in this maze of relations can easily get confused responses about their marketing plans. After all, those other professionals see exporting differently. And why not, for their reward systems vary, as do the politics of their operations. However, it's not an impossible situation. Good credibility pays great dividends. Those who recognize others and give them credit gain. Those who share problems and concerns, willingly accepting failures and blame, establish their own networks. If those networks include reputations for fair play and openness, along with hard word and persistence, then more is likely to happen inside the corporation and outside through channels of distribution.

Just as the process works internally, so too it works internationally. Managers must pass on their own culture inside the Korean culture. They should develop systems of "recruitment, training and development, and career path management to help individuals cope with diversity and complexity."[10] What Barlett and Ghoshal found was that sometimes the internal market mechanism is more powerful than the organizational structure itself. In decentralized operations, product managers for Korea soon discover that informal networks provide the climate for becoming regional vice presidents. If individuals can survive fifteen years with little formal power, surely a formal power base would increase their effectiveness.

One example is Matsushita. This Japanese firm uses two approaches for facilitating greater learning and motivation. Its uses two groups of research labs, one for company projects and one for smaller projects. To access the first, the research labs, product divisions, and top managers must approve particular projects. To access the second, product divisions make suggestions. In both cases the labs and the divisions must cooperate in marketing new products. That forces them to be market sensitive about what's selling or working. Annually Matsushita hosts an "internal trade show" to get everyone together. "Relying on their sense of their own markets, the managers pick and choose among proposed models, order modifications for their local markets, or simply refuse to take products they feel are unsuitable."[11]

CONCLUSION

Henry Mintzberg, Professor of Management at McGill University, changed our thinking about what managers do. He disputed four misconceptions. First, folklore had it that managers are reflective. Mintzberg found they were active and followed an unrelenting pace. Second, folklore assumes that effective managers have no regular duties; Mintzberg found that false. They follow prescribed patterns of duties, including rituals and ceremonies. Third, folklore says that senior managers use aggregate printed information to make decisions. Not so. They favor verbal communication—calls and meetings. Fourth, they are like scientists following a rigid course of action. Contrary to belief, their craft is delicate, almost an art. Certainly they don't act as scientists or technicians, who operate in laboratories.[12]

More recently Mintzberg took yet another angle to explore how top managers actually employ strategy. To communicate his findings, Mintzberg used the metaphor of a potter who shapes a lump of clay into something useful. Managers are craftsmen and strategists working with their own clay. The clay, or strategy for global networks, is molded through a process whereby managers use a plan (intended course of action), a ploy (maneuvers intended to outwit competitor), a pattern (consistency), a position (finding a market niche), and a perspective (a way of perceiving the world).[13]

Should we consider viewing our world as a garden? That question has broader implications than we realize. Western models are conceived of as technological metaphors such as simple machines, but to assume that the world is a simple machine means it has no emotions, culture, or differences. To assume that the world is a complex system, like cybernetics suggests, is to view the world as a living organism. Were we to think like the Japanese, the world would be seen differently from either of these models. To them the world is like a garden, a delicate ecosystem. What do these metaphors have to do with a book on exports to Korea?

Western models of the world are

largely technological. Whether a simple machine, a complex system, or a hologram, these metaphors are abstract, intellectual, and technical. This is not the case with some of the other cultures with which we are in direct and intense competition. If anything, the Japanese, for example, seem to operate with an overarching metaphor of the world that combines the global garden and the complex systems. What will it take to shift our society's predominant metaphor so that it can truly compete in a global environment?[14]

The Korean export market is part of one world market. It includes everything from automobiles to peanuts. If you are successful in Korea, it is possible that other markets will be available in this region. Ours is a world of global interdependence. Consequently, more U.S. companies need employees who think internationally. The recent trend of mass marketing all products toward all markets failed. Too many international markets were lost with increasing specification of the market segments. While thinking globally is important, it's not enough. CEOs must feel comfortable in those markets. Only in that way can they select country-area managers, keep up with scheduling of products, coordinate the construction of new facilities, and tailor products to life-style categories within those markets. Think globally, but respond locally.

NOTES

1. E. B. Gurman, "The Effects of Foreign Travel on Creativity," *The Journal of Creative Behavior* 22 (1989):281. Diversity and variety of experience contribute to creativity. Of two student groups, one studying in the United States and one in London, the latter showed more creativity.

2. Geert Hofstede and Michael Harris Bond, "The Confucius Connection: From Cultural Roots to Economic Growth," *Organizational Dynamics* (Spring 1988):5.

3. Ian Mitroff, *Business Not as Usual: Rethinking Our Individual Corporate and Industrial Strategies* (New York: Josey Bass, 1987), 161.

4. Melissa A. Berman, "Global Management Structure," *Perspectives* 8 (November 1987):1.

5. Berman, 1.

6. Berman, 3.

7. Christopher A. Bartlett and Sumantra Ghoshal, *Managing Across Borders* (Boston: Harvard Business School Press, 1989).

8. Bartlett and Ghoshal, 67.

9. Bartlett and Ghoshal, 67.

10. Bartlett and Ghoshal, 71.

11. Bartlett and Ghoshal, 123–24.

12. Henry Mintzberg, "The Manager's Job: Folklore and the Fact," in *Designing and Managing Your Career*, ed. Harry Levison (Boston: Harvard Business School Press, 1988):47–51.

13. Henry Mintzberg, "The Strategy Concept I: Five Ps for Strategy," *California Management Review* 30 (Fall 1987):9.

14. Mitroff, 179.

22

Consumer Markets

According to a recent survey conducted by Price Waterhouse, selling overseas isn't as difficult as people might think. Of those companies surveyed, over 60 percent reported profitable foreign sales within the first year. Another 28 percent reported profits within three years. Yet only 10 percent of domestic manufacturers who could sell overseas, in fact, do. That may explain why only 250 U.S. companies account for 85 percent of all U.S. exports.[1]

McKinsey & Company and the American Business Conference offer sound reasons for exporting. For nine months these consultants worked with one hundred fast-growing firms. Their revenues, growing at an annual rate of 21 percent (1984–86), were between $10 million and $2 billion. These firms wanted to start exporting. Although these successful companies were not alike, they had five common characteristics for success internationally: (1) product excellence—good products potentially sell anywhere; (2) marketing excellence—finding where to sell them is the problem; (3) high initiators—these companies were prudent risk takers who didn't wait until they were multinational operations (Milli-pore's total sales were $10 million; Analog Devices, $1 million); (4) in-cremental expansion—they moved slowly and deliberately with sound facts. Even so, profits came with this sound strategy—64 percent of the 100 companies recorded profits in one year, 76 percent in two years; and (5) organizational commitment, it takes time and money to export. "One-half of all ABC executives spend more than 20 percent of their working hours on international business matters; for one out of ten, the proportion exceeds 40 percent."[2]

Poor quality is costly. Research by the Technical Assistance Research Programs (TARP) demonstrated just how costly. The majority of those consumers with complaints (45–60 percent) don't complain to business. Rather they complain to friends. The average consumer with service or product difficulty tells nine to ten people. That's why it costs five times more to attract new customers than it does to keep old ones satisfied. That ratio of costs is even higher on exported goods or services. Since overhead costs are higher, greater attention should be directed toward all aspects of consumer markets.[3]

KOREAN MARKET POTENTIAL

Accounting for 1.81 percent of the world markets, Korea ranks thir-teenth as the largest world market.[4] According to data from *Business International*, the USSR (second) and China (third) comprise about 25 percent of world markets, while the United States (first) accounts for about 20 percent (19.41 percent). Using those statistics, we find that South Korea (thirteenth) accounts for 1.81 percent of the world markets. In the East Asian region only Japan (fourth) ranks higher. Japan (8.07 percent) ranks ahead of West Germany (fifth, 4.21 percent). Other Eu-ropean countries follow—Italy (sixth, 3.58 percent), France (seventh, 3.34 percent), UK (ninth, 2.81 percent), Spain (eleventh, 2.09 percent). Brazil (eighth, 3.00 percent) ranks just behind France, while Canada (twelfth, 1.99 percent) follows Spain.

Table 22.1 shows not only the size of consumer expenditure but also the strength of particular country markets compared to other countries. Beginning with column one, size of the country, we see just how small Singapore and Hong Kong are compared with other Asian countries. The largest country is Indonesia. Though it purchases a large number of trucks or buses, it has the smallest number of telephone lines. Even though Indonesia is much larger than Korea, this Southeast Asian coun-try has fewer TVs than Korea ($7.11 billion versus $8.64 billion). Indo-nesia imports fewer computers (N/A) and does about a tenth of the importing that Korea does from the United States ($966 million versus $8.78 billion).

Table 22.1
Asian Private Consumption Expenditure

Country	Size total (mil)	cars >8 seats	trucks buses	tel. lines	TV	computers mainframe	imports from US (mil)
		---thousands-----		--thousand-----		--thousands----	
Korea	64.1	664	645	6,517	8,643	109	8,781
Japan	122.1	28,654	19,319	48,840	30,250	7,540	31,957
Taiwan	53.2	1,047	440	4,228	6,085	50	7,627
Hong Kong	5.7	178	97	1,742	1,357	29	4,141
Singapore	2.6	241	138	797	538	43	4,778
Indonesia	172.5	937	1,291	602	7,114	--	966
Malaysia	16.3	1,165	351	959	1,565	15	2,376

Source: Business International Indicators of market
size for 117 countries, weekly report, July 3, 1989.

Table 22.2
Imports by Commodity

(US$ million, %)

Type of Commodity	1985	1986
Industrial Supplies	17,406(55.9)	17,134(54.2)
Crude Petroleum	5,589(18.0)	3,373(10.7)
Chemicals	2,865(9.2)	3,546(11.2)
Metals	1,776(5.7)	2,278(7.2)
Wood, Lumber & Cork	538(1.7)	549(1.7)
Raw Cotton	532(1.7)	403(1.3)
Capital Equipment	11,097(35.6)	11,359(36.0)
Machinery	3,573(11.5)	4,926(15.6)
Electric & Electronic	3,013 (9.7)	4,350(13.8)
Transport Equipment	4,052(13.0)	1,465(4.6)
Consumer Goods	2,633(8.5)	3,019(9.8)
Cereals	1,180(3.8)	1,138(3.6)
Domestic Use	17,641(56.7)	18,864(59.7)
Export Use	13,495(43.3)	12,720(40.3)
Total Imports	31,136(100)	31,584(100)

Thus we can conclude that within these seven countries, there are considerable differences. However, one comparison is worth noting here. Japan exceeds Korea in all columns. The Japanese, of course, have more people. But the ratio of difference here is far less than the number of cars, buses, telephone lines, TVs, and computers and the size of imports from the United States. In fact, the three countries of Korea, Japan, and Taiwan account for most of the imports, 3.9 times more than the other four.

Table 22.2 shows the strength of various markets inside Korea. The two columns show growth rates for a two-year period. Comparing all rows across columns reveals the increasing growth rate in all commodities except two. Only the crude petroleum ($5.58 billion to $3.37 billion) and transport equipment ($4.05 billion versus $1.47 billion) showed losses. In 1988 and 1989 (not shown) both Korean import items rose slightly (petroleum, $3.70 billion versus $3.69 billion; transport equipment, $1.85 billion versus $1.04 billion).

In 1986 the industrial supplies—crude oil (54.2 percent) and the capital equipment (36.0 percent)—accounted for most of the imports to South Korea. Consumer goods accounted for the rest (9.8 percent). Most of these items—raw materials and capital goods—came from the United States and Japan. Some imported commodities (40.3 percent) were for export use; others (59.7 percent) for domestic. This table shows the small consumer market compared to industrial supplies and capital equipment. Consumer goods accounted for less than 10 percent of the total imports; cereals amounted to 3.6 percent (1986).

By 1989 the import items on Table 22.2 rose in volume (chemicals, $4.25 billion; metals, $2.28 billion; wood, $1.87 billion; cotton, $.72 billion; machinery, $7.91 billion; electric, $7.18 billion; and consumer goods, $1.32 billion). Since 1986 Korea has become a leading industrialized power, with a nominal GNP of $223 billion (projected 1990). With the advent of democratization in 1987, Korean labor obtained wage increases of about 60 percent from that year until 1990. That has eroded Korea's advantage in exports of labor-intensive manufactures. The ROKG is now encouraging structural adjustment toward higher value, technology-intensive products.

Ironically Korean planners, once occupied with building a labor-intensive exporting economy, now face new challenges. Production losses from labor disputes and wage increases, along with currency appreciation, contributed to the slowdown in Korea's economy. For three straight years Koreans had double-digit real growth (over 12 percent in 1988). In 1989 that growth slowed to 6.5 percent. South Korea's private sector (16 million of the 42.8 million) recently produced a per capita income of over $5,000 (1989) with projections for per capita GNP of $5,230 for 1990.

AN IMPORT ISSUE AND SOLUTION

Korea imports large quantities of raw materials for use in manufacturing finished products which they, in turn, then export. Korea is the world's leading exporter of manufactured leather goods. So it would naturally also be the leading importer of hides and leather to supply this industry. Bilateral trade issues prompted Korea to increase its imports of U.S. hides and leather. Shoe component imports from the

United States totalled $7.8 million (1987); untanned leather accounted for 95 percent of that total.

Beef is a luxury food item for Korean consumers. From the Korean perspective, importing beef was a sensitive, volatile domestic issue. In the early 1980s, when imported beef was allowed, the act of importing beef created a stampede among Korean farmers. The problem for the United States was how to get the beef back into Korea.

Korea is watching other developments. If the United States insists on fair treatment with Japan and the EC, what would happen to a small country like Korea? The Koreans realize two facts about this issue: the beef interests in the United States are powerful political forces, and beef may not be the real issue. It only symbolizes the strong sentiments about trade imbalances worldwide. Ironically, Japan supplies about 50 percent of Korea's leather imports and cattle hides, while the United States accounts for only 20 percent of the market. In 1987 Korea imported $579 million of this item, 44 percent of the total U.S. exports of cattle hides. This figure represents an increase of 536 percent from the 1980 figures.

In 1988 the Koreans agreed to import beef, which did not, at that time, seem to bother Korean farmers for two reasons. Koreans prefer domestic beef anyway; it's cheaper. Only luxury hotels, accommodating foreign guests, buy high quality U.S. beef. Koreans had already directed their fury at another, larger domestic issue, that of mismanaged farm policies. So they haven't bothered about imports of beef.

Korea's liberalizing of beef imports is significant. The American Meat Export Federation projects that by 1994 the market should reach $313 million. Presently Koreans consume about 10.1 pounds of beef per person annually. That figure is compared with Japan's 100 pounds, Western Europe's 50 pounds, and the United State's 100 pounds annual per capita beef consumption.[5]

There is an irony, though, to this story—Koreans import more beef from Australia than from the United States. In fact in 1989 Australia had 48 percent of the market, compared to the United States (43 percent), followed by Canada (6 percent) and New Zealand (4 percent). These other sources of beef are cheaper. U.S. beef sells for $4,451 per ton on a CIF basis; Australian beef sells for $2,581. Since all beef purchases come through an open bidding system, U.S. beef exporters lose out on this volume market. The United States is also beginning to lose out on the high quality market as well. Australian ranchers now feed their cattle grain only for the last three months before slaughter, yet they are beginning to compete for the hotel business as well.[6]

IMPORTING CAPITAL EQUIPMENT

Several factors are crucial to exporting capital equipment. U.S. exporters need information about the product potential before taking action on the critical issues as they enter the markets. Initially, the specific type of capital equipment must be identified. It should have a potential for the business. Is it an economically assessable and stable market for the next three to five years? Once the criteria are established, marketing experts begin their work.

The market demand for metalworking equipment has increased remarkably. Heavy industrialization has grown because of facility investment, as has the demand for metalworking. But the sophistication and precision of imported equipment must also keep pace with these heavy industries. Specifically, the demand for controlled machine tools seems the greatest (metal cutting machine tools and metal forming tools). From the 1986 figures of $672 million, they have increased to $1 billion (1988) and $1.4 billion (1989), respectively.

Korea needs more sophisticated types of metalworking equipment. That is good news because this industry, which is technologically intense, gives high net profits with high added value. Local industries cannot provide this quality machinery. Korean industry has problems supplying high quality forged machine tool parts and components such as spindles, bearings, gears, pumps, and chucks. Their industries do not have the capacity for heat treatment technology necessary for manufactured durable precision parts.

Since metalworking equipment is closely linked with other heavy industries, exporters should contact Korea's heavy industrial companies: (1) Iron and steel industries. The Pohang Iron & Steel Company produces an annual 9.1 million tons of crude steel within an integrated steel mill. Some of their productions (5.4 million tons crude) are located at Kwang Yang, where a facility is under construction—estimated completion date, 1991. (2) Automobile industry. Contact Hyundai, Daewoo, Kia, Asia, and Ssangyong. All of these firms plan to expand their capacities of production. (3) Electronics products areas. Major companies here are Samsung, Daewoo, and Lucky Gold Star. Production for 1987 was $10 billion; 1988, $13.7 billion; and 1989, $17 billion.

Find specific names of these industrial customers by location, size of operations, and product application. Then determine the marketing mix, product distribution, and promotion price for the equipment. Don't put all your efforts in this one basket, though. Look for new untapped applications in wholesale, retail, and even service. Determine the supply conditions. Korean companies want technology to produce more sophisticated equipment. They want technical licensing agreements, for they hope to improve their precision range.

There are certain additional issues. The U.S. share is only about 13.4 percent. Japan dominates this market (75.9 percent) because of good quality, fair prices, faster deliver, closer proximity and quicker after-sales services. Popular Japanese producers are Okuma, Mitsubishi, Toshiba, Makino, Yamajaki, and Osaka Kiko. Koreans lack qualified design engineers and the technology demanded for metalworking equipment parts and components. So opportunities are there for numerically controlled operating machines, precision boring machines, and machining centers.

U.S. exporters must enter the market with technological abilities. They could show a strong Korean commitment first by getting and keeping customers, and second by sending high-caliber engineers and technicians to Korea. They should face Japanese competition head on with strategies for gaining entrance (a few Korean companies), adding other firms later.

Since the ROKG liberalized the import of metalworking equipment, U.S. suppliers should emphasize the versatility of their products in sales promotions. They could send qualified technicians and agents to their Korean branches and recruit Korean agents to assist in marketing activities. Sales agents and U.S. technical representatives should make personal sales calls to potential end users.

The Korea Machine Tool Manufacturers' Association is located at 35–4, Yoido-dong, Youngdungpo-ku, Seoul, Korea. This association has annual exhibits. Contact Manager Jin, P. O. Box Yoido 581, Seoul, Korea, for information about trade shows or technical seminars operated by the U.S. Embassy in Seoul.

AGRICULTURAL MARKETS

The Bush Administration places agricultural markets high on its Korean policy list. Market access is the issue, including bulk commodities, forest products, and high value agricultural products. To get that access, Washington presses Seoul for concessions, including lower tariffs, fewer quantitative restrictions, and more import licensing.

The Korean liberalization through 1991 includes a few agricultural products. While Korea has made some concessions, they still have high tariffs on U.S. agricultural products: wine, 100 percent; fruits, 50 percent; almonds, fresh lemons, and chocolate confectionary, 40 percent; and feed products, 20 percent. The ROKG announced a 1989 beef quota of 39,500 metric tons. When combined with the Japanese quota of 60,000 metric tons for three years, these figures add up to some major changes for this import market.[7]

Agricultural imports include corn, wheat, and soybeans. The U.S. share of the market is highest for soybeans (90 percent), followed closely by corn (89 percent), then beef (43 percent), and woods (30 percent). If the Korean government lowers crop and fertilizer subsidies, that would further reduce the incentives for agriculture, as well as the output per

Table 22.3
Fastest Selling Agricultural Products

HS	Description	List of Korean Importers
0304	fish fillets	Chunil Foods Manufacturing C.P.O. Box 1927
0306	crustaceans	Daewoong Lily Pharm. LTD. 820-8 Yoksam-dong
2106	food preparation	Beverage Industries Korea C.P.O. Box 5365
2301	flours, meals,	Oyang Fisheries LTD. 76-3 Taepyongno 1-ga Chung-gu Seoul
4102	raw skins sheep lambs	Wonduck Trading LTD. Chongnyangni P.O. Box 191

Table 22.4
Largest Volume of Agricultural Products

HS	Description	List of Korean Importers
1001	cereals wheat and meslin	Miwon Company LTD. C.P.O. Box 2156
	maize (corn)	Korean Feed Association C.P.O. Box 3473
1201	soya beans	Dong Bang Corporation C.P.O. Box 3031
4101	raw hides	Taejon Leather Industry LTD. C.P.O. Box 4238
5201	cotton	Choongnam Spinning LTD. C.P.O. Box 1539

crop. The fastest selling agricultural and wood products are found in Table 22.3.

The largest volume of agricultural products are found in Table 22.4. As in the other tables this also came from listings published by the KFTA. Since Korean importers were randomly selected, consider other Korean firms. These listings show possible connections for prospective U.S. exporters.

To conclude, it is estimated that restrictions on import licensing and de facto import bans cost U.S. exporters millions. Richard Bank, formerly with the Department of State, believes that "feed grain imports could increase as much as $62 million a year if government quotas were lifted."[8]

PROMOTION IN THE MARKETING MIX

Effective advertisement for international markets requires three conditions. First, the company should have its own internal affairs properly organized. Second, it should have both money and patience for long-term commitments. Third, it should identify its most profitable products and suitable Korean markets before matching its product with advertising agencies capable of worldwide operations.

Three types of international advertising allow for alternative choices. Corporate advertisers either make decisions at headquarters before sending them to target markets, allow national advertising staffs to make their own advertising decisions, or combine the two through centralizing advertising strategies and decentralizing applications regionally.[9]

Peebles does not agree that the world is a global village. Assuming that a firm has one uniform product, he suggests four steps: "(1) select one advertising agency worldwide with a worldwide account coordinator reporting to client headquarters; (2) establish multinational client/agency group planning meetings and a multinational creative team; (3) guide the brand headquarters to conduct or supervise consumer research and advertising pretesting; and (4) direct the resulting global campaign to desired product quality, allowing for the life styles and cultures intended."[10]

There are three possible sources of contacts. (1) International Advertising Association, 342 Madison Avenue, 20th Floor, Suite 2000, New York, New York 10017; (2) International Chain of Industrial and Technical Advertising Agencies, 201 Littleton Road, Morris Plans, New Jersey 07950; (3) International Federation of Advertising Agencies, 1605 Main St., Suite 1115, Sarasota, Florida 33577.

Promotion establishes response. Four types of marketing activities stimulate demand: personal calls (sales), advertising, sales promotion, and publicity through message and media. Having a proper mix of these activities is as important as having a proper marketing mix.

Table 22.5 lists some of the many marketing and advertising agencies available in Korea. Usually these firms provide media research for nationwide analysis; consumer research, which tests advertisements, concepts, packages, and products; omnibus surveys covering housewives and other special market segments; industrial research on certain markets; in-depth interviews of consumers; and store index research about distribution and purchasing behavior of consumers and sellers in supermarkets and retail stores.

The Korean advertising market will be totally open by 1991. Beginning in 1987, U.S. advertising firms entered into joint ventures with Korean firms. In 1988 the ROKG agreed to eliminate limits on equity participation by 1990, with the possibility of branch offices by 1991.

In promotional strategies, U.S. exporters want to create a favorable climate for future sales by increasing an awareness of their products. Promotional strategists should be sensitive to cycles as well as flavor, style, and emotional impulses.

Table 22.5
Marketing and Advertising Agencies

Price Waterhouse CPO Box 5940 Room 602 Baikcho Bldg 1 1-KA Uldchi-Ro Chung-ku Seoul 100	Peat Marwick Mitchell Room 1819 Daewoo Bldg. 541 5-KA Namdaenum-Ro Chung-Ku Seoul 100
Korea Survey (Gallup) Polls 221 Sajik-dong, Chong-ro Chongro-ku, Seoul 110	Pacific Projects, Ltd. International P.O. Box 5361 Tokyo 100-31, Japan
A. T. Kearney International Sumitomo Tamuracho Bldg. 1-15-1 Nishi Shimbashi Minato-ku Tokyo 105	ASI-Intech Research 9th Floor, Onarimon Bldg. Minato-Ku Tokyo 105
Hankook Research Co 696-18 Yeoksam-dong Kangnam-ku Seoul	TV Guide/ Korea Publications 40-1 Shinkye-dong Yongsan-du Seoul 140

In conclusion, consumer markets can be viewed from two perspectives. For U.S. exporters, the future looks good by necessity and desire. According to one Korean trade official, "In order to sell to West Germany, the United States, the United Kingdom, Italy, and Sweden, we have to buy from them."[9]

And they do just that. Wealthy Koreans new prefer brand-name consumer goods that sometimes cost six times the imported prices. These items include the BMW 750 model sedan, a Sony 19-inch color television, Dunhill lighters, Italian furniture, refrigerators, kitchenware, chinaware, golf kits, wrist watches, and rugs. The 1989 imports for Westinghouse refrigerators totalled about $14 million. All together, imported consumer items account for 10 percent of Korea's total import volume, and that figure is increasing substantially. The 1989 consumer goods figures increased 49 percent from the previous year.

For many Koreans, however, the future looks grim. Their surplus of exports over imports is decreasing. For the first nine months of 1989, imports were at $44.98 billion versus imports at $45.16 billion. But a more problematic concern has to do with a growing social issue. Many Koreans perceive that only a few of their numbers control the wealth, wealth that is often obtained through questionable means. The largest issue is the distribution of the desirables: Who gets what? How do they get it? Is the system fair? That issue will not affect U.S. exporters unless or until these sentiments precipitate into action. But already about 81 percent of Koreans consider "the current system of wealth destruction unfair."[10]

NOTES

1. *Boardroom Reports,* New York: Price Waterhouse Publications, February 1989.

2. John Endean, "The ABCs of Export Success," *Business America* (Special Issue), 109, 1988, 28.

3. Eugenia S. Hunter, "Quality: A Consumer Perspective," *Business America,* May 9, 1988, 10–11.

4. "Indicators of Market Size for 117 Countries," *Business International,* July 3, 1989.

5. Michael Copps, "America's Beef," *Business Korea,* December 1989, 71.

6. Articles recently appeared in *Business Korea,* March, and in *Business America,* July 4, 1989.

7. Richard K. Bank, "A Tough Row," *Korean Business World,* May 1989, 15.

8. Bank, 15.

9. Richard M. Diaz, "Advertising Effectively in Foreign Markets," *Advanced Management* (August 1985):12.

10. Dean M. Peebles, "Executives Insights: Don't Write Off Global Advertising," *International Marketing Review* 6 (1989):76.

11. "Consumer Consumption Blasted by Criticism," *Business Korea,* December 1989, 41.

12. "Consumer Consumption," 41.

23

Service Outlets

Distribution, prices, and the ability of Koreans to pay—all of these factors affect service outlets there. "We always had a policy of responding to all export leads within 24 hours of receipt," said an executive from Electrical South (Greensboro, North Carolina). But shipping transformers to Inchon from Providence takes longer than shipping them from Juneau to Olympia. Channels of distribution, mainly distance and type of stores, impact service outlets. So do prices. "We held our prices, even reduced some of them just to hold on," said the marketing director, Belco Industries (Carizozo, New Mexico). "We knew the situation would get better."

And it has gotten better with the devaluation of the dollar. But service outlets also depend upon product demand. Presently the United States is Korea's largest market (40 percent exports) and source of supplies for investments. Korea ranks eleventh among trading nations. Translated that means export opportunities.

In 1989, American exporters responded to product demands at these four Korean events: (1) U.S. Auto Parts Exhibition in Seoul (exceeded $6.6 million); (2) Korea Trade Show (Korean firms switching suppliers from Japan to U.S.); (3) U.S. Pavilion at Weldex, and (4) Products Show Seoul '89 (scientific instruments, computers, electronics, industrial process control, materials handling, telecommunications). If you are interested in any of these contact KOTRA, COP Box 1621, Seoul.

The ability of Koreans to pay for U.S. exports is reflected by the 12.2 percent growth of Korea's GNP this past year. Although that percentage decreased in 1989, there are possibilities for the future. The automobile market—300,000 cars a year—should double in 1990.

There are also strong demands for U.S. industrial raw materials, heavy machinery, electronics, and high-technology scientific products, as U.S. firms contribute to Korea's product upgrading. Sales continue in medical equipment and supplies, communications equipment, analytical and scientific instruments, electronic industry production and testing equipment, electronic components, food processing and packaging equipment, industrial controls, special machine tools, and special-purpose computers and peripherals. Already Korea is a major market for agricultural commodities and industrial materials such as coal, chemicals, scrap metals, logs, and lumber. As agriculture expands, demands increase.

Since service outlets depend upon product demands, prices, and distributions, look for increased exports. In 1987 Korean companies signed 637 technical licensing agreements with foreign firms. The United States accounted for 180 of the total (28 percent). In 1988 those figures increased by 15 percent. Royalties paid by Korean business on technical licensing agreements totalled $249 million, of which the United States received $95 million, followed by Japan with $92 million, and France with $18 million. By industry the electrical and electronics sector accounted for $82 million, followed by machinery ($59 million) and petrochemicals ($34 million).

Recent developments—higher Japanese yen, lower oil prices, trade surplus, lower interest rates, government policies—positioned Korea internationally for more service outlets. Korea's strength is found deep in tradition, but the 1988 Olympic Summer Games visibly transformed Korea. Those who are culturally aware still see beneath internationalization to the people.

These cultural roots shape Korea's national character, the Koreans' enthusiasm for life and diligence. Osgood says the Chinese are intelligent, the Japanese aesthetic, the Koreans survivors. They are survivors who work fast and ferocious—yet with respect, cooperation, and a desire for harmony. Although the Korean decision-making process lacks consensus-building like the Japanese, Korea's implementation of five-year plans beginning in 1962 serves as a model for developing countries. And while their planning strategies are good, their implementation is better. "Koreans are said to excel at implementation rather than planning and policymaking."[1]

The people complete the marketing elements. The Koreans establish the service outlets through product demands, pricing structures, and channels of distribution. Not to learn how that works is to risk making serious mistakes and losing potential markets. Kim and Mauborgne validated that assumption by identifying six trade aspects of successful entrance into country markets: (1) knowing how the local economy works (pricing), (2) understanding product demands and differentiation, (3) switching costs (pricing) successfully, (4) accessing the distribution channels, (5) knowing the true market value of products, and (6) knowing their cost disadvantages independent of scale and local capital requirements.[2]

PRODUCTS IN THE MARKETING MIX

Products define the value. That is why getting the facts clear helps in product selection. But that can be tricky, indeed. Only 5 percent of Korean families have microwave ovens. This makes marketing microwaves in Seoul seem easy. That is, until we realize that over 20 percent of Korean families in Seoul own one. Or, take the questions about the breadth and depth of product line, or the ones about when to make product additions or deletions. Providing packaged food adds value, but correctly identifying the customer is once again rather complicated. Statistics show that 54 percent of Korean households own refrigerators. But that doesn't say anything about the type. The older models have less space and no freezer. So the original estimates on frozen food products are over estimated if you assume that the 5.2 million homes with refrigerators are similar to those in the West. Other questions about products concern how to package, how to identify them, and how to service those distributors who sell them.

Products affect sales growth, capacity utilization, and improved market share. Exporters should examine per capita GNP for age groups. Older Koreans like traditional food, younger ones eat at McDonald's, drink Coca-Cola, and smoke Marlboros. Identify the ultimate users, the target market segments, and the specifications of the target market. People in the Cholla provinces have their own identity; they're more traditional and old-fashioned. Selling in that area is different from selling in Seoul.

Determine the resale specifications of wholesalers and dealers, then match both user expectations and reseller requirements with the design

Table 23.1
Import by Industrial Sectors for Japan

($1,000)

Sectors	Number of Items	Imports by countries '86		
		Total Amounts (A)	Japan (b)	B/A(%)
Machinery	93	1,642,115	983,177	59.9
Electrical & Electronic Machinery	48	1,589,580	911,352	57.3
Chemical Products	71	1,373,828	503,308	36.6
Drugs and Medical Equipments	16	292,802	100,430	34.3
Others	107	2,044,621	1,243,843	60.8
Total	335	6,942,946	3,742,110	53.9

perform and cost specifications of the product (appearance, performance, costs). An American executive put it this way: "You have to decide when you come into this country (Korea) whether you want to control your business or give it away to your partner. If you want to control it, you must do your own distribution; it's harder, but we decided it was necessary to retain control over marketing."[3]

Broad statistics like those in Table 23.1 don't show exporters what to do about product identification, trademarks, and how to fit immediate product decisions into a long-run product line program. They don't help U.S. suppliers estimate the cost of product strategies or prepare a preliminary budget. They don't even give them insights about how to test new or improved products, certainly not by Korean engineering, manufacturing, and marketing criteria. But this table does show imports by industrial sectors for Japan.

The data in Table 23.1 provide baselines for comparisons. In 1987 U.S. exports to Korea totalled $612 million (235 U.S. high potential items). This figure was up (42.1 percent) from those a year earlier. It compared with an increase rate of 29.4 percent for all U.S. imported goods. U.S. machinery recorded the fastest growth rate (62.7 percent; $203 million) of exports to Korea in early 1987. The electric/electronic and chemical industries posted moderate increases (30 to 40 percent).

Table 23.2
Competitiveness of U.S. Products by Industry

	Machinery	Electric Electronics	Chemicals	Textiles	Steel Metals	Total
U.S. products less expensive	7.0	8.3	24.6	16.7	5.3	10.5
No difference	25.4	40.0	47.4	23.3	26.3	30.5
U.S. products more expensive	67.6	51.7	28.0	60.0	68.4	59.0
Total	100.0	100.0	100.0	100.0	100.0	100.0

Note: This 1987 data illustrate pricing competition of U.S. products. Devaluation affected perceptions.

PRICE IN THE MARKETING MIX

Establishing a product price is the most challenging aspect of the marketing mix. More uncertainty surrounds price than any of the other elements. Pricing in Korea is not an exception, for Korean suppliers evaluate U.S. products compared to some subjective standard. Table 23.2 reveals, from a 1987 Korean supplier survey, something of the delicate balance of pricing. The majority of those surveyed believed that U.S. products were more expensive than products from Japan or other sources.

This survey confirmed one fact—that while consumer responses may be unknown, the competitive pricing is not. Price, along with quality, remains a constant factor and consumer concern.

Pricing decisions are complicated; they depend on so many other factors. Korea's tariff rates show that the agricultural and fisheries imports have the highest tariff rates (25.15 percent, January 1988). Exporters will want to inquire about their particular products and their average tariff rates.

Manufactured goods are now 11.2 percent (1989); by 1993 these tariff rates will drop to 6.2 percent. Average rates are now 12.7 percent and should be 7.9 percent by 1993. In the last two years, the Koreans have reduced rates on 1,873 items: passenger cars, tobacco products, cosmetics, electrical goods, and paper. In February 1989, tariffs on 203 items were reduced, including chocolate, refrigerators, and computers.[4]

Whatever the particular pricing strategy, executives should identify their products' users and purchasers. After all, market segments determine the relation of price to demand. Take the industrial processing equipment in Korea. The demand is great. According to Korea Electric

Power Corporation (KEPCO), its operations divisions are planning a series of expansions to include twenty-four thermal plants (coal, bunder C, LNG). Already eight nuclear power plants and fourteen hydraulic power plants are operational, while three nuclear and two hydraulic power plants are being built.

At present thirty-five petrochemical manufacturing companies are known to be operating at 100 percent of their production capacity. Honam Petrochemical completed the expansion (from 80,000 tons/year to 100,000 tons/year) of polypropylene production capacity. Knowing these figures should, in turn, facilitate your own pricing strategies. You may want to sell volume at lower prices.

Korea still imports about 65 percent of its total electrical demand. Japanese firms have geographic advantages. The prices of many varieties of Japanese manufactured goods make them almost irresistible to Korean industrial users.

Deduction margins and discounts of channel components also determine the manufacturer's net sales price. It is a good idea to estimate the total fixed and variable costs of price/volume alternatives, deduct total costs from total revenue for each price/volume alternative to obtain profit estimates of various pricing options. Future sales of industrial process controls are directly dependent upon: (1) successful bidding by U.S. consulting and engineering firms in designing plants, (2) the availability of U.S. funds to finance projects, and (3) the ability of U.S. suppliers to identify projects at early stages of development in order to follow through with effective sales campaigns.

U.S. suppliers who sensitively evaluate pricing strategy components should also complete their rough drafts in Korean for end users. Preliminary decisions for pricing components and pricing decisions will obviously differ depending upon the CIF value of the shipment. Current tariff rates for industrial process controls are 15 percent of the CIF value of shipping.

DISTRIBUTION CHANNELS

Distribution determines product availability. Shipping channels, wholesale distribution, retail distribution, facilitating agency, warehousing, internal transportation, and marketing—all of these affect product availability. Basically, distribution refers to either marketing logistics or marketing channels. On the one hand, logistics are defined as arrangements (storing, breaking bulk, delivering) for maintaining and moving physical products for resale in Korea. Physical distribution is usually separate from marketing, especially to Korea, because of its transporting costs. On the other hand, marketing channels are defined as any facilitating agency services required to deliver the products.

The Korea Maritime and Port Administration operates facilities for unloading, storage, and transportation of the cargo at Inchon and Kunsan on the West Coast; Pusan, Ulsan, and Masan on the southern and eastern coasts. Inchon uses a lightering service, whereby large ships are unloaded in the outer harbor and barges feed the cargo into the harbor for unloading.

The term "distribution" refers not only to marketing logistics but also to marketing channels. Marketing channels have to do with agency services required to deliver products. U.S. suppliers should determine their distribution objectives. First, they obtain distribution in the Korean market, in order to maintain (possibly improve) their Korean market share in existing channels. Second, they also try to achieve predetermined patterns of distribution (department stores, mass merchandisers, specialty outlets). Third, and finally, they try to improve channel performance of distribution.

Regardless of the particulars, your exports to Korea follow four distribution channels—(1) industrial goods, (2) unprocessed agriculture products, (3) consumer goods, and (4) government purchases.

In the first channel, Koreans buy industrial goods—raw materials and capital goods—from suppliers. Exporters chose six approaches: (1) direct to end users; (2) to agent, then end users; (3) to agent, importer, then end users; (4) from importers to end users; (5) from agent, then leasing companies, to end users; (6) from leasing companies to end users. Agents with offers register with the Association of Foreign Trading Agents of Korea (Foreign Trade Transaction Act). In their active modes, agents want import recommendations (nonrestricted items) from various associations; in their passive ones, they comply with the Import Deliberation Authorities. To do both, agents first study the list of imported goods and how they are classified (restricted items) in the Annual Export-Import Notice.

For the second channel (unprocessed agriculture products), suppliers go through eligible agents (bidding) to the end users' organizations before going to the end users. They could even go with a general trading company (bidding) to the end users' organizations and end users. Both of these procedures require them to go through the four major end users' organizations: Livestock Cooperative Federation, Korea Feed Association, Korea Corn Processing Industry National Association, and Korea Agriculture Cooperative. Sometimes the government purchases goods directly through the ROKG Office of Supply.

Whether exporting industrial materials or agricultural products, suppliers retain eligible agents registered as end users' organizations (The

Office of Supply). These agents see the invitation notices three days before closing. If participating in any tenders, they deposit an advanced security (2 or 3 percent). Upon winning that tender, and including security with it, they then deposit a 5 percent performance bond.

U.S. exporters have two other channels—consumer goods and government purchases. Consumer goods include durables and nondurables, along with processed food. From a Korean perspective, consumer imports have both positive and negative effects upon consumers. Positively, these imports satisfy consumer demand for high quality goods. But they are often diverted into black markets. Further, these import channels are complicated. The longest channel is from U.S. suppliers to importers, to exclusive purchaser, to brokers, to wholesaler, to retailers, and then to consumers. Based on the latest polls, the consumers find these foreign goods at specialty stores (33.4 percent), general stores (24.4 percent), department stores (23.1 percent), and small shops (19.1 percent).

Finally, the fourth distribution channel is the Korean government itself. Government agents, like those with agricultural products, purchase a variety of import products. If agents do not have trade licenses, importers must be involved because of government policy. Remember, however, government agents do not directly engage in the importing process.

Recently, Armstrong revamped its distribution strategy for Korea. They developed a new Korean marketing system for their acoustical ceilings and vinyl floor products. Before this development, Armstrong's distributors acted as subcontactors. For several years this worked. However with increased spending for housing, Korean buying practices changed. This meant that their old distributor system was ineffective to new markets. So they implemented their new system. They chose well-established dealers to run their expanding business more profitably. Armstrong changed their distribution system by working with a local affiliate, Samyoung. These Koreans now promote Armstrong products.[5]

By identifying channel issues and problems, they made significant changes. And as a result of these changes, their strategy reaches more end users, the ones who insist on higher quality products and buy them. They now use dealers who make proposals, maintain close supervision over installation, and control all aspects of the production. By improving their new distribution system, they also increased their sales. Their old system was not responsive enough to the changing Korean markets. Under their new system, Korean dealers sell directly to architects and builders, as well as to Korean consumers.

U.S. suppliers aren't the only ones concerned about distribution, so are the Koreans. In marketing U.S. products, Korean trade experts think that U.S. suppliers are at a trade disadvantage on prices and quality products. In order to evaluate this issue, KFTA conducted a survey (1987) to find out about competition and channel access. Realize that these are not actual comparisons, only perceptions by Korean consumers and suppliers. These are the Koreans who know about U.S. suppliers' access to appropriate channels of distribution. Therefore, this is valuable information, which suggests improvements.

Most of these Koreans think the access is good (52.3 percent). A few even said they have no access to information on U.S. suppliers (5.1 percent). What these figures suggest is that U.S. firms could improve public relations with Korean consumers and information services. Prices must always be competitive. However they could become more consumer oriented by maintaining services and producing products designed specifically for Korean consumers.[6]

Another team of academic researchers studied export effectiveness. According to their work, about 250 U.S. companies account for 85 percent of all U.S. exports. Along the same line of research, Prahalad and Doz studied 500 multinational corporations to explore distribution strategies. Generally speaking, they found senior managers of the business units doing their jobs. These international managers responded correctly to local market demands and to globally integrated requirements. By means of their bifocal visions, these same managers maintained the strategic advantage by making organizational changes where necessary. Based on that study, the researchers isolated three key strategies.[7] These three strategies—demands, requirements, change—appeared to make the difference between success and failure.

U.S. suppliers should know how to identify the Koreans who can access the appropriate channels of distribution. These Koreans are quite useful, but they do not necessarily guarantee ready-made success. What matters is what works best. Some argue for wholly owned subsidiaries in Korea, such as joint ventures (JVs); other U.S. exporters disagree. U.S. managers in Korea who favor JVs give eight reasons for using JVs: (1) access to local markets through well-established Koreans, (2) control and protection of U.S. products and markets, (3) tax incentives, (4) delegation of accounting systems, (5) access to ROKG's programs, (6) terms of agreements, (7) skilled Korean workers, and (8) moderate labor costs. Those who argue against JVs do so because they limit control (a potential problem with nationalism); they create too many cultural and language problems; they require too much red tape; and they restrict business expansion.[8] You should experiment with the uniqueness of your product to see what might work.

NOTES

1. Kwang-Suk Kim,

2. W. Chan Kim and R. A. Mauborgne, "Becoming an Effective Global Competitor," *Journal of Business Strategy* (January/February 1989):33–38.

3. David O'Rear, *New Consumer Markets in Korea and Taiwan* (Hong Kong: Business International, 1988).

4. Seung-Soo Han, *Responsive & Responsible: Korea's Trade Partnership with the United States* (New York: Reid & Priest Law Firm, 1989), 5.

5. "Armstrong Revamps Strategy for Distribution in Asia to Tap Building Boom," *Business Asia*, January 16, 1989, 18.

6. Ministry of Trade and Industry, *Free and Fair Trade: Korea's Record and Commitment* (New York: Reid & Priest Law Firm, 1989), 60–61.

7. Yves Doz and C. K. Prahalad, *The Multinational Mission: Balancing Local Demands and Global Vision* (New York: The Free Press, 1987).

8. "JVs in Korea: Points to Consider Before Taking the Plunge," *Business International*, May 16, 1988, 150.

24

Business Prospects

Before the Republic of Korea National Assembly, Seoul, on February 27, 1989, President Bush gave his first major address on foreign soil. The president reminded Koreans of their heroic struggle for economic prosperity. President Bush recognized the Koreans' industrial base of international trade. The president encouraged open bilateral trade, unrestricted by political barriers, for increased business prospects. Throughout it all, "Korea [has become] the seventh largest trading partner, larger than many of our traditional European trading partners."[1] President Bush thinks that, "now in the 1980s, human aspirations for basic political and economic freedoms have become almost universal."[2] Such dynamics are nowhere more evident than with Korea's economy, one which benefitted from the free flow of international trade.

This chapter sums up both the outlook for business prospects in South Korea and the book. To be more specific than the president, Korea shows significant progress in electronics, manufacturing, and biomedicine. The Ministry of Trade and Industry (MTI), in conjunction with Samsung,

Lucky-Goldstar, and Daewoo, will jointly develop high-definition television (HDTV) by 1993. The cost for development is estimated at between $4.5 million and $7.7 million for each of the three companies. Samsung will undertake research on HDTV systems, Lucky-Goldstar on peripheral equipment, and Daewoo on the cathode ray tubes.

Korean companies—Sinyong, Chinyong, and Tanhae—are developing solenoid valves. Sinyong designs the general technology, Chinyong the high-precision manufacturing technology, and Tanhae the heat processing and materials production. Together they have invested over $2.5 billion, as they move toward completion in 1992. Technology transfer comes from two Japanese companies—Kuroda Precision Industries and Shiloku Electrical Construction. When completed, the project should lower consumer prices, save on imports, and result in substantial savings.

Another major project is at the Korea Chemical Research Institute, where twenty researchers have developed an antibiotic one hundred times more effective against virus strains than any existing product. The drug, KR–10664, is a substitute for penicillin, whenever viruses becomes resistant. Hoechst, the multinational pharmaceutical company cosponsoring the research, has applied for patents in over fifty countries. Before they market this drug (within three to five years), plans call for extensive testing. Conservative estimates are that the profits from this drug should exceed $25–50 million annually. These developments are the tip of the iceberg.

The international roles are reversed. For decades Korea accumulated a massive trade debt, while the United States achieved economic dominance. Now that the roles have been reversed, the relationship has become more strained. Korea continues to "ease previous restrictions affecting trade with the United States. Korea has already taken [steps] and plans to open its markets with the United States . . . to preserve and strengthen the vital relationship between the two countries."[3]

Any business prospects should be analyzed from the perspective of time—past, present, future. Certainly exporters should identify obstacles and opportunities facing their Korean business ventures. They need to forecast and budget, conduct periodic reviews, and, if need be, modify plans with contingency plans.[4]

PEAKS AND VALLEYS OF PRODUCTION

Today Korea actively pursues world trade, for only through international trade can Koreans enjoy higher standards of living and greater abundance of consumer goods. To appreciate the drastic changes that have taken place in Korea, one must realize that during the Korean War every major city was destroyed; the country was in ruins. The true strength of these people is evident, as we evaluate their achievements.

The Korean experience is truly a miracle. Korea has few natural resources, a small population, and a small labor force. They work 20 percent longer hours than Japanese and 30 percent longer than Americans. But their success comes from two sources.

First, against the backdrop of current prosperity, broad changes have occurred in the occupational base. The major change from 1920 until today has been a reduction in the primary sector from 57 percent to 13 percent in agriculture, forestry, and fishing. Likewise, there has been a change in secondary sectors, or manufacturing, from 20 percent in 1920 to just over 34 percent today. In direct proportion, the tertiary, or service, sector has also gone from 23 percent (1920) to over 53 percent today.

Essentially, Korea has now reached the stage of development that America obtained about thirty-five years ago. The Korean service industry is rapidly growing with more professionals, scientists, and engineers. This means there are more white-collar workers. This also means that the service revolution expanded, even as the fishing and farming industries declined. The last developmental phase includes tertiary sectors, such as restaurant chains, retail or wholesale, and fashions.

Second, current prosperity is reflected in the two-tier system of internal structures: one is the very large business operation, the other is the small-sized business operation. Korea now has many legal corporations operating in the country, but fewer than 50 corporations employ more than 5,000 workers. The majority of the corporations are small and account for most (80 percent) of the workers.

The larger tier of major companies is represented by the chaebol. Chaebols control almost a quarter of all paid-in capital in Korea. In 1988 the top three recorded sales of almost $30 billion. The next six largest Korean corporations combined also recorded $30 billion in sales. The eleven largest Korean corporations employ approximately 450,000 Koreans. Their sales now account for over 30 percent of the paid-in capital. The total sales of these firms now account for about 25 percent of Korea's GNP, or about half of the nation's foreign trade.

At the other end are the smaller companies. These represent the second half of this two-tier system. Most of these smaller companies are subcontractors for larger companies. They are linked with the bigger companies, but the employees do not reap the same benefits as employees of the larger companies. Nevertheless, their productivity is impressive. These small- to medium-sized companies account for some shipments of manufactured goods.

Their productivity was not always high; their failure rates were disproportionately high. These companies failed to attract good workers, lacked the capacity to improve, and produced inferior products. The government now assists these companies with financial loans, management consultations, and some protection from failures.

The effectiveness of the organizations is found in their productivity. Productivity in Korea has been especially high over the past few years. During this time the GNP per person employed increases substantially. While hospitality industries and agriculture and retail operations are much lower in productivity, the large companies compete with American companies.

OPPORTUNITIES AND RESTRICTIONS

Economic opportunities for exports to Korea have begun (1989) to slow. This trend should be seen in a broader context, along with Korea's trade advantage and the $10 billion-plus bilateral trade surplus. To commemorate these developments Washington removed these newly industrialized countries (NICs) of Asia from the Generalized System of Preferences. That means harder U.S. negotiations on beef, tobacco, and insurance. This comes at a time when the ROKG seems to have less political clout than ever before.

President Roh and the ruling Democratic Justice Party are more sensitive to constituents and social issue. Roh himself campaigned for equity of all Koreans—the poor, small businesses, and farmers. Yet if Roh is pushed too far, he could be identified with the United States, creating more anti-American sentiments. He cannot move too fast under Washington's pressure without tilting the delicate balance of a pluralistic ruling system and democracy. Tariffs have decreased on consumer goods and industrial raw materials, but there were less related to the Roh administration and more a function of long-term policies.

Roh spends more money on social welfare programs than his predecessors. Regional and city governments recorded increases (12–15 percent) in funding. At the same time, wages have increased 18 to 40 percent for three years. Higher wages were long over due, yet their effects have repercussions for multinational corporations (MNCs) and U.S. investors in manufacturing and services sectors. The ROKG is trying to cool the labor unrest, but the unions have gained considerable power. Their true, long-range political power is yet to be tested.

The financial system of Korea is undergoing considerable changes as well. The sixth Five-Year Social and Economic Development Plan (1987–1991) maps out extensive revisions, such as a prime rate system, new financial instruments, and a better credit-rating system. The overall purposes for these and other financial changes are to (1) attract foreign direct investment and advanced technologies, (2) improve the domestic investment climate and simplification of administrative procedures, and

(3) raise direct investment flow from countries other than the United States and Japan.

Some state-owned banks will be privatized to spear head commercial and industrial development. Other liberalizing policies give greater management autonomy. Koreans can establish savings accounts outside Korea; they can even take more money outside Korea for reverse investments.

The Ministry of Finance eliminated income tax breaks for expatriates, foreign investors, and interest received on international financial institutions or earned on foreign currency loans. Korea still has some of the highest tax rates (second to Japan) in the Asia Pacific region.

Venture capital thrives in Korea. It is rooted in the well-established policy of the ROKG. Through it the government stimulates and supports domestic technological research and development. This approach is consistent with the strongly held values of independent self-reliance and the entrepreneurial role. Industrial conglomerates (chaebols) were supported both by favorable government-sponsored financing and by grants of effective monopolies in certain industries considered as necessary for ambitious business expansion programs. Beginning in the 1980s, however, the ROKG also began promoting small- and medium-sized enterprises. Established programs provided them with managerial support and greater access (R&D in technology). By giving greater priority to this second sector of businesses, the ROKG restricted conglomerates from exploiting them.

The dual strategy is paying off. The ROKG has achieved cost-efficient manufacturing (technology), a favorable exchange rate, a cost decline of imported fuel, the overhead of Korean debts, and the increasingly favorable credit rating accorded Korean borrowers. Because of that climate, even small firms are obtaining easy financing.

The Ministry of Finance (MOF) has reduced bureaucratic application procedures and operational management rules. Foreign investors can now import domestically produced capital goods. These transactions are on the automatic approval lists of no restrictions. Specifically, joint-venture partners (less than 50 percent ownership, under $1 million with no tax exemptions) need only report their intentions when they produce a new product in the same industrial category. Before now foreigners obtained approval from MOF.

Such action reduces overheads on exports to Korea. Another strategy is to reduce personnel. Loctite Corporation, a U.S. manufacturer of adhesives and solvents, derived 50 percent of its profits ($337 million) from international operations.[5] Those profits don't tell the full story. Throughout the early and mideighties, corporate executives determined that staff operations were too restrictive and costly. So beginning in 1987, top executives began to reorganize their global operations by decreasing the

U.S. headquarters staff to three. Simultaneously, they increased the authority of their country managers. These elevated country managers worked in one of three world regions: the Pacific, Europe, and Latin America. As decentralized operations, country managers gained control over their own operations, the ones they knew best. This gave them greater flexibility to coordinate regional marketing.

This independence is not to be equated with insubordination or neglect of corporate plans. Local country managers had headquarters training and experience. They acquired the necessary language skills. They frequently traveled within and between their regions to the corporate headquarters in Newington, Connecticut. These travel costs weren't exorbitant but could be cut. The corporation cut costs through greater use of video communication capabilities. Based on the bottom-line results, they know it worked. It has paid off to the tune of $337 million. The Loctite team—hundreds of workers in twenty-eight wholly operated subsidiaries, four joint ventures, and distributorships in fifty countries—did their work. They successfully implemented these changes based on product demand.

Successful exporting is more than merely gathering information on financing, marketing practices, and distribution networks. Successes depend upon competent export managers who travel to Korea and demonstrate their abilities.

To demonstrate one's international abilities is, as we've shown, quite a challenge. International management is no easy job, for the role changes in direct proportion to our world. At one time domestic markets were big enough. In the 1960s, and even early 1970s, country managers had considerable independence; they made decisions about the company products, market strategies, and selection of indigenous staff. Then many multinational companies shifted away from country focus to product line focus. Now with satellite communications, supersonic transports, fax machines, and global computer relays, it takes networks of coordination to market successfully to Korea.

Competitive advantage, more than ever, depends on an integrated team effort. Any competitive advantage these days requires the support of all facets of the exporting process. U.S. firms simultaneously evaluate their export capacities (internal aspects of strategic marketing), even as they develop their Korean markets by using carefully devised, individualized strategies. Each step of exporting to Korea means key decision makers must know their particular country environments and product capabilities. Thus corporate strategies include two broad sets of variables—the internal (the company strengths and capabilities) and external (market opportunities and risks).

In concluding the book, we should probably once again ask whether exporting to Korea is profitable. The answer is both yes and no. It all depends upon firms, the products, and a host of other factors. The answer is qualified by whether firms find niches and sell appropriate products. But for those who can answer yes, Korea is a profitable export market, they have probably gone beyond negotiations to the supplier and the distributor. They have already established intermediaries and Korean importers.

Edwin Watson is a middle-aged business man who lives in Seoul. He compares his Saturday drives to his Inchon factory with earlier international experiences. He contrasts Korea with Pittsburgh where he grew up, or with Rhode Island where his factory is located, or with Saudi Arabia where he last worked. His cost of living is high in Seoul. Hotel rooms cost 144,000 won, with an extra 30,000 won added for the executive floor.

After leaving the Seoul metropolitan area behind, Edwin Watson listens to a George Winston tape while viewing rice paddies, family farms, *ginseng* tree sprouts, oxen-driven plowing operations, and small clusters of primitive huts. At the end of his ride, and while going down an old dirt road, he suspends his momentary delight. While still captivated by the beautiful rural scenery, he shifts his attention to the noise of chattering workers. Then he hears Mrs. Shin. "Do you care for some cool barley tea?" she asks. After drinking some, he goes off to eat a Korean lunch with his Korean workers.

In answering the question about whether exporting to Korea is profitable, Watson talks about finding market niches and selling appropriate building materials to Koreans. He's gone beyond negotiations to supplying products for the Olympic Cultural Center and finding distributors who will further market his product. He experienced the Korean environment first hand and, therefore, can offer five specific suggestions for would-be exporters.

He suggests, first of all, that exporters to Korea adapt their products, if necessary. He did that. His Inchon factory manufactures an insulation board. It is a high demand product because electricity is expensive and the ROKG wants more insulated products. These factors, when combined with the building boom, make his product quite attractive. The product is fake stucco put on rough or smooth. In Korea the rough texture collected pollution particles; therefore, the factory makes only the smooth finished products.

Second, he suggests that exporters should look for the best in Korea. But, at the same time, they should be prepared for the worst from this Asian country. There is a lot of labor unrest right now. Korea is undergoing rapid change because of international trade activities. Breaking old traditions creates problems in Korea. Not everyone is happy with those changes. "The people who are going to get hurt will resist as much as they can," he says.

Third, he suggests that exporters be sensitive to business practices. While his Korean employers are dedicated, business is conducted differently in Korea. Watson is impressed with the twelve Koreans who work for him. They have contributed to his successful enterprise. But business is much different. Americans are impatient. They "barge in and expect things to happen overnight. It doesn't work that way," he says. Marketing is different too. Most of the customers come from contacts with old friends and classmates. It was through contacts that he signed some rather large contracts within the Seoul area. Even despite these successes, Watson says that "it's tough breaking into this market."[6]

Fourth, he suggests that travelers to Korea merge themselves into the Asian culture. He himself has adjusted to the living and working conditions there, and he likes . . . almost all of it. He has learned to speak some Korean, but usually carries a Korean-English dictionary along just in case. While at the factory though, he communicates with his workers through an interpreter. He's even learned to like the hot Korean food kimchi.

Fifth, and finally, he suggests that exporters consider the attractiveness of Korean joint ventures. Watson owns 60 percent of the joint venture known as The Hyosung-Dryvit Incorporated. Presently, the business is booming. In his periodic drive from Seoul to Inchon, his observations and reflections about this experience are now and again disrupted by thoughts of new projects and sales opportunities for his operation. While his company sales for 1988 were $4 million, he hopes they will reach sales of $10 million by 1991.[7]

NOTES

1. George Bush, "Remarks before Republic of Korea National Assembly, Seoul, February 27, 1989," *Korea and World Affairs* (Spring 1989):213.

2. Bush, 213.

3. Seung-Soo Han, *Responsive & Responsible: Korea's Trade Partnership with the United States* (New York: Reid and Priest Law Firm, 1989), 1.

4. David Hopkins, *The Marketing Plan* (New York: The Conference Board, 1981), 53.

5. Ann Blumberg, "Management Practices: How Loctite Prospers with 3-Man Global HQ, Strong Country Managers," *International Business*, May 2, 1988, 129.

6. Nora Lockwood Tooher, "Rhode Island Business Plays by South Korea Rules," *The Business Providence Journal Bulletin*, September 13, 1988, 1.

7. Tooher, 1.

Resources

Korean Government: (1) The Korea Trade Promotion Corporation (KOTRA), Korea Foreign Trade Association (KFTA) Bldg., 159, Samsong-dong, Kangnam-gu, Seoul 135–729, CPO Box 1621. There are nine of these organizations alone in North America. For the past several years KOTRA has assisted the Korean Ministry of Trade and Industry in hosting the U.S. Products Show in Seoul, South Korea. (2) Offices for KOTRA are found in New York, Dallas, Los Angeles, Miami, Chicago, and Washington, DC. The New York office is located at 460 Park Avenue, Suite 402, New York, NY 10022. Be sure and ask for the book *Guide to the Korean Import Market*. This book includes information about South Korea's economic background, import policy, import trends, procedures, and distribution systems, as well as how to be successful in the Korean market. KOTRA provides information on export products, business investment, and joint ventures. They also arrange meetings and contacts with Korean importers. Once in Korea, they can be contacted at the Kimpo International Airport. (3) World Trade Center Korea, 10–1, 1-ka, Hoehyon-dong, Chung-gu (CPO Box 117). The Korea World Trade Center is located on a 200,000-square-meter site in the Yongdong area, south of the Han River. Its facilities total 564,639 square meters of floor space, including an exhibition complex, the trade tower (office building), a hotel, a convention center, a shopping center, and a city air terminal. The KFTA operates the World Trade Center. It also links over 11,000 companies for the purpose of promoting beneficial trade relations, monitoring changes in trade laws, and dispatching foreign trade missions.

U.S. Government: (1) The first stop that a U.S. company should make in preparing to export to South Korea is the U.S. Department of Commerce. This government agency operates a U.S. and Foreign Commercial Service network. This network is about overseas market opportunities that have been developed both by commercial officers in Korea and by industry and desk offices in Washington, DC. The many export services of the International Trade Administration include agency/distributor service, export counseling, *Commercial News USA*, comparison shopping for custom made service, foreign buyer program, trade opportunities, world trade data reports, overseas catalog and video-catalog shows, overseas trade missions, overseas trade fairs, and matchmaker events. (2) For a good general resource about these and other U.S. government agencies, get a copy of the book titled *Exporter's Guide to Federal Resources for Small Business*. This was written by an Interagency Task Force on International Trade; write the U.S. Government Printing Office, Washington, DC 20402, for a copy.

Private Economic Organizations: (1) The Korean Chamber of Commerce and Industry (KCCI), 45, Namdaemuno 4-ga, Chung-gu, Seoul (CPO Box 25). In their Korean Business Directory KCCI publishes a list of cooperatives by business and trading companies. (2) The Federation of Korean Industries (FKI), 28–1, Youido-dong, Yongdungpo-gu, Seoul (CPO Box 6931). (3) Korean Federation of Small Business (KFSB), 16–2, Youido-dong, Yongdungpo-gu, Seoul (Youido POB 1030). (4) Korea Foreign Trade Association (KFTA), 159–1, Samsong-dong, Kangnam-gu, Seoul (CPO Box 1117). (5) Korean Traders Association, World Trade Center Korea, 10–1, 1-ka, Hoehyon-dong, Chung-ku, Seoul. This office assists with visiting trade missions and buyers.

Offer Agency Association: *Trading Agents Directory*, Association of Foreign Trading Agents of Korea, 45–20, Youido-dong, Yongdungpo-gu, Seoul (Youido CPO Box 337).

Market Research Agencies: (1) Korea Survey (Gallup) Polls, 221, Sajig-dong, Jongro-gu, Seoul. (2) S. H. Jang & Associates, Seoul (CPO Box 737). (3) Frank Small & Associates, Rm. #706, Samhwan Bldg. 17–3, Youidodong, Yongdungpo-gu, Seoul. (4) South Korea, Business International Corporation, One Dag Hammarskjold Plaza, New York, NY 10017. (5) Foreign Economic Trends Korea, International Trade Administration, U.S. Department of Commerce, Washington, DC 20230. (6) Survey Research Group, Facts on File Publications, 460 Park Avenue South, New York, NY 10016.

Business Consultants: (1) Pacific Consultants, World Trade Center Korea Bldg. 159, Samsung-dong, Kangnam-gu, Seoul. (2) S. H. Chang & Associates, WTCK Bldg. 159, Samsong-dong, Kangnam-gu, Seoul. (3) Kim and Chang, 4th Floor,

Seyang Bldg., 223, Naeja-dong, Jongro-gu, Seoul. (4) *Partners in Export Trade*, printed by the U.S. Department of Commerce, ITA, Washington, DC 20120. It contains over 4,500 banks, export trading companies, export management companies, manufacturers, service organizations, and producers. Order: Superintendent of Documents, U.S. Government Printing Office, Washington, DC 20402. (5) The U.S. Embassy, Consular Section, in Seoul also provides a list of attorneys in the consular district of Seoul.

Credit Survey: (1) Korea Credit Guarantee Fund, 254–5 Gongdeok-dong, Mapo-gu, Seoul. (2) Korean Management Credit Rating Corp., Korea Development Bank Bldg., 27th Floor, 10–2, Gwancheol-dong, Jongro-gu, Seoul. (3) Korea Investors Service Inc., 16–1, Youido-dong, Yongdungpo-gu, Seoul. (4) Korea Information & Credit Evaluation Inc., 98–4, Oonni-dong, Jongro-gu, Seoul. (5) Sachan Data Bank, 29, 1-ga, Myung-dong, Jung-gu, Seoul (CPO Box 5040).

Directories: (1) World Trade Academy, 50 East 42nd Street, New York, NY 10017. (2) *The Korea Directory* (CPO Box 3955), Seoul. (3) Korean Traders Association, 460 Park Avenue, Room 555, New York, NY 10022. (4) *U.S. Business Directory for Korea.* Published by U.S. and Foreign Commercial Service, American Embassy, 82, Sejong-ro, Chongno-gu, Seoul. (5) *Korean Trade Directory*, Korean Traders Association, 460 Park Avenue, Room 555, New York, NY 10022, or CPO Box 1117, Seoul.

Products: (1) *A Guide to the Korean Import Market*, KOTRA (CPO Box 123), Seoul. (2) *New Opportunities for Exporting to Korea*, KFTA, World Trade Center, 159–1 Samsung-dong, Kangnam-gu, Seoul. (3) *What to Sell to Korea*, KFTA, 159–1, Samsung-dong, Kangnam-gu, Seoul (CPO Box 1117).

How to Do Business with Koreans: (1) *Doing Business in Korea*, Seihwa Accounting Corp., Royal Building, 9th Floor, No. 5, Dangjoo-dong, Chongro-ku, Seoul (Price Waterhouse). (2) *United States-Korean Trade Issues*, American Chamber of Commerce in Korea, Chosun Hotel, 3rd Floor, Seoul. (3) *South Korea: An Export Market Profile* (by John Dyck and Don Sillers), Superintendent of Documents, U.S. Government Printing Office, Washington, DC 20402. (4) *1989 National Estimate Report on Foreign Trade Barriers*, Office of U.S. Trade Representative, Department of Agriculture and Department of Commerce, Superintendent of Documents, U.S. Government Printing Office, Washington, DC 20402. (5) Investment Promotion Section, International Financing Bureau, Ministry of Finance, 1, Chungang-dong, Kwacheon, Kyonggi. (6) Investment Promotion Center, Korea Chamber of Commerce and Industry, 111, Sokong-dong, Chung-ku, Seoul,132 They provide information and guidance on foreign capital investment and joint ventures, they introduce potential Korean partners to foreign investors, and they investigate and recommend certain investments in South Korea.

A Korean Perspective on Trade Issues: (1) *Free and Fair Trade* and *Responsive and Responsible: Korea's Trade Partnership with the United States.* Write: Reid and Priest, 1111 19th Street, N.W., Washington, DC 20026. (2) *Korea's Policies to Increase Imports*, KFTA, 159–1, Samsung-dong, Kangnam-gu, Seoul (CPO Box 1117).

Background, Economic, and Social Factors in Business: (1) *Background Notes on Korea,* U.S. Department of State, Washington, DC 20520. (2) *Korea 1989 Guidebook,* Eurasia Press, 108 State Street, Teaneck, New Jersey 07666. (3) *Facts on Korea, 1988,* Samhwa Printing Company, CPO Box 4218, Seoul. (4) *Venturing Abroad in Asia* (by Robert Moran), International McGraw Hill, 1988. (5) *Korean Etiquette & Ethics in Business* (by Boye De Mente), NTC Books, Lincolnwood, Illinois. (6) *Managing Cultural Differences* (by Philip R. Harris and Robert Moran). Video tapes are available from Gulf Publishing Company, P. O. Box 2608, Houston, Texas, 77252. (6) *Korea: the Tiger Economy,* London: Euromoney Publications, 1988. Order at the Nestro House, Playhouse Yard, London EC4V5EX. (7) *The International Business Handbook: Republic of Korea,* Global Quest, Inc., 2101 Crystal Plaza Arcade, Suite 238, Arlington, Virginia 22202. (8) *Business Korea Yearbook 1989–90,* Business Korea, Yoido, P. O. Box 273, Seoul 150–602 Korea. (9) *Foreign Economic Trends and Their Implications for the United States* (1988), FET 88–111, and *Marketing in Korea* (1985), Overseas Business Reports (OBR 85–02). Write either U.S. Department of Commerce, Washington, DC 20230 or the Superintendent of Documents, GPO, Washington, DC 20402. (10) *The Quarterly Economic Review: South Korea,* The Economist Intelligence Unit Ltd., Spencer House, 27 St. James Place, London SWIA INT, England or 75 Rockefeller Plaza, New York, NY 10019. This review is about Japan and Korea.

Selected Bibliography

Axtell, Roger E. *Do's and Taboos Around the World*. New York: Parker Pen Company, 1988.

Brislin, Richard. *Intercultural Interaction*. Beverly Hills: Sage, 1985.

Burmeister, Larry L. *Research, Realpolitik, and Development in Korea*. Boulder, Colo.: Westview Press, 1988.

Carvounis, Chris. *The United States Trade Deficit of the 1980s*. Westport, Conn.: Greenwood Press, 1987.

Chung, Kyung Cho, Phyllis G. Haffner, and Fredric M. Kaplan. *The Korea Guidebook*. Boston: Houghton Mifflin, 1989.

Clifford, Mark. "Korea Inc. on Trial." *Far East Economic Review* 4 (August 1988):44–45.

De Mente, Boye. *Korean Etiquette & Ethics in Business*. Lincoln, Ill.: NTC Business Books, 1988.

Furnham, Adrian, and Stephen Bochner. *Culture Shock: Psychological Reactions to Unfamiliar Environments*. New York: Methuen, 1986.

Grayson, James Huntley. *Korea: A Religious History*. New York: Oxford University Press, 1989.

Griffin, Trenholme J. *Korea: The Tiger Economy*. London: Euromoney Publications, 1988.

Harris, Philip R., and R. Moran. *Managing Cultural Difference.* Houston, Tex.: Gulf, 1987.

Hoare, James, and Susan Pares. *Korea: An Introduction.* New York: Kegan Paul International, 1988.

Howell, Russell Warren. *The Koreans: Passion and Grace.* San Diego, Calif.: Harcourt Brace Jovanovich, 1988.

Kim, Kihwan. "Korea in the 1990's: Making the Transition to a Developed Economy." *World Development* 16 (1988):7–18.

Landis, Dan, and Richard W. Brislin. *Handbook of Intercultural Training.* New York: Pergamon Press, 1983.

Lautensach, Hermann. *Korea.* New York: Springer-Verlag, 1988.

Lee, Chong-Sik. *Korea: Land of the Morning Calm.* New York: Universe, 1988.

Leipziger, Danny M., ed. *Korea: Transition to Maturity.* New York: Pergamon Press, 1988.

Leipziger, Danny M. "Editor's Introduction: Korea's Transition to Maturity." *World Development* 16 (1988):1–5.

Macdonald, Donald Stone. *The Koreans: Contemporary Politics and Society.* Boulder, Colo.: Westview Press, 1989.

Merrill, John. *Korea: The Peninsular Origins of the War.* Newark: The University of Delaware Press, 1989.

Moran, Robert T. *Venturing Abroad in Asia.* New York: McGraw-Hill, 1988.

Moskowitz, Karl. *From Patron to Partner.* Lexington, Mass.: D. C. Heath, 1984.

Nahm, Andrew. "Modernization Process in Korea: A Historical Perspective." Pp. 25–68 in *Modernization of Korea and the Impact of the West.* Edited by Chang-Soo Lee. Los Angeles: East Asian Studies USC, 1981.

Nahm, Andrew. *Korea: Tradition and Transformation.* Los Angeles: Holloway, 1988.

Petri, Peter A. "Korea's Export Niche: Origins and Prospects." *World Development* 16 (1988):47–63.

Whitehill, Arthur M., ed. *Doing Business in Korea.* New York: Nichols, 1987.

Index

About the Author

LARRY M. HYNSON, JR., is Associate Professor of Sociology and Faculty Associate at the Center for International Trade Development, Oklahoma State University. He has written over 30 articles, monographs, and book chapters on topics relating to East Asia, international trade, technology transfer, and organizational culture.